HOME BEFORE DARK

A FAMILY PORTRAIT OF
CANCER AND HEALING

HOME
BEFORE DARK

A FAMILY PORTRAIT OF
CANCER AND HEALING

David, Kate, Michael, and Sam Treadway

UNION SQUARE PRESS

An imprint of Sterling Publishing Co., Inc.

New York / London
www.sterlingpublishing.com

STERLING and the distinctive Sterling logo are registered trademarks of Sterling Publishing Co., Inc.

Library of Congress Cataloging-in-Publication Data
Home before dark : a candid family portrait of cancer and healing / by David, Kate, Michael, and Sam Treadway.
    p. cm.
  ISBN 978-1-4027-6071-6
  1. Treadway, David C.—Health. 2. Cancer—Patients—United States—Biography. 3. Psychother-apists—United States—Biography. 4. Cancer—Patients—United States—Family relationships. I. Treadway, David C.
  RC265.6.T74A3 2010
  362.196'99400922—dc22
  [B]
                         2009034822

10 9 8 7 6 5 4 3 2 1

Published by Sterling Publishing Co., Inc.
387 Park Avenue South, New York, NY 10016
© 2010 by David, Kate, Michael, and Sam Treadway
Distributed in Canada by Sterling Publishing
c/o Canadian Manda Group, 165 Dufferin Street
Toronto, Ontario, Canada M6K 3H6
Distributed in the United Kingdom by GMC Distribution Services
Castle Place, 166 High Street, Lewes, East Sussex, England BN7 1XU
Distributed in Australia by Capricorn Link (Australia) Pty. Ltd.
P.O. Box 704, Windsor, NSW 2756, Australia

Manufactured in the United States of America
All rights reserved

Names and identifying characteristics of some individuals depicted in the book have been changed, and all patients of the author depicted in the book are composite characters.

Sterling ISBN 978-1-4027-6071-6

For information about custom editions, special sales, premium and corporate purchases, please contact Sterling Special Sales Department at 800-805-5489 or specialsales@sterlingpublishing.com.

CONTENTS

"For all those who wake, or watch, or weep this night."

—Augustine of Hippo

A NOTE FROM THE AUTHORS

This book is our shared story of confronting the sudden catastrophic illness of a family member. It recounts our experience as we tried to find new ways of holding each other and sharing our fears and frustrations while trying to stay connected. We wanted to embrace whatever time we would have fully and, amidst the stress, find laughter, love, and even joy.

The challenges were overwhelming for each of us separately and for us as a family. How would we come together and encourage each other, while simultaneously needing so much support ourselves? How would each of us manage the challenges of our individual lives while trying to pull together as a family? And how would we go on without David if we had to?

Our book is ultimately not about cancer or death. It's about living as well as one can with the sharp, sudden awareness of an everyday fact: we are all on borrowed time. It is our way of trying to make meaning of a situation that all families either have faced or will face. Ours is not a unique story. It is the human condition, simply intensified by circumstance. We all live on the knife's edge. This is our family's experience of it.

◇◇◇

David has survived so far. While preparing for the worst, we've been blessed by the best. We know that there are no guarantees that there won't be a recurrence of cancer, but our chances, once so bleak, are excellent. Compared to how much suffering and loss other families face, we know how fortunate we've been.

We hope to share with other families our struggle to stay close despite our individual differences in life stages, understanding, and coping styles. What it's been like for each of us. What we've learned, what we've lost, and how we've changed for better and for worse.

Writing this book together has changed us both individually and as a family in surprising and unexpected ways. We offer you our story in the hope you will feel less alone with yours. All families, each of us in our own way, are trying to find their way home before dark.

David, Kate, Michael, Sam
Boston, October 2009

Spring 2005

David

On Saturday, I play tennis with abandon and I lose, as usual. I check in with my distraught client, whose daughter was killed in a car accident just the week before. Kate and I go out to the movies. We hold hands. Sunday afternoon, I go to hear my Buddhist teacher talk about how to maintain equanimity in intimate relationships. No small challenge. That evening, I host a book group that read my new book, a collection of short stories about how the lives of therapists and clients impact each other. They are kind enough, couching their criticisms carefully. It is a good weekend. I kiss Kate goodnight and roll over, content. My life feels like it's flowing rhythmically along, moment to moment, like the ocean rolling gently beneath me on a long sea passage.

In the middle of the night, I am jolted awake by what feels like a knife digging into my left shoulder. I wake up the physician in bed next to me, and Kate immediately grills me for signs of a possible heart attack. It's good to be married to a doc.

"You're okay. Take a Tylenol." She pats me reassuringly as she rolls away from me.

"We're having a failure to communicate," I insist. "This really hurts."

"Well, maybe it's a little tear in your rotator cuff. Do you need a Percocet?" she asks with more concern.

Despite the Percocets, the pain spreads down my whole left arm. My right shoulder begins to hurt, too. I am scared. Dr. Kate has gone back to sleep, and I don't want to wake her again. A half hour later, I take another Percocet and wonder if I should cancel tomorrow's appointments and head first thing for Massachusetts General Hospital, where Kate works.

In the morning, Kate agrees that I should see my doctor and, of course, then I resist. "Kate, I can't cancel a morning's worth of clients just because my shoulder hurts."

"Can you imagine really listening to your clients with your shoulder feeling the way it does now?"

"Well, no." I suddenly realize how scared I am. I've never been in such pain.

2

The tests and scans begin. Over the next ten days, hypotheses swirl around me. It is the rotator cuff. It is a Lipitor allergy. Maybe even a rare disease usually found only among Ashkenazi Jews. I keep canceling my clients to go to doctor appointments and, with increasing frequency, to take naps. I am eating Percocets like M&M's. When my sons, Sam and Michael, call, I can barely focus on their news. We're not telling them anything yet.

The following week my doctor calls me between my clients and tells me briefly that my shoulder is full of tumor. He thinks it started somewhere else but doesn't know where. I know it probably means I have very advanced cancer, maybe lung or kidney or pancreatic. Regardless, it's probably a death sentence. I am too stunned to talk and thank him for calling without asking any questions, knowing Kate can fill me in later. I put down the phone in disbelief, both in hearing the incredibly harsh news and at my utter lack of response to it. It is as if I had asked him about the weather. I open the door to my next clients and smile my hellos, still utterly numb.

◇◇◇

Finally, Kate's home.

She tries to talk about the tumor without scaring me. "We still don't really know anything," she says, trying to be reassuring. I can tell she is really worried, which is more frightening than anything else. "Are you okay?" She asks, reaching for my hand.

I feel utterly frozen. Dead already. "I'm fine," I lie.

A few nights later, I feel excruciating pain in my jaw. My docs decide it is time to hospitalize me. My days in the hospital, flattened by pain meds, leave me even more adrift, floating though the hours, day blurring into night, interchangeable moments under the fluorescent lights and random visits from nurses, doctors, and technicians. It's obvious from the hushed voices, the averted eyes, and the worried exchanged glances that I am in serious trouble.

Three days after my admission, the shoulder biopsy results come in. The doctor says, essentially, that I am riddled with cancer in virtually every organ and throughout my bone marrow. The very first thing that pops into my head is the Air Force Academy fight song, "Off we go into the wild blue yonder, climbing high into the sun. . . ." What neuron has diligently stored that in my brain all these years, and why fire it off now?

There's a chance to beat this thing, the doctors say. They seem tiny, as if I'm looking at them in their white coats through the wrong end of a telescope. I nod politely, not actually hearing much. I can't imagine beating anything. And frankly I couldn't care less about putting up a good fight. I have already assumed the worst.

"I don't want to lose you," Kate says with tears in her eyes, when everyone has left.

I feel like she already has.

As a therapist, I know what is going on in me. In the face of a traumatic experience, most people flip into the fight/flight response. I am having the "freeze" response, in which one stops reacting emotionally. It's a state of shock. I have been prone to numbing out as a way of protecting myself from being overwhelmed by feelings ever since I was a little boy growing up in my emotionally dangerous family. Going numb and dissociating feels old and familiar and safe, as if all this were happening to someone else.

Kate, however, is flooded with feelings and wants to connect with me desperately. I look at her as lovingly as I can, reach for her hand, and say gently, "It's going to be okay, sweetie. We'll get through this." The words taste like sawdust in my mouth.

Kate

"OH, MY GOD. MY SHOULDER!" THE URGENCY AND PAIN IN DAVID'S voice pull me from a deep sleep. It is 2 a.m., Monday, May 2. In the fog of awakening, my doctor self clicks in. *Is he having a heart attack? Could this be an aortic dissection?* "Are you having any chest pain? Any difficulty breathing?"

"No." His voice communicates his excruciating pain.

"Does your shoulder hurt if you move your arm?"

"Yes."

I breathe a sigh of relief. If it hurts to move his arm, then it must really be in his shoulder. Nothing too serious. After some more questions and a brief look at his shoulder, I give him a Percocet left over from some recent surgery I had had. He seems better. I fall back asleep. I am not worried.

The next morning, his shoulder seems better but it still hurts, and we agree he should call his doctor. I have relegated this to some muscular or joint problem. It should be readily fixable. Relieved the crisis is over, I head to the medical school, where I spend Mondays. It is the height of spring in New England. The leaves are fresh and new with the bright green of the season. The sky is clear and sharp and blue. I am relieved that winter has passed. As I drive to work I smile to myself in anticipation of the long, golden days of summer ahead. Later that day David calls after seeing Harvey Simon, his internist. Harvey had found a spot of extreme tenderness near David's shoulder and thought it was bursitis. He ordered a shoulder x-ray, which was normal, and gave David a corti-sone injection. David thinks it helps, I am relieved, though somewhere in the back of my mind, I can still hear David's cry of pain in the night. It didn't quite seem like bursitis.

The next day he sees Diane Plante, his regular physical therapist, at the hospital. "Hi, hon. It's me," says David, who always announces himself as if I wouldn't recognize his voice after thirty-eight years. "I told her about the shoulder, and she called an orthopedist that specializes in shoulders. He thinks it might be a calcium leak into the joint, which would explain the pain."

"Well, that makes sense. Those really hurt." I am relieved again.

Maybe this really can explain that awful pain. A little while later I get an e-mail from the orthopedist, Dr. Perlmutter, saying he would be happy to talk about it, so I call him. This is one of those times when it's such a gift to have easy access to colleagues and friends who are at the top of their fields.

On the phone, I briefly describe what had happened two nights before. We talk about the calcium leak hypothesis. "You know, given that he is the spouse of a physician," he says, expressing the half-believed myth that doctors' families always have unusual complications, "I'd get an MRI." It seems like a good idea, and the MRI is scheduled for the following Tuesday, a week away. There is no rush. Briefly, I wonder if he suspects something much worse than a calcium leak. I don't ask.

On Thursday, David wakes up and says, "Boy, my arms and my thighs really hurt." How does this relate to the extreme pain of Monday morning or to his localized shoulder problem? I ask him other questions, to which the answers are all no. I am perplexed. David seems otherwise well, but something is not right. I am not able to come up with a unifying hypothesis to explain his symptoms. I suggest he take ibuprofen during the day and push my vague uneasiness to the back of my mind.

By Friday night, the pain in David's arms and legs is much worse. He canceled patients in the afternoon to sleep—a very unusual behavior for him. I am mystified. His blood work was normal on Monday, except for a slight elevation of one enzyme. There was no evidence of infection, and he doesn't have any other symptoms. "It's Friday night, and I don't think there is anything to do immediately," I say, despite my growing anxiety. "This will probably just go away. There's likely nothing serious to worry about."

"I'm not going to start worrying until you do," David says, smiling at me. We are both scared and pretending not to be. I wonder why I haven't been pushing harder to find out what's going on. I feel an odd passivity, thinking I should be doing something but not knowing what. As a doctor, I have often dealt with complicated problems. I have learned not to leap to conclusions, letting a careful history and examination and tests help determine which of the many possibilities is the correct explanation. For an internist like me, this often means allowing time for symptoms to change or become more definitive in order to reveal the underlying problem. I am trying to be patient, practicing the old treatment plan of "wait and see."

Finding the right balance between being a wife and mother and being a doctor has been an issue all of my professional life. I am trying not to be David's doctor. I have asked questions, but I am trying to be a spouse. I do not want to overreact. But still, some part of me knows I am in different territory. I am frightened and unable to think clearly.

On Saturday morning, David and I come up with the idea that this is all a reaction to Lipitor, his cholesterol-lowering drug. It seems like a stretch to me, but at least it is a theory of some sort. But on Sunday, David sleeps most of the day, and I decide he needs more blood tests.

Tuesday morning we are lying in bed drinking coffee and preparing to face the day ahead. The check-in has become the beginning of every conversation. "How are you feeling?" I ask, as I did innumerable times over the past week.

"Really tired. My muscles still hurt. And there's a new wrinkle: yesterday I felt so weak, it was hard to get up the stairs." I feel a deep jolt of fear. This is something more than Lipitor or some transient muscle aches. Something progressive and serious is going on. The MRI scheduled for this afternoon seems irrelevant now. This is well beyond a shoulder problem. I say nothing to David because I don't want to worry him. So far he seems to be taking his cues from me, but there is an unusual passivity in him that bothers me.

The next morning I go off to a community-based cancer support organization where I have been teaching second-year medical students how to give bad news to cancer patients for the past eight years. I enlist the expertise of cancer patients who come to the center and who generously give their time each year for this exercise. At midday, I return to my office at Mass General. "Harvey Simon was looking for you," my secretary tells me.

He must have the MRI results, I think as I walk down the hall to his office. I don't expect it to answer any of our questions.

Harvey is with someone. While I wait for him to be free, I log onto the computer in the hall to pull up David's MRI report: "Multiple T2 hyperintense lesions measuring up to 4 cm filling the marrow consistent with metastatic disease." *Whose MRI is this?* I check the name on the report. David Treadway. I read it again. *Wait a minute. What are they talking about? This can't possibly be David. Where is the calcific bursitis? Where is the muscle tear?*

I feel my chest constrict. I can't breathe. I actually log off the computer and start all over again with the completely illogical hope that a different report is going to be there. As I read the same words over, I can't believe they are talking about David. This can't be happening. Metastatic disease means advanced cancer; incurable cancer. He will die. This can't be happening to one of my own.

I drag myself away from the computer screen and walk into an empty room, where I pace back and forth. I cannot bear to think of David, my dear husband for whom the yearly blood draw for his cholesterol is a major event, going through what medicine will put him through in an effort to buy time. I do not want him to suffer the things that I know lie ahead, much less be confronted by certain death. Then I think of our two sons, twenty-year-old Sam and twenty-seven-year-old Michael. My father's death when I was fifteen had been a devastating loss, and I'd spent most of my adult years dealing with it. This was the single event that I had prayed my whole life as a parent would never happen to my children, and now here it is. The thought is simply unbearable. And me — how can I live without this man whom I love so fiercely, whom I have known since I was eighteen; the person who supports me, who nourishes me, the one and only person on the planet on whom I am utterly dependent? It is beyond possibility.

Harvey stands at the door. "I guess you saw the report?" He is in as much shock as I am. "I went over this with the radiologists. They really don't know what it is. It is in an unusual location. In fact, they said they had never seen anything quite like it. They have no idea where the primary tumor is." In medicine one never wants to be something unusual; it is never good to be "interesting." But it was clear we were well into the very interesting and highly unusual. "To be honest, I'm not sure what the next step is." Harvey says.

We call an oncologist friend and I read him the report. "Oh, Kate, I'm really sorry to hear this. It is very unusual. I suppose renal cell could do this, or maybe a GI tumor. We need more information. He needs a PET CT scan. That should help locate a primary." Locating where this is coming from will help to know how to treat it. The PET CT is scheduled for Friday, two days from now.

All of these conversations take place in dead calm, as though we are talking about someone else, some "interesting case." I am in shock. My stomach is a clenched fist of fear. All I really want to do is find someplace to go and start screaming, but, just as patients and family often do in this setting, I maintain the appearance of calm.

"Kate, do you want to tell David, or would you rather I call him?" Harvey asks. I can't think. I want to be with him, but I don't want to tell him. It just does not feel right for me to call—I would be acting as his doctor, not his spouse. I ask Harvey to talk with him.

I cancel my afternoon. I am desperate to be home. I pull into the driveway of our antique gray colonial. A client's car is there, so I know David is still in a session. I want to run into his office and yell at them, "Don't you know he has cancer and he is going to die? Get out of here." Instead I go sit in our backyard and wait. The sun is golden through the trees, the sky crystal clear. The daffodils are out in force. Some tulips are about to bloom. How can it be so beautiful?

I hear the footsteps of his clients as they leave, and then there he is, standing in the doorway with a slight smile on his face. He is wearing a blue-and-white striped shirt and khaki pants, and in that golden light, he looks perfectly well. We look at each other and then he steps outside. "So when doctors use the term *tumor*, we're really talking cancer, aren't we?" David says lightly, still smiling.

"Yes."

He sits down next to me. We both look across the grass into the sunlight, sitting together in silence. I am thinking nothing, just being with this man whom I love so much. We are here together at the top of the roller coaster in that moment of calm before the drop. Finally David asks, "So what happens next?"

"Well, the question is: where is this coming from? They want to do a special kind of scan called a PET CT. It's scheduled for Friday morning." He doesn't ask any other questions. I am relieved. I don't want to answer questions about what this means. We decide there is no point in telling our children until we know more and have a plan.

On Friday, I take David to the PET scan area. The waiting room is cold and David asks if I can find a blanket. This from a man who is never cold, whose hands are always warm no matter what the temperature, who stands at the helm of a boat in wind and rain for hours without complaint. I find two blankets and put one across his legs and wrap the other over his shoulders. I look at my watch and realize I have to go. My first patient is already waiting. I stand in the hall looking back at him and see him suddenly as he is: tired and weak, hunched in a chair wrapped in blankets, looking years older and incredibly ill. It feels impossible to leave, but I do.

I do not know how I see patients or concentrate on their problems. It is as though I am in two parallel worlds. Part of me is seeing patients, and part of me is in a state of panic about the PET CT results. From very early in our medical education, we are trained to leave behind our own lives when we enter the examination room. So despite my panic, there is a certain comfort in being at work, some sense of the normal when my own world is falling apart.

Somehow I get through the morning. In midafternoon, I get a call from Dr. David Kuter, the oncologist on call for the weekend. I am enormously relieved that it is someone I know well and have high regard for. We were interns together twenty-seven years earlier. "Hi, Kate," Dr. Kuter begins calmly, the practiced voice of someone who has had this conversation innumerable times. "I just got through reviewing the PET scan with several radiologists. To be honest, they are all baffled. It looks as though whatever this is involves his lungs, his kidneys, his spleen, his bones, and his retroperitoneal nodes. We don't see a primary. Has he had an LDH level?" This can be elevated in lymphoma.

"No." We decide I should call David and ask him to go get this extra blood test today at an MGH satellite clinic near our house. We talk briefly about the scan. I try to be as vague as possible, and David does not push for answers. In the evening, David mentions that he has a dime-sized area of numbness on the left side of his chin.

Saturday morning, I log onto my computer to get David's blood results. His LDH is very elevated. I also read the final report on the PET CT, which was not available the night before:

Marked diffuse osseous metastatic disease.

Metastatic disease is also present in the lungs and mesentery.

No primary site is clearly identified.

Symmetric abnormal renal FDG activity, which is unusual for metastatic disease.

His kidneys are diffusely involved, and his kidney function is impaired. I call David Kuter with the LDH results.

"Well, then, it's likely this is lymphoma." He says he will arrange a bone marrow biopsy early next week. I tell him about the dime-sized area of numbness on David's face, a neurologic symptom that could mean that this disease might be in David's spinal cord or brain. I can tell he is concerned. I am, too. He tells me to call if anything changes.

The weekend crawls along. David is getting sicker. He sleeps most of the morning. When he comes downstairs he sits, saying little, looking awful, too exhausted to talk. He watches a baseball game on TV for an hour and then goes back to bed. He eats almost nothing. I am frozen with fear. On Sunday, the numbness has spread along David's lower jaw. He is even more fatigued, if that is possible. He sleeps all day. He comes down in the evening about 8 p.m. holding his jaw. He has intense pain along the lower side of his face—exactly in the location of the trigeminal nerve, which carries sensation from the face to the brain.

I put my hand on his face; his skin is hot and dry. I get a thermometer. His temperature is 102. I call David Kuter. "He needs to be admitted now," he tells me. "I know there is a bed on Ellison 14 because I just discharged a patient. Take him in and I'll arrange it."

An hour later, we walk onto Ellison 14, the cancer floor. David is taken to his room and given his hospital johnny and the inevitable forms and questions. The nurses are full of kind efficiency, gentle in their duties, smiling, though their eyes convey other knowledge. David will have an MRI of his brain sometime during the night. I stay for a few hours and then go home to our empty house. Maybe this will be my new reality in some relatively short time.

The next day I spend at David's bedside. The head MRI showed dural enhancement, meaning that the outermost covering of his brain looks abnormal and thickened, but no one knows what it means. Otherwise his brain is normal; there is no obvious explanation for his trigeminal nerve involvement.

Despite how much of David's body is involved by this disease there are no easy places to get tissue, which is needed to actually make a diagnosis. They decide to biopsy the bone marrow in his arm. Later in the day I walk behind David as he is wheeled to the procedure room for the biopsy. I am sure this is going to be painful because they are going to have to go through his humerus to get to the marrow using CT guidance to help them find the right place. David is in a fog of narcotics and anti-anxiety drugs. He is unnaturally calm, but I am intensely anxious, consumed with wanting an answer. Any answer will do, because an answer will lead to a plan, and a plan is what we need more than anything.

In the middle of the night, I wake up in a panic: I did not call my insurance company. I'm in an HMO and need approval for David's admission. I know I have good health insurance, but I am still terrified they will not cover his stay because I did not call before David was admitted. In the morning, I call as soon as I think they are open. Rather than the hassle I expect, I talk to an incredibly kind woman who assures me that everything is fine. I have nothing to worry about; it will all be covered. And then she tells me to be strong and that she hopes everything will work out. I hang up the phone astonished by how nice she was. I feel incredibly lucky not to have to worry about paying for David's care while I am so worried for his life. I cannot imagine having to worry about that on top of everything else.

We wait. Two days later Dr. Kuter calls me. "It is probably lymphoma," he says, his voice conveying his relief. "The final read will be out tomorrow." Improbable as it seems, I, too, am relieved to hear this. Lymphoma, even one this far advanced, is the only cancer that has even a small chance of being curable. Anything else this widespread might only be temporarily halted, if at all. It is the best news I can hope for, all things considered.

I dread telling our children, but it is time. The call will change everything for them. "Let's keep this simple and positive," David says.

"I agree. Do you think we should have them come home?"

"I think if they want to come they should, but I don't think they should feel they have to." My rational self agrees, but another part of me desperately wants them home.

David calls Michael. I call Sam.

◇◇◇

The next day the diagnosis is finalized: stage 4B, highly aggressive, diffuse, large B cell, non-Hodgkin's lymphoma. Stage 4 of anything is what you don't want to have. It means that the cancer has spread over many sites, and the chance of successful treatment gets lower as the stage gets higher. B means that in addition to having cancer everywhere, it has caused fever or weight loss or other overt symptoms that mean it is widespread, another marker of more advanced disease. By this time, I have begun to read the medical literature on advanced lymphoma. It is not a happy experience.

In addition to the fact that David has the worst stage, there are several other factors that make his prognosis even more dismal. From what I read last night, we will be lucky if he has a 26 percent chance of surviving. I try to tell myself that the statistics are only meaningful applied to a group, not an individual, but it is cold comfort.

It is time to transfer David's care to a lymphoma specialist. I ask David Kuter whom he would recommend. "Well, Kate," he says. "There is a wonderful young doctor who has been here at MGH for the past few years. He trained at Dana-Farber, and I really think he is excellent." The Dana-Farber Cancer Institute is an outstanding cancer center in town, and I have tremendous respect for David Kuter's opinion. I immediately find comfort in his confidence. I know what a gift this is. So many patients have to face these terrible circumstances with strangers.

Dr. Ephraim Hochberg, whom we will come to know as Effi, walks into the room. He looks incredibly boyish, a look reinforced by his white coat, which is too short in the sleeves. He sits at the end of David's bed. Dr. Kuter is standing slightly behind him, and I am sitting near David's head, facing them. David has his now familiar, somewhat vacant, drugged expression. He looks at Effi and says without preamble, "I want to know the best-case scenario and the worst-case scenario."

As a doctor, the thought of answering that question from a patient he just met and in the presence of a senior colleague makes me cringe. I watch this young man to whom I am entrusting my husband's life. I can barely breathe. He leans forward and says earnestly, "Well, this is not a conversation I usually have on a first meeting. I, ah . . ." I am sure he fervently hopes that David will let it pass.

David doesn't. "Look, I get that this is really difficult, but I will do better with the hard and cold facts. Even if they're bad." Propped up in the hospital bed, David is trying to be brave, but I know he doesn't have a clue about what is going on and probably won't take in much of what

Effi says. I realize it is going to be my job to help David understand his situation. And my job to protect him from knowing what the rest of us in the room know altogether too well: how difficult and torturous this disease and treatment might be.

Effi takes a deep breath and says, "There's a new drug called Rituxan, which will be given to you six times with a cocktail of other medications that we call CHOP, so the combination is called CHOP-R. This can be incredibly effective with this kind of cancer, so there's a chance that you could be cured. Of course, there are some people who either aren't responsive to that drug or their bodies can't tolerate it, in which case we would try other kinds of chemo, which might be less effective. Usually the treatments lead to a remission, but if there is a recurrence, then we will do a different kind of intensive treatment. And, of course, there's a small possibility that you won't respond to treatment and—"

"What then?" interrupts David.

"Well," hems Effi. "In some cases, I guess that means some people die. Truthfully, it means you could die."

"Thanks." David gives him a weak grin, "You passed the first test with me."

"How so?"

"I don't feel like you bullshitted me. I'm a shrink. I needed to get a read on you."

I breathe a sigh of relief. Effi had given him the respect and honesty that was so important to David. His face relaxes as he settles back into his pillows. I can tell he is relieved about Effi becoming his doctor, as am I. It isn't just David's life we are putting into his hands. It is all of ours.

In the late afternoon, I leave the hospital and head for the train station. Michael wanted to come home, and I'm going to pick him up. Thank God he is coming. I want to be there to help him through this, and I know his presence will be a comfort for me. Driving along the river, the sun filters through the trees and shimmers off the water. The light is golden. I can't believe its still spring.

Sam

I AM HEADING TO THE REC CENTER ON THIS BEAUTIFUL WEDNESDAY afternoon with one thing on my mind: girls. I hate them. Okay, being a heterosexual twenty-year-old male, I obviously don't hate them. Actually, I'm obsessed with them. Three of them, to be exact.

First there is Sarah, my girlfriend. We've been together for a year and half, and she's been a life-saver through college. She essentially is my whole world. Besides her and my roommate, Kurt, I've made few really good friends here. I adore Sarah, but there is trouble ahead. I am a junior at Carleton, and she is a senior, soon to be graduated. Now here's the quandary I'm mulling in my mind today: what do you do in a relationship when it looks like it's coming to a natural ending point? Do you:

> (a) end it on good terms, try and to stay in contact, but slowly drift off into a superficial friendship because you're living in different places and living different lives?
> (b) be indecisive about what to do next and end up increasingly agitated with one another because of your uneasiness with the situation?
> (c) force the relationship to continue, even though all signs point to ending?

Naturally, option (a) is out because it's way too logical and mature. I've chosen (b), and Sarah is all about (c). You can see why we might have some problems.

For the sake of keeping us together, Sarah has volunteered to live in Northfield for a year while I finish school. Her family lives in L.A., which is a much more exciting place than Northfield, Minnesota, where the town motto is "Cows, Colleges, and Contentment." (It's too good for me to make it up!) Except for its two colleges, St. Olaf and Carleton, Northfield is a typical small Midwestern town where everyone is very polite at four-way stops. It's one claim to fame is that it's the site of the Jesse James Gang's last robbery.

The second girl on my mind is Lisa. She is the main reason

I'm going into the gym to work on my abs. I'm going to see her this weekend. Lisa was, is, and probably always will be the love of my life, though I have no clue why. I had a crush on her in high school, and then we became friends. When we talk, the sexual tension—for me at least—is through the roof. For her, talking to me seems to rate up there with washing the dishes. She tells me everything, unfortunately, including her most intimate secrets about the boys she's dated. Yeah, I'm *that* friend.

The third and final girl who occupies obsession time in my brain is Kat, a friend of a friend. She represents all the girls in this world I can't have. She's a beautiful, fun party girl and smart enough to be going to one of the best liberal arts schools in the country. Way out of my league. On the occasions she gives me the chance to talk to her, all sorts of flirting goes on. She even told me once that she had a crush on me freshman year. But now she has a boyfriend. And I, of course, have Sarah.

Pondering girls takes a lot out of a guy. What's the point of even bothering with the gym? Oh, thank God, my cell phone's ringing. Maybe someone wants to go grab a late lunch with me. But no, it's my mom. Were cell phones created just so moms could keep track of their children?

"Hey, Mom."

"Hi, honey." She sounds strange. "Where are you?"

"I'm outside the rec center. Why?"

"I have some distressing news."

"What's up?" My mom sounds very worried, but I remain nonchalant. There is a broad range of possibilities that could be distressing. She could have had a car accident, or maybe Michael broke up with Kristin—or worse, he hasn't.

"Your dad has been diagnosed with lymphoma."

She just says it. No beating around the bush. "Like, cancer?"

"Yes, about two weeks ago he woke up with pain and—"

I can't listen to her. My dad has cancer. "Is he going to be ok?"

"He's starting treatment this weekend. And he—"

"Should I come home? I could catch a flight tonight."

"No, no honey, that's all right, but if you did have time to fly home this weekend, that'd be nice. Your brother has decided to come up this weekend. It will be your dad's first dose of chemotherapy."

"This weekend? All my high school friends and I are supposed to go to New Orleans, but, of course I can come home." I say the right things, but I'm thinking about missing out on New Orleans. I can't believe I'm thinking that.

"What? New Orleans?" My mom blurts out.

"Didn't Dad tell you? I told him last week. It's Jared's graduation."

"No, Sam, he didn't tell me. But he's been very sick for two weeks now."

Jesus, this must be really serious. "But he's going to be okay, right?"

"Well, there's this new kind of drug that can be incredibly effective, and your dad has an excellent chance . . ."

Nothing sinks in. I want to talk to Sarah. I want to pretend none of this is happening. I want to see Lisa this weekend. I need to talk to my brother. He's going home this weekend? When did he hear the news? "Wait, Mom," I interrupt her. "When did Michael find out about this? Why haven't you told me? I talked to Dad on Sunday, and he said everything was fine!"

"We didn't want to alarm you. Your father called Michael earlier today."

She's on the brink of tears. My mom, the doctor, is on the brink of tears. This isn't good. "Mom, I already have the tickets to New Orleans. I can change them if I need to, but I'd rather not. I'm going to be home in a few weeks anyway. If Dad's going to be all right till then, then that should be okay, right?"

"I guess so, sweetie. I'll talk it over with your father." This obviously wasn't the answer she was expecting or wanted. "But I don't want you to worry about not seeing him. He's not going to die soon."

He'll be fine. I know it. I try to conjure up a picture of my dad being really sick, and I can't. I'm going to go have fun this weekend. And then I'll finish school. And then I'll be home all summer. Why make myself crazy with worry? I tell Mom I love her and that I will talk to her soon. Then I walk into the rec center, ready for a thorough, kick-ass workout. I want to feel some muscle burn.

The next day my dad calls. He doesn't sound that bad at all. He says he's doing fine. He tells me that he definitely wants me to go to New Orleans. Everything is going to be all right, he says. If that's the case, I guess it's okay to meet up with my friends. When I get off the phone with him I try to ignore my guilt for not going home. Instead I think about my upcoming weekend. I'm headed for New Orleans!

17

Michael

I AM WAITING OUTSIDE THE NEW ROCHELLE TRAIN PLATFORM ON A HOT afternoon in mid-May, pacing the narrow cement corridor. Dad told me about his condition less than twenty-four hours ago, and I decided to take the train up to see him before his first chemo treatment begins. The train is late. I repeatedly call Amtrak for updates, engaging in long, one-sided conversations with Amtrak's automated computer, "Julie." Pressing my phone tightly against the side of my face, I carefully enunciate each question: "CUR-RENT STA-TUS?" Julie patiently explains to me that my train has already left Penn Station, that it is between twenty minutes and two hours late, and that there is no more information at this time.

The sun is high, and one of my would-be fellow passengers is lazily fanning himself with a folded magazine. I walk laps around the platform guided by the yellow lines on the concrete that mark off the areas where I shouldn't walk. I don't know what to think of my father's cancer, his prognosis, or the consequences. My father primarily talked about going through chemo and losing his hair. My mother attempted to brief me on the positive and negative aspects of his diagnosis. It is stage 4 cancer (bad), but likely to be lymphoma (good), but the presentation is atypical (bad), and the inflammation of the dura mater may suggest involvement of the central nervous system (very bad).

Between my phone calls to Amtrak's automated Julie are calls to my mother, during which we reassure each other by discussing my travel plans: making guesses at how late the train will actually be, reviewing how I will get from the station to the hospital ("Will it be faster if I take a cab?" "Depends on when you get in." "Maybe you should just walk." "Forget it. I'll just pick you up."), repeating jokes already made several times about the situation, the train, anything, until concluding that we have exhausted any reason to stay on the phone. After we hang up, Mom returns to avoiding her deskwork, and I call Julie again. I would rather stay on the line with my mother, even if only in silence, holding the phone as if I could put my arms around her, than return to the concrete desolation of the train platform.

The train station is familiar to me, having moved to New Rochelle from Manhattan less than a year ago. Every day I spend an hour on the train commuting to and from Columbia University, where I have been working as a research assistant. The decision to live outside the city was not entirely my own. It was part of a compromise with Kristin, my girlfriend, who needed a place closer to Connecticut.

Kristin and I dated for only six months before we decided to move in together, which has been a mistake. After almost ten months of rocky cohabitation, Kristin and I both wanted to end the relationship but were equally unable to summon the will to leave.

Then came the phone call from my father, who gently described his diagnosis. As I listened, I felt very calm and very small. I relayed the news. Kristin listened with her head down, her large hazel eyes focused on the floor, her hands held tightly between her thighs. As I began to cry, she approached me awkwardly. Her arms around me felt strained and unsure.

I think we both instantly recognized that this family crisis would provide the opportunity for the clean break we had been waiting for. We could leave without ever having to admit to one another how bleak our relationship had become. I would be the dutiful son moving back to Boston to be close to his father, and she would be the generous lover, understanding that this was best for me and my family. We would exchange warm hugs and gracious words and then disappear.

Being really disappointed in the person I was in my relationship with Kristin, it's reassuring to know I can be there for my father. I know how to give him love—we have always been close. I'll be free to love him with open abandon. Despite my terror at my father's illness, when I board the train I feel an odd sense of relief.

I doze through most of train ride as it wends its way up the New England coast, passing through New London, Kingston, and Providence before arriving in Boston. When I arrive, Mom picks me up, we have a long hug, and then we head over to MGH, where Mom's always worked and now Dad is a patient. As we get to the bustling main entrance, she turns to me again, and I throw my arms around her. We hold each other for a long time. "Are you ready to see your dad?" she finally asks. I nod, suddenly aware that I wanted to see him desperately. We walk slowly to the elevator.

When I walk into the hospital room, I barely recognize Dad. He looks sunken into the bed, like a statue carved in partial relief. His normally tan skin is pale and ghostly, with a tinge of green. His eyes are listless, and his cheeks hang slack, making his face seem pinched and contorted. "Hi, Mike. Good to see you," he says vacantly. He's not himself. Normally he's incredibly attuned to others around him.

"Hiya, Pops," I say with a weak smile. "How are you doin'?"

A nurse walks in.

"This sucks," he says as he turns his attention to the nurse. The nurse wanted to remind Dad about his next blood draw. He nods and then looks away.

"Are you nervous about the chemo?" I ask, searching for something to say.

"No." He closes his eyes. My dad has always been generous in his attention and concern for others. I never really thought about it as something he did or something that might have been effortful; it was just who he was. His eyes usually cast a warm glow over you as he listened. It was easy to feel his caring presence. That presence isn't there now.

We stay for a few hours, and say little. Mostly, I just want to hug my dad, but I can't. Around nine o'clock we go back to our house in Weston—the house where I grew up—and make some dinner. My mom and I discuss my plans. I will return to New Rochelle on Monday, begin packing up and then move back home to Boston in a few weeks. Mom mentions that Sam will be driving across the country around that time. She suggests that he could meet me in New York to help with the move. Soon afterward, Mom goes to bed. It has been a long time since I've seen her look as tired as she did today.

I sit alone in our family room. It's a big room with high ceilings and large bay windows looking out onto the yard. On the mantle of the fireplace is a hollow glass cylinder filled with seashells that my mom collected on beaches when we were young. I should call Kristin, but I don't really want to. I feel very alone. There is a leaden feeling in my chest that is hard to identify. I flip through the movie channels and find nothing to distract me. All I can think is that I'm not ready to lose my dad; there's so much I haven't said to him. I go to my suitcase and grab my laptop. I sit down and begin to write.

David

MICHAEL LOOKS AT ME IN MY HOSPITAL BED. HE HAS A TWO-DAY growth of beard, his blond hair looks unkempt, and his eyes are filled with fear and love. "I wrote something for you, Dad. I'd like to read it to you, but I don't have to now if you're not up for it. I mean, if you're not feeling okay enough." He's taken time off from work and the train up from New York to be with me yesterday when I started chemotherapy. I'm still a mess from my initial severe reaction to chemo. I had a violent response to Rituxan, a recently developed drug that might be effective but not everyone can tolerate. Despite being quite ill, I got through my first treatment.

"Not to worry," I say to Michael, worried myself that I'm too drugged, too numb to be able to respond to him. Ever since I entered the hospital, I've been poked and prodded, just a limp body carted back and forth on a stretcher from PET scans to CAT scans and MRIs. I'm in a haze of disbelief, disassociation, and pain meds, exhausted from the chemo, but I've got to rally. Michael wants so much to reach me, love me. I want him to feel good about this letter he wants to read me. He looks at me anxiously, and I remember when he was seven years old and gave me a picture he painted of my sailboat. He'd been so proud and shy, leaning over my shoulder as I unwrapped it. "Do you like it, Dad?"

Now, twenty years later, the little boy has morphed into the young man with kind blue eyes and a furrowed brow by my bed. After all the years of my being his cheerleader, sounding board, and giver of advice, here Michael is, earnestly wanting to switch roles and take care of me. I doubt anything he can say will touch me at all, but at least I can show him appreciation for his effort. I ramp up my bed. "Go ahead, Mike, I really want to hear the letter."

"You're sure?"

"Yup." He begins to read.

To my father on the day after his first chemotherapy treatment

Dad,
Slowly I have tried to make sense of the dim noises that have echoed in the back of my mind since last Wednesday. Mostly, there has been

a thick, deadening fog. At other times, all the terror and fear of your sudden departure from this earth grabs me with full force. I find myself focusing on memories of the way I used to experience your presence when I was a child. I know that in the past, I have painted some bleak pictures of my childhood and our relationship at that time. But now what I remember most is your calm, your strength, and your warmth.

Most of my images of you are not of particular times, places, or events. They are simply recollections of the tenderness of your hand holding mine or the compassion in your eyes. I remember so often hearing your voice as you entered your bedroom, long after I was supposed to be asleep. Just knowing you were home made the darkness around me turn into a warm blanket.

To realize I might lose the person in these memories is what I have now been forced to face. Of course, this has always been the reality, but it seemed incomparably remote. Even if our prayers are answered, and you receive a full cure, this new reality will not change. I hope that life is kind enough to treat this whole thing as a warning and then give me back my dad. But either way, I want you to know now how grateful I am for you, for your life, for your friendship, and for the privilege of being your son.

I love you, Pops,
Michael

He looks at me, tears in his eyes. My chest heaves, and I start sobbing. "Oh, Dad." Michael clambers onto the bed like a little boy. But he's not. He's a man, a man who takes me in his arms and holds me. My heart breaks open. After a long time, I lie back on the bed and smile at him.

"Are you okay?" he asks.

"Not really. But I am really glad you're here."

SUMMER 2005

Sam

"HONEY, I JUST DON'T KNOW IF THIS IS REALLY WHAT YOU WANT TO write," my mom says over the phone. She's talking about my submission for Dad's big birthday present. Instead of a birthday party for my sick father, mom's been collecting letters and pictures from all his friends and family to put in a book for him. "It's sweet and nice, but I think you want it to be a little more serious. Say what you truly feel, maybe not in poem form."

"You didn't give me a lot of time, and I'm dealing with finals right now." I punch the air as if she can see my gestures. "You told everyone to write something about Dad, right? This works. And it's even funny. What's wrong with it?"

"Well, first of all, it seems more about me than your dad. And I think it's not quite the tone that other people have been writing."

"It's the best I can do right now. That's all I'm writing."

"Well, I just hope you'll give it a little more thought."

After the usual niceties, I get off the phone, but I'm still pissed. What does she expect? She tells me not to worry, to focus on finishing my finals, and then she gets all like that with me. I just can't get things right with her! My little poem might be kind of lame, but it is the best I could do in the half hour I spent on it. And now I'm stuck trying to rationalize that that is all I need to do.

I pace in the small space in my room between the bunk bed, desks, chairs, and heater kicking dirty clothes in annoyance. I climb onto the top bunk, take a deep breath, and try to see things from my mom's point of view. She's probably scared about Dad. She's a doctor, so she has seen cancer before. And her mother died of lung cancer. I know she just wants me to get in touch with my feelings about Dad. Uggghh.

I hate "getting in touch with my feelings." My mom is almost worse than my dad when it comes to wanting me to "really talk" about things. When she asks how I'm doing, she always expects me to recite all the issues I'm facing, what they mean to me, and how they make me feel. Instead, I close up and just say that I'm fine and don't want to talk about it. It doesn't help that my brother has graduated from the residual teenage anger phase. At least once a week he talks to Mom or Dad and sometimes both of them on the phone at the same time! In comparison, I look like a jerk, when really I'm more in touch with my feelings than most kids I know. I'm like a psychologist for all my friends, able to evaluate their relationships and give them advice. If only I could communicate my self-awareness to my feelings-hungry parents.

Now my mom wants me to put touchy-feely thoughts on the page and write something meaningful for Dad's birthday. The guy has cancer. I wish he didn't, but he does. Nothing I do is going to change that fact. What's the point of worrying? I'll deal with his illness when I get home. Right now I have to focus on school.

I need to make a to-do list. I look over at my desk. The papers, books, and odds and ends look like a pile of knocked-down bowling pins waiting to be mechanically reorganized. No matter how many times I rearrange it, it always explodes, like a perfect strike. I stretch over the edge of the bed to reach a pen and some paper on my desk. After discarding eight pens that don't have ink and finding three pieces of paper unsuitable for a to-do list (I'm oddly finicky about the way my to-do lists look), and after almost falling off the bed twice (it would make too much sense to actually get down from the top bunk), I finally get settled and write my list.

To Do
- Differential Equations final (hard)
- Presentation for History of Math
- Complex Numbers (not till Monday)
- Bartend at the Tavern on Thursday and Friday night
- Help Sarah move to her new Northfield apartment
- Store everything I don't need for the summer
- Pick Moses up from the airport
- Watch Sarah graduate
- Pack the car

The first three items make me cringe. This term has been a constant reminder of my bad choice of a major. At the end of sophomore year, math was the only subject I had taken more than one class in, and I had done pretty well in the calculus series. I thought it would be easier to stay with math than scramble to figure out another major. I tend to take the easy way out, but now I'm stuck taking three math classes this term. I wish there were enough time left to change my major, but that would be a lot of work. Hence, the easy choice of sticking with math. The wise choices, I'm finding, are rarely the easiest ones.

At least I made the wise decision to help Sarah move and stay here to watch her graduate. She doesn't graduate until a week after the term ends, so she appreciates that I'm sticking around after all my friends leave for home. Unfortunately, they leave right before my twenty-first birthday, which lands on my dad's sixtieth. It's been frustrating, sharing the same birth date with my father. Birthdays should be the one day of the year when it's all about the birthday boy. A day of special breakfasts, special presents, and special parties. Instead, when I was little I resented sharing the attention with my dad, having to think about gifts for him while I contemplated what I would receive. This year is no different, dealing with that poem.

David

KATE AND I ARE CURLED UP TOGETHER ON THE SOFA, PRETENDING TO watch TV on my first night home from the hospital. I am wearing a wool nightshirt, socks, slippers, and a heavy winter bathrobe. It is 80 degrees outside. Every few minutes one of us asks, "Do you think we should check it again?" We agree to wait a few more minutes. Finally she pops the thermometer in my mouth. 100 degrees. We both sigh, having dodged another bullet. At 100.5, my temperature would be considered an emergency and I would have to go back to the hospital.

I desperately don't want to go back to MGH. The twelve days there are a blur. I remember a nurse holding my hand and stroking my forehead during a difficult spinal tap. I was crying and she cooed to me as if she were soothing a two-year-old. A few days later, I had my terrible response to the Rituxan; my temperature spiked to 105 and my blood pressure skyrocketed. I became delirious. Kate and Michael were visiting, and I heard one of them say "oo-be-joo-be-woo-be" and laugh. I accused them of making fun of me, but Kate and Michael patiently insisted that it was actually me who had said "oo-be-joo-be-woo-be." I angrily denied that and retreated into a sulky silence.

"If I have to go back to the hospital, I'll just have to find a way to kill myself," I said.

"Not to worry, honey, I'll do it for you." Kate said, teasingly.

We limbo under the 100.5 bar all evening.

The next day I am standing at the sink, just out of a hot bath, looking at my scrawny body in the mirror. I have lost fifteen pounds in two weeks. I feel hot and dizzy. Suddenly I am falling into the tub. On the way down, I smash my forehead on something. I end up lying with my head and torso facedown in the tub, my pelvis balanced on the rim, and my bare butt poking up in the air.

"Kate!!!" I scream. "Kate!!!"

She is there in seconds. She pulls me up and walks me toward our bed. I am incoherent, trying to tell her what happened. Halfway across the room, I pitch forward. Kate can't hold onto me, and I fall smack on my face. I desperately try to keep my eyes open and talk, with the wild idea that as long as I can see and talk, I won't die. Kate quickly takes my blood pressure—70 over 40. She looks scared, which scares the hell out of me.

"It's not good but not likely to be fatal. Just lie still. I'm going to get some tomato juice. The potassium and salt might bring up your pressure."

"Let me get this straight, I'm dying and you want to give me tomato juice. What's this, a Campbell's commercial?"

"Hush yourself. If you're making dumb jokes, you're hardly dying."

The tomato juice works. Kate hauls me into bed and calls the emergency room. She and her colleague decide the tomato juice treatment, though somewhat unconventional, is probably better than waiting for hours in the emergency room, as long as Kate keeps a close eye on me.

"I can't believe how lucky I am to have you," I whisper.

She is looking at my head. "Wow, you've got a big goose egg on your forehead right above your left eye." She touches it.

"Ow! Stop that!"

"You must have smacked into the soap dish on the way down. There's no blood or discoloration. It's just swollen."

I touch it gingerly. It feels like the size of a golf ball, "This isn't going to look so great for the Lancaster workshop."

"Honey, I wouldn't count on you being able to lead a full two-day training just two weeks from now. You just might not be well enough."

"I've got to be able to do it. There are two hundred people signed up."

"You're only going to do it if Effi okays it." Kate says firmly.

◇◇◇

A week after falling, I am sitting on the porch off our kitchen on a warm early summer evening. Despite the lack of attention, our yard looks resplendent with tulips, rhododendron, and azaleas in bloom. The yard looks bright and fresh. Today is June 8, my sixtieth birthday and Sam's twenty-first. Kate is bustling about in the kitchen fixing my birthday dessert. Sam will be partying hard with his friends tonight out at Carleton. Legally.

Earlier in the day I went into town to the Masterworks Hair Design. "So what can I do you for, Dr. Treadway?" asked Renee, my hairdresser. She sounded more chipper than usual. I could tell that she had noted how pale and sickly I look.

"Here's the deal. I'm going to have to have a lot of chemotherapy, and all my hair is going to fall out, so I thought I'd get it over with rather than wake up with it every morning on my pillow. Today's my birthday, and this is my treat. Let's take it off. All of it. Michael Jordan me."

"You mean you want me to shave it?" she asked incredulously.

"Actually, don't go that far. Just a Marine buzz cut will do."

I sat there with my eyes closed as she ran the razor over my head. I hadn't been given a crew cut since I was ten. I liked the idea of a preemptive strike against the debilitating effects of the chemo. It felt a little like Doolittle's raid on Japan after Pearl Harbor. Didn't mean a thing militarily, but at least it was us on the attack. For a moment sitting in the chair, I felt my scrawny ten-year-old self sitting up straight, squaring his shoulders, squinting off into the distance, trying to be John Wayne tough.

"So there you go," said Renee as she shook my gray clippings out of the cape she'd fastened around my neck. "How do you like yourself so far?"

As I paused to contemplate the unintended enormity of her question, she moved on breezily and said, "I have a friend who has breast cancer, and she's done really well with the chemo and wears scarves instead of a wig, which works for her. You're lucky. You have a nice-shaped head. Besides, Nikki said that the nausea from the chemo wasn't half as bad as morning sickness. So you'll be fine. But since it's your birthday, why don't you consider this as on the house? My treat."

Renee has been cutting my hair for twenty years. I turned toward her and looked into her big brown eyes. They held such concern and kindness. I turned away hurriedly. "Best birthday present ever," I mumbled back at her. "Here, let me at least give you a tip."

"Nah, not on your life. You just get well soon, you hear."

Like Renee, my friends and clients have been solicitous and sweet, and I am soaking it in. The love and kindness comes in cards and flowers, meals, and e-mails and phone calls. It buoys me up as if I were wearing a life preserver. Even when people do say dumb things like, "I know you'll beat this thing because you have such positive energy," I don't mind. They are trying the best they can. Each gesture is a moment of grace.

When I get home, I take a nap. Kate has rushed home to do the birthday dinner and is already frazzled and out of sorts. I can hear her in the kitchen fussing under her breath about the "goddamn pie crust" and the burnt butter. Normally, I would jump up to offer help, but I just want to go back to bed. I couldn't care less about blueberry pie and Häagen-Dazs vanilla ice cream, my favorite dessert. How are we going to make it through the time ahead, if this is just the beginning? Kate slips the pie into the oven and yells out that she is going upstairs to change before giving me some birthday cards.

I was supposed to have a big sixtieth birthday bash tonight. We planned to invite friends from every stage of my life to a square dance. It was going to be great.

Suddenly, I remember my fifth birthday party. It was during the more stable time in my family, before my mother's smile made me wince and wonder. Long before the silences and the pretending everything was okay. Long before my family's descent into alcoholism, mental illness, and, finally, her suicide.

Back in 1950, we were the only family in Sturbridge, MA, with our own swimming pool. All my friends from kindergarten had come for a pool party. I remember my delight with my birthday present, which stood next to the pool: a green Schwinn bike with no training wheels. A big-boy bike. Before the cake and ice cream, we were supposed to dive for pennies in the shallow end of the pool. My mother had lent my bathing trunks to a boy who had forgotten his. She told me that I would have to go in with just my white jockey shorts on. "You're the host," she said, with a cajoling smile. "You don't want Sammy to be uncomfortable, do you?"

"But, Mom, everything will show once I get wet."

"Honey, trust me, nobody cares. It's just little boy bits. I bet they don't even notice."

"But there'll be girls, too."

"Do what you want, David," she said dismissively as she stood up. "After all, it's your birthday. You don't have to go into the pool at all if you're too shy."

In the water, my underwear became completely transparent. When I got out, everybody looked at me down there. Even my mother. I could tell.

I am lost in this painful memory when Kate comes out to the porch with cards and a large, gift-wrapped present. "Hey," I say, "I thought we agreed to skip presents given everything that's been going on."

She gives me a coy smile. "Well, it's just one."

In the box is a green, leather-bound binder embossed with "David C. Treadway June 8, 2005" in gold lettering. My hand trembles as I open it. It's filled with pictures of me going back to infancy, with Kate and the kids, letters from a lifetime of friends and family, favorite poems and quotations. It holds my life on its pages. The letters share funny anecdotes, startling affirmations, and declared love. Tears run down my face as I read every word. Believing that I really matter to other people has been a challenge for me my whole life. I look up at Kate. "I have never felt so known and loved in all my life. I am speechless."

"Well, honey, it's about time you figured out that you really matter to a whole bunch of people. And we all want you to be well." She reaches across the table and takes my hand. "Starting with me." She watches as I read through the pages, each letter from family and friends filled with teasing humor and declared love.

"The whole thing is amazing, Kate. It's the best birthday present I have ever received." I reread the letter from my friend Barry out loud:

I discovered the essential David on the tennis court. It was the second time we played—after exchanging a few witticisms ahead of time. The air was a little cool, we thought, but nothing that wouldn't yield to some manly motion and sweat. We began by whaling the ball at each other. This seemed good. A worthy opponent, serious and competitive but not mean, applauding good shots of mine and clearly appreciating his own.

Then it began to snow, a sign for sane people to step off the ever more slippery courts. Not us. Without so much as a word, we just continued. As the snow grew more intense, so did our tennis, as though we might not have another chance for ages to come, and so did our laughter. We laughed at our silliness—secretly thinking we weren't really silly, just strong and determined. We laughed at the beautiful scene. The sheer exuberance of it all was almost perfect. And we laughed because we had the first inkling that we had found in each other, true companions.

We've played—

"Sorry to interrupt your reading, birthday boy, but I've got to get to the dishes."

"You know what's amazing? Barry's one of the few who actually mentions the cancer. It's just like our good WASP friends to not mention the rather gigantic elephant in the room. And yet, I can still feel their caring and worry for me. I have to say I really like Barry's directness. By the way, Barry and I are going to the tennis court this weekend. Even if I can barely stand up and it only lasts for five minutes. It's my version of raging against the dying of the light. And he gets it."

Kate smiles and pats my newly bald head as she gets up. Bending down to kiss me, she says, "I know, dear, and some of us just think you're nuts. So it's good you have Barry."

Later that night, Kate lies curled up beside me, gently snoring. I listen to the whoosh of the occasional car going by on our street. The moon lights the shade and I can see silhouettes of branches and leaves moving in the breeze. I return over and over to the outpouring of affection I received. Each of the letters was so loving. Like eulogies, I think. Reading the book felt a little like I was attending my own funeral.

My thoughts turn dark and I imagine my life summarized, acknowledged, even wept over; people kicking the dirt off their shoes as they get back into their cars, murmuring regrets before turning to other questions of the day. That beautiful book is the sum of my life. And not even accurate, of course. Every contributor focused on the best of who I am, leaving out the countless ways that I had been a difficult or disappointing presence in their lives. *Get off the pity pot, boy*, I scold myself. *People are trying to love you as best they can. Let it in.* But I can't. Death feels near. Like the roar of a huge waterfall, it drowns out the love of others.

One summer years ago I sailed across the Atlantic Ocean alone. On one stormy night, I lay in my bunk, filled with a cold, creeping fear, and listened to the boat crashing through the seas. I was listening for something wrong, for something breaking. I wondered if I should go up on deck, look around, and check the sails. The night seemed so long. I snuggled down in my sleeping bag, waiting for sleep or the first hint of light on the horizon while I listened to the rush of the big waves rising behind me. Now, lying in bed next to Kate, I remember the darkness and the waiting and the being alone. It is going to be a long, long night.

Dawn doesn't bring much relief. I am still seeing clients, so I get ready for work. "And how are you?" used to be my greeting to clients. Now it belongs to them. When I open the door to the waiting room, Sandy and Eliot jump to their feet, startled like all my clients by the sight of me. As if they'd seen a ghost.

"How are you?" Sandy asks in hushed tones, like they are visiting me at the hospital. Ever since I got sick, she's been solicitous of me. A soccer mom in her forties, Sandy is a perky, attractive ex-cheerleader type. Despite three kids, she is in great shape and very pretty without appearing to be wearing any makeup. Elliot is a lawyer at one of the old-line Boston firms. He is dressed in a suit and wearing a jaunty bow tie that belies his somewhat reserved personality. They're here because Sandy is hurt and disappointed that Elliot doesn't seem to have the slightest interest in a sexual life.

I give them as concise and optimistic report as I can.

"Dr. Treadway, it just doesn't seem right for us to launch into our difficulties around intimacy when you're dealing with something really enormous. Our issues seem so petty, by comparison," says Sandy in a hushed tone.

It is true, I think. But what my clients don't know is what lifesavers they are. They don't know that I spend the hours between sessions in bed, dozing when I can, but mostly staring at the ceiling, wishing I could enjoy what may be my last summer. Sometimes I review my whole catalog of regrets, remorse, disappointments about myself as father, husband, therapist, son, brother, man, citizen of the human race. You name it. My clients are a huge distraction from that. It is better to be mucking about in their sex lives than drowning in my fears and failures

"Listen, guys, my illness does put regular everyday problems in perspective. Hopefully, you can utilize that awareness to be more tender and appreciative toward each other. But the other lesson is that my office should be the one place where you feel like you can truly open up about the pain you carry and the struggles you have." I pause. "And besides, while we're having this conversation about whether my cancer is more important than your issues, how many children on the planet have died of starvation just in the last few minutes? Everything really is relative."

"Thanks for the food for thought, Dr. Treadway. Now I *really* don't want to talk about sex!" Elliot laughs.

Starving kids? What am I thinking?

My clients also distract me from how worried I am about Kate, Michael, and Sam. One of the things I love most about Kate is that she is an absolutely straight shooter, incapable of dissembling. You always know where you stand with her. Unfortunately, that means that her efforts to shield me from her worries don't work at all. Despite trying to sound positive, it is pretty clear that she is very pessimistic about my chances. She tries to reassure me, but she sometimes gets lost in her own anxiety about going on without me. Over our thirty-eight years together, we have become incredibly emotionally dependent on each other. Kate doesn't have a coterie of close, intimate friends. I am it for her, not just husband but also best friend, as she is for me. It is disconcerting when we try to talk about what we each are going through. My core issues are worries about what will happen to her, Michael, and Sam, fear of pain, and to a lesser degree the likelihood that I probably won't live out the year. That is tough for her to take. She is not focused just on losing me but also on going on alone and trying to be strong for the boys.

To cope with all this, I have insisted on our using the "taking turns" technique that I teach the couples I treat. So we set aside regular, scheduled time when each of us has a turn exploring our feelings, fears, and frustrations with each other. The other just listens and tries to understand and be as empathic as possible. Kate doesn't much care for what she calls my "therapy gimmicks," but having cancer gives me a little extra persuasiveness. She humors me.

One morning after the birthday, we are in bed. It is her turn to talk. "I'll be like Mother after Daddy died. She was so lonely. I won't be able to stand it." She starts to cry. I reach over and put my arms around her. "And I know that I will just come home to this house and I won't know what to do with myself. I can't imagine doing anything but getting into bed and then," she gulps, "and then, you won't be there." She starts sobbing. I feel like I am holding that fifteen-year-old girl whose daddy has just died. I ache for her. I stroke her hair, murmuring acknowledgments.

"And what's worse is you're the only one who I would want to talk to about this." She lets her feelings come out without worrying about me. And I hold her and love her without worrying about me, either. It isn't my turn. The two of us are paying attention to one of us at a time. My time will come later.

The thought of my sons losing a parent early haunts me. My mother killed herself when I was twenty, and Kate's dad died of a heart attack when she was fifteen. Neither of us had a chance to say good-bye. We have either grieved (Kate) or avoided grief (me) our whole lives.

Michael and Sam are responding in different ways to my illness. Michael is scared and solicitous. He has always relied on me for emotional support and advice. Most of the time, Sam is frustrated by me, impatient with my idiosyncratic habits and endless efforts to help him manage his life better. Sam retreats into humor and optimism and very determined denial.

I have difficulty focusing on my own circumstances. My denial is of the Alfred E. Newman, "What? Me worry?" variety. But I am really afraid about Kate and the boys not being able to go on well in their lives. I feel a desperate determination that we all somehow work through my death together in advance. I know my death will leave gaping holes in their lives, but I want to make sure they will feel the strength and resilience and support from each other to carry on. I don't want them to be crippled by my death. Somehow we have to live as well as we can, loving each other as best we can, and ready ourselves to let go and move on as best we can if I die. I pray I will have enough time to help them be prepared for the worst. Enough time to truly say good-bye.

Michael

WHEN I ARRIVE AT THE PARTY, I IMMEDIATELY REGRET COMING. IT'S filled with people from high school I haven't seen in years. I offered to skip the party. Twice. But my parents insisted I go, arguing that it was important for me to take a break and try to enjoy myself. After a few greetings, I make my way through Doug's apartment to the back porch, where a cluster of people are standing by the grill. I cringe in anticipation.

"Is that Mike Treadway?" cries out Alex, a classmate a few years older than me. He is the gregarious type: a popular, easygoing jokester whose social skills I had admired in high school. In other words, he is the last type of person I would want to bump into at this party. The group turns and looks. I recognize a few faces and smile awkwardly.

Ever since I moved back home from New Rochelle, I have been anxious about running into old friends and acquaintances. I have always been preoccupied with being a big success story. When I graduated from college in 2000, working at a dot-com seemed to be a good way to get on the fast track. At the time, it didn't even really matter to me what the company did, as long as I seemed like a success. There hadn't really been anything I *wanted* to do, other than to be impressive.

But now, at twenty-seven, I'm living at home again, between careers and unemployed. To compensate, I often bring up the subject of my dad's cancer preemptively, and awkwardly. I always pictured myself as having made my first million by now, not living at home. I want to justify it, to keep myself from feeling like a screw-up.

"How are you, man?" Alex asks, "It's been like, what, six years since I've seen you?"

"Great," I say with a forced smile, not wanting to answer any more questions. My eyes wander to the cooler filled with beer.

"What are you up to these days?"

"My dad has cancer." There is a pause. Everyone looks at each other quietly. Alex's eyes widen; he starts to say something but seems to change his mind. Even I am dumbfounded that I blurted it out like that. "So I'm living at home now," I finally continue. The few people who are still listening nod.

"I'm sorry to hear that, man," Alex says with surprising sincerity.

"Thanks." I say, and mean it. I grab a beer and move back inside, where there are fewer people. I am struck by the warmth in Alex's voice. It's amazing to me how much people's sympathy has made a difference. Any time in the past that I was told that someone had a gravely ill family member, I thought it was best to change the subject. I was afraid that talking about it would somehow remind the person about their sadness. Now I realize that when you are going though a situation like this, it's all you ever think about. Even in the brief moments when I somehow forget— when I have that vague sense that something dreadful has happened but I can't quite remember—a stranger's words of sympathy are still welcome. No one could remind me of my dad's cancer faster than I can.

I drink a beer quickly and continue to try and avoid people. I open a second beer. I start to feel calmer.

After the dot-com boom turned to a bust in the first few years after I graduated, I managed to get a job at a venture capital firm. In hindsight, I only got the job because the general manager was friends with my dad, but at the time I was too arrogant and insecure to admit it. Instead, I took it at face value when I was told that I had a lot of the necessary skills to be a great private equity investor, that I would bring an important perspective, and that I would be an invaluable member of the team. I'm not even sure if anyone ever said those things to me, but I wanted to believe it. So instead of recognizing that I was entering the firm at the lowest level, my attitude was that I was something special. I think many of the senior members of the firm didn't think well of me but weren't sure what to do because I had personal ties to the boss. After two years at the firm, I realized I needed to figure out what I would want to do with my life if impressing other people was not the priority. I finally recognized the importance of doing something because I really wanted to do it, not just so I could feel important at a high-school reunion.

About a year ago, I decided to abandon the goals of being rich, powerful, or important and follow my dad into clinical psychology. I had often admired the way helping others had played such a significant role in the lives of both my parents and decided to take a gamble that it would be meaningful and fulfilling for me, too. As part of moving back home, I am applying for research jobs and preparing to apply to graduate school this fall.

I am just finishing my second beer when two girls who were a few grades ahead of me arrive. We introduce ourselves, and I discover one of them is a therapist at a local school. She is much cuter than I remember from high school. I offer to get her a beer and in the process grab another for myself.

"So, how do you like working in the schools?"

"I love it!" she gushes, "It's been a great fit for me."

"Cool. I'm just switching into the field. I used to work in finance, but now I've decided to get a degree in clinical psychology."

"Wow!" she says with the enthusiasm reserved exclusively for awkward small talk at parties. "What made you want to switch?"

"Well, I had been thinking about it a lot, because I wasn't happy in finance, and well, then my dad got cancer, and so now I'm living at home, but—"

"Your dad has cancer?" she says with genuine warmth. "I'm really sorry to hear that."

The kindness in her voice almost makes me feel as if I could marry this girl. "I just realized, you know, working in finance, I was spending all my time helping these five rich partners get richer," I say, putting an idealistic spin on my decision to leave finance. "Like, this is not what I want to do with my life," I say emphatically. "I really want to help people, not just spend time making money."

I am speaking as if I made a clear and confident choice. This is almost a complete fabrication. My decision-making process has been anything but decisive. In general, I hate making choices. When I was little, my father would offer me a choice of vanilla or peppermint ice cream for dessert, and I would burst into tears, terrified that I would make the wrong choice. I still feel that way. My father used to tell me, in his therapist voice, "Now, Michael, there's no way to know in advance if a choice is right. Sometimes you just have to make them and then make them right," but I didn't believe him.

Even when I was older I didn't. It seemed like the kind of self-consolation that I imagine people use with themselves after they've discovered that they're forty-five, stuck in a loveless marriage with three children and a mortgage, and have blown any chance they ever had of doing something important with their lives. So then they simply start saying things to themselves like, "There are no right choices" and "It's about the journey," and then they sit back and admire themselves for having become so wise before their fiftieth birthday. But deep down they know the truth. They made the wrong choice. They blew it. They chose peppermint. Or vanilla. Or whichever they weren't supposed to take. It was right there in front of them. All they had to do was to make the right choice, and they didn't, and now there was no place to go but sideways, puttering onward. I am constantly afraid that I will become one of those people.

My parents and most of my close friends have always responded to these anxieties by telling me that I am incredibly hard on myself. I generally agree with them but have never quite figured out how to be less hard on myself. Instead I simply interpret my tendency toward harsh self-appraisal as yet another reason why I'll probably make the wrong choice.

"Yeah, well, I think that's great," she says. She excuses herself to grab another drink, and I am left alone.

My thoughts immediately return to my dad, who is in the hospital tonight; Mom is staying with him, and Sam is at a party of his own. I want to go home, but the house is empty.

Kate

WE ARE FINALLY ON THE PLANE TO PENNSYLVANIA. DAVID SITS NEXT TO me, his head back, eyes closed. For my part, I cannot believe he is going to lead a two-day workshop in this condition. The long lines of check-in and security left him exhausted. He is wearing a hospital mask over his nose and mouth. I made him wear it, a flimsy protection from the passengers around him, who seem to be nothing but vectors of disease. Completely bald, he looks pale, weak, and thin. I am sure half the plane thinks he is a carrier of some dread disease, the mask being worn to protect them rather than the other way around.

David has given workshops around the country for thirty years on a variety of topics—substance abuse and families, family therapy, couples therapy, therapist burnout. This one is on therapist self-care. They are typically one or two days long, with David on his feet, talking, engaging the audience, laughing, full of energy. Teaching is his greatest gift. But now, of course, things are different. He finished round two of his chemo a week ago, so we are traveling at the nadir of his white blood cell count, putting him at serious risk if he develops an infection. Since the beginning of chemo we have been told infection can become life-threatening in a matter of hours.

This trip is crazy. He should have cancelled it but wouldn't. He has been clinging to this trip as though it were evidence that he is still David—sick but really okay. Aside from my fear that doing this is a significant health risk, he is also utterly exhausted. He is sleeping half of every day. But it is impossible to say no to him, because of the unstated obvious: This could be his last workshop. I decide that the only way I could possibly let this happen was to go with him. At least I can recognize signs of infection and get him to a hospital. As a precaution, I set up a contact with an oncologist and infectious disease specialist through one of my medical school buddies at Penn. I feel so fortunate that I can get excellent treatment quickly if I need it.

"Are you scared about doing this?" I ask, reaching for his hand.

"The idea of you watching me perform for the next two days scares the hell out of me, frankly," he says, giving me a small smile without opening his eyes.

"You know what I mean."

"Okay, kidding aside, I know if I get in trouble, you'll do whatever it takes. I am not afraid."

"Oh, great. Your life is in my hands. I think you're nuts to be doing this," I tease, carefully not saying what I truly feel. *You, my darling husband, don't know enough to be afraid. And I do. And I am really scared.* But my fear scares David, so I try not to let it show. He looks over at me and opens a book, which he reads for less than a minute before closing his eyes again. I look out the window at the thick wall of clouds. Raindrops are streaking across the pane.

Being a doctor when a family member is ill is a difficult balance. My mother was diagnosed with lung cancer in 1986, when I was thirty-nine. I remember standing in the kitchen when she called. "I saw Dr. Brown today. You're not going to like this. They found a spot on my lung." She had been a heavy smoker for years. In that moment, the future opened up before me. I knew this was almost certainly lung cancer and that over the next months to years it would kill her. I could see her wasted and dying the way so many of my patients with this diagnosis had done over the years. This was not an abstraction to me. Obviously, I said none of this to my mother.

My brother and I decided to have her move in with David and me in Boston rather than stay in New York. It also seemed easier to have her cared for in my hospital, even though she had excellent doctors in New York. Like most doctors, I feel more in control when dealing with my own colleagues.

The morning of her surgery, when they put her on the stretcher to take her to the operating room, I had the distinct feeling they were taking her to her execution. It was the first time that I felt the fear and anxiety I am sure many of my patients and their families feel during all the invasive and difficult procedures we do to patients. I was so used to being on the other side, to taking all this in stride, that it was a jolt to recognize how hard it can be.

She got through the surgery and radiation, but she had stage 3 disease, and the prognosis was not good. Her doctor told me that most recurrences happened in the first two years. If we could get to the two-year mark, the chance of cure would go up dramatically. (I would hear this exact statement repeated about David years later.) My mother survived to the two-year mark, but not much farther. She developed a small, painless, pea-sized lump on her neck. She asked me to feel it, and I knew immediately from its appearance and rock hard consistency that it was her lung cancer, now spread to her skin. I did not tell her what I thought, but the biopsy results confirmed my suspicions.

Mother decided she did not want chemotherapy that might extend her life only a short while. She wanted to die at home She took to her bed. Over the next few days, she asked me to help her edit an obituary she had already written and select who should get which ties for Christmas. That was the beginning of July. I virtually never left her bedside, watching as she slowly slipped away. She died ten days later.

She had a gentle death, but one never knows who will be so spared. I hate the idea of the dreadful ways David might die. I try not to think about it, but when the thoughts come, unbidden, I feel as though I am falling into blackness. I have an image of a psychiatric hospital filled with locked cells with heavy steel doors. Inside one of the cells, a woman kneels, her arms wrapped tightly around her chest, screaming "NO! NO! NO!" In some deeply buried cell inside me is a woman who is just howling and shrieking. I slam the steel door shut; I cannot go there. Despite my terror, I feel some comfort knowing I will be with David to the end, just as I was with my mother.

Some of my colleagues in similar circumstances have become intensely involved in every decision, sometimes almost usurping the role of the doctor. I did not want to second-guess Effi. I was confident that he would make the best decisions possible. Still, I found myself frantically reading everything available, trying to learn as much as I could. Most of my patients who had an advanced cancer like David's died. Reading gave me a sense of control, as if by knowing, I could somehow prevent the worst from happening.

David wakes up when the plane lands. Jay Lappin, an old friend, picks us up at the airport. We drive to his home in New Jersey, within striking distance of Lancaster and nestled on the banks of a lovely river. His backyard is full of shade-loving plants, with a path meandering down to the river's edge, where we sit under a huge weeping willow. Watching the river and feeling the gentle, cool breeze, I can almost forget. Until, of course, I look at David, which makes it impossible to forget anything.

Jay and his wife, Joyce, drive us the two hours to Lancaster that night, a long trek for them and an act of great kindness for us. We listen to Jay's favorite tunes, reminisce, tell old jokes. All the while I feel enveloped by their care and concern. It is one act among many that I have been profoundly grateful for in these first few weeks.

I have always had problems asking for help. When I was little, I was a real tomboy and assumed the creed of toughness and self-reliance prevalent in the John Wayne era of the 1950s and embedded in the WASP culture of which I was a part. That might have changed when I was older, but after my father died, when I was fifteen, I found that talking to my friends about what had happened was impossible. Even though they tried, I knew they didn't understand, and it was simply too painful to share the depth of my grief and loneliness. I stopped trying.

Without my asking, our friends made meals for us when David first came home from the hospital. One of his colleagues asked if I would mind if she planted a perennial garden along our front walk. Mind! It has become David's victory garden for me—watching those plants grow and thrive makes me feel that David might, too. Another friend hired a gardener to help with the weeding. People volunteer to drive David to his chemo infusions when I cannot. They bring flowers, baskets of tomatoes, fruit. They write and call, send videos for us to watch. I do not know if the people who do these things really understand how much it matters. Each gesture sustains me. It surprises me how grateful I feel. I hope I will remember this generosity the next time one of our friends is going through a hard time.

David is slumped in the backseat of the car, asleep again. I feel a rush of love for this man to whom I have been married for thirty-eight years. We met in Philadelphia, and now here we are again. I was eighteen and a freshman in college. He was twenty and on academic leave. He had come down from Boston for a fraternity party. Although I had come to the party with someone else, David and I sat on the big oak table in the main living room and talked most of the night. I just remember sitting side by side, our shoulders touching, simply grinning at each other. I felt immediate connection and comfort, which happened only rarely for me. Afterward, we saw each other occasionally at parties but did not go out until my junior year. Almost immediately, we starting seeing each other every day, finding the same attraction and connection we had felt two years before. We talked endlessly about everything and anything—anything, that is, except the most important events in each of our lives.

One night, in a bar, it came up in conversation that David's mother had committed suicide the preceding year. It felt as though we had suddenly dropped into territory that, until that moment, I had been in alone. Now, David was there, too. I remember thinking, *Oh, so you understand.* I felt a lock click into place; we were linked, deeply and irrevocably. David confronted me, made me think in different ways, but, perhaps most important, he was the most compassionate person I had ever met. He accepted people's foibles and weaknesses without judging them. He inspired me and challenged me to be a kinder person.

In that way, he was similar to my father. My father adored me. I felt loved and safe in his gaze. When I was twelve, we began having talks about life that had a profound impact on the person I wanted to be. He talked about my duty to use my talents to make the world a better place, about being kind, about doing my best. I felt as though he was entrusting me with some precious knowledge passed down over generations. A few years later, when I was away at boarding school, he ended a letter he had written in answer to inquiries about my Scottish ancestry with the following admonition: "The measure of you, Katharine Conrad Kennedy, is what you give to life, the kindliness and thoughtfulness with which you give it, and the joy you create in the giving." A few months later, he would be dead of a ruptured aorta. It was an unspeakable loss. I have spent my life trying to live, however imperfectly, those words.

Out of the deep bond forged by our shared experiences of loss, David and I have been connected at many levels. We have been like Hansel and Gretel facing the dark forest, like two teenagers rebelling against the grownup rules, and we have also been colleagues providing powerful support to each other's careers. Our early marriage was not easy. Each of us was traumatized by the loss of our respective parent and afraid to be that vulnerable again. But David was never one to let things go unsaid, and gradually, like the Little Prince and the fox, we tamed each other. David has been the only person in the world who knows all my thoughts. There is nothing I have not or would not share with him. He is my bulwark against the pain of the world. He is my safe harbor and my deepest refuge.

◇◇◇

The next morning, the workshop begins. The large auditorium slowly fills. David is introduced and starts his workshop, not with his usual upbeat riffs but with the story of what is going on. The room grows quiet and somber. Then, having given a brief and basically optimistic summary of his illness, David switches gears and says, "This reminds me of the *New Yorker* cartoon when the tall, smug man says to the short woman looking up at him, 'Well, now, that's enough of me talking about me. Why don't you talk about me?' The audience bursts into laughter and the energy quickens. David gets them to start talking with each other about their own concerns and questions about the next two days.

I quietly leave and go back to our room. I sit down to work on a new course I have been asked to direct for all incoming first-year medical students at Harvard called Introduction to the Profession. Its purpose is to help students make the transition into medical school — to understand that not only are they responsible for their intellectual growth but their moral, emotional, and professional growth as well, to understand that who they are is as important as what they know, and that both are critical to their success as physicians. I have already been working on it for a year, and thanks to the help of wonderful colleagues, the rough structure is in place, but there are innumerable details yet to be decided. Although it will not begin until August of 2006, I am in a panic because I have been unable to work on it at all for the past two months. I pick up my course outline and read through my list of next steps, carefully adding details as I go. At 10:30 I go down to check on David at the break.

He comes out looking exhausted. I take his temperature and he lies down on a cot they provided for him in a little room off the stage. We repeat this ritual at lunch and midway through the afternoon. At the end of the first day, he says wanly, "Maybe I'm not doing such a great job modeling self-care."

"You think?" is my somewhat tart reply.

On Friday, David is no longer walking up and down like an animated talk-show host. He sits in an armchair, clutching his microphone, clearly exhausted but gamely taking the audience to their own inner struggles, helping them share their stories and find strength from each other. I look at the clock—six more hours. I can't watch. I go back to the hotel room and try to go back to work. We've agreed with the organizers of the event to end early.

Finally, it's over. The audience cheers and gives David a standing ovation. They seem to know how much this effort has cost him. And there is David sitting and smiling. I am proud of him. Even though it was a dumb idea, maybe I needed the reassurance that he could do it, too.

Sam

I'M STANDING ON THE PORCH OF MY PARENTS' HOUSE, WATCHING MY DAD climb out of the car after his workshop in Philadelphia. He looks frail in a tan suit that hangs off him. He looks like a thirteen-year-old wearing his father's clothes. Patches of pure white fuzz are all that's left of his hair. He's hunched over, as if standing is too much effort. Isn't this supposed to happen when you're, like, eighty? He's only sixty. And I'm only twenty-one. My dad shouldn't be a stooped, shriveled wreck. How could he have given a two-day workshop? It seems crazy, looking the way he does. If I barely want to see him bald and sick, why would an audience of strangers? The strength he must have mustered is admirable, or stubborn, or a mix of both.

I rush to give him a hug and take his bags inside. My mom looks like a mess. The woman who is always in charge now seems locked between fear and sadness. She smiles when she sees me, but her eyes look worried and distracted. Maybe I should have come home earlier.

My best friend, Moses, and I had driven from Minnesota to New York City, where we met up with Michael for a night to enjoy being twenty-one. Moses hopped a train back to Boston, while I stayed with my car to help Michael make the final move out of the apartment he shared with his now-ex-girlfriend to live with our parents while he sorts things out. Then, together, we returned to our childhood home.

The car ride was cancer free. We talked about my girl troubles and his breakup with Kristin. Michael, six years older than me, is the classic big brother—meaning "older equals wiser"—but he's been able to listen to my advice in recent years. Finally being on a more level playing field has been a good bonding experience for us. I gave him the rundown on my junior year at Carleton—what was interesting and what wasn't. He told me about the classes he was taking and his transition out of the business world. I'm proud of him for taking a leap into the unknown. Starting fresh must be scary. I admitted that I was nervous about the great unknown after college. We talked about anything and everything that wasn't infected with mutating cells.

When we got home, the house was empty. I helped my brother get settled and then unpacked my stuff. It was both strange and good to be home for a day sans cancer; a day of hanging with Michael and high school friends before dealing with the inevitable reality of my dad's illness. Now it is staring me in the face with sad, puppy-dog eyes. A puppy that might have to be put down

I carry my dad's suitcase into the kitchen, where Michael and Moses are sitting. Moses came over not knowing that my dad would be arriving home. He knows about the cancer; I dropped that bomb on him in New Orleans. For the first time in our twelve-year friendship, he was speechless.

My first memory of Moses is from thirteen years ago, when he tripped me in the second grade. It was a classic moment you see in a movie. I was the awkward little kid, late to class, running down the hall. The bully carefully extended his leg at just the right moment, so that I flew through the air and landed in a heap next to the classroom door. Not surprisingly, I didn't much like Moses that year. The next year, he was in my third-grade class with Mrs. Eberhart (top three best teachers I've ever had). After hitting it off in class, he invited me over to his house one winter day.

I showed up, a little nine year-old with a backpack of essentials: my favorite stuffed animal, a pocket knife, a pair of winter gloves, and a juice box in case his mom didn't have apple juice. After my mom drove away, I walked up the frozen driveway toward the front door. His older sister popped up from behind a pile of snow and hit me in the face with a snowball. The war began. His driveway was a battleground with huge snow forts on all sides. I ran for cover, got out my gloves, and was ready to fight. It was a crazy day of warfare, finished off with walking around the coolest house I had ever been in, and an epic pasta dinner. We've been best friends ever since.

My dad slumps into a kitchen chair. Moses doesn't know what to say. After my own shock wears off, and knowing my dad can't stand the pity in the room, I lighten the mood.

"You really don't look that bad. I think you're faking."

Moses picks it up right away. "Yeah, DCT, you look fine to me. Dr. Kate, are you sure he has cancer?"

"You just wanted an excuse to cut off your last couple hairs." We all laugh a little, but it's forced. Moses knows his time is up; he says his good-byes and heads for the door. He hugs my dad. He hugs me. Cancer affects us all.

JULY

David

"ARE YOU GOING TO GO TO YOUR SUPPORT GROUP WHILE I'M IN NORWAY?" Kate asks while she packs.

"If I get a clean PET scan," I remind her of our deal.

We agreed that if I successfully completed two rounds of regular chemotherapy and two weekends of my special preventative treatment and if my first scan is good, it would be okay for her to keep her scheduled hiking trip with her women friends in the fjords and mountains of Norway. We held onto the plane tickets and reservations, figuring that if things went poorly we wouldn't be worrying about losing the money.

She needs the break. Frankly, giving her this feels like reciprocating in a small way for all that she has done for me. But we're in the midst of a killer heat wave, and I just wish I were strong enough to go up to my boat while she's gone. I can't remember the last time I arrived in mid-summer without spending time on our boat, the *Crow*.

I don't know if I will force myself to go to my cancer group. Right after I came home from the hospital in early June, Kate began encouraging me to join a cancer support group. I responded with my usual maturity: "Why the hell would I want to join the fraternity of the lame and the halt leading the blind?"

"You are such a jerk," Kate said, not inaccurately. "Most cancer patients really seem to appreciate having people who truly understand. Besides, at least one study showed that people who do groups do a little better in terms of outcome. Although, to the best of my knowledge, nobody has been able to replicate those results. Anyway, forget that. It just might help you get to know some cancer *survivors*, if you get my drift."

Kate knew perfectly well that the only people I'd known with cancer, besides my clients, were my best friend, John, my extraordinary therapist, Barbara, and my beloved mother-in-law, Fran. All of them had died, and I had been with them to the end. Fran had died in the addition that we had built for her on our house before her cancer came back. We had surrounded her bed and read prayers as she completed her last ragged, slow breath and was still. Barbara had died shortly after, bravely throwing a big birthday party for herself. We had remained very close after my therapy, and her husband had called me on her final day to see if I wanted to come over. I was seeing clients and didn't think I could cancel them. I wish I had.

My lifelong friend, John, died on Ellison 14—the same place I go for my treatments. John was the sweetest, most self-deprecating man I've ever known. As little boys in elementary school, we staged endless battles of toy soldiers indoors and then more endless wars with toy rifles up and down the alleyways and cobblestone streets of Beacon Hill. He was an unfailingly good sport and loyal friend. We went to boarding school together and encountered the casual meanness of *The Lord of the Flies* male culture. John was gawky and uncoordinated, and the jackals went after him. They were relentless in their biting wit. He always took it well, responded with his own self-deprecatory remarks and a goofy smile.

I remember not standing up for John, afraid that the barbs would be turned on me, willing to look the other way and leave my best friend behind. Cowardice. I've often taken the easy way out, learning at an early age to simply not "care" about things that made me feel vulnerable or needy. From the age of six or seven, I created an outgoing social persona that helped me navigate growing up in my family and survive the harsh male culture of private school. I still hide behind my smile, but I always fear that when truly tested, I will shirk my duty. Now, as I've faced the grim visage of this disease, I've felt the urge to capitulate to it. Secretly, shamefully, I've felt afraid to fight for my life. Afraid to care.

When we were adults, I apologized to John for having abandoned him. He responded, "Not to worry, Dave. At least you never joined in. I always appreciated that."

John was surrounded by visitors on his last days. Kate and I were lucky to have a little time with him alone. His face was gray and gaunt and his belly hugely distended with tumor and fluid. A familiar sight for Kate but a shock for me. (No wonder she looks at my possible future with terror. She can so clearly imagine me where John was.) John still had his shy smile. Despite all the pain meds, he was lucid. He said to Kate with a worried whisper, "So I don't see exactly how it happens. I mean, do I just go to sleep and then not wake up?"

Kate took his hand and said, "Yes, John, that's the way it happens."

"But what if it doesn't? I mean, I actually don't feel so bad. What if I just sort of linger here? All these people have come to say good-bye, and nothing's happening. I don't want to waste everyone's time. I mean, what if I'm still here at Christmas?"

We couldn't tell if he was kidding. It was July. Kate said with a tender smile, "Not to worry, John. You'll just be here until you're not. It will be okay whenever it is."

"I just don't want to be a bother," he mumbled.

I was holding his other hand and gave it a squeeze. "You could never be a bother, John."

Today's the first anniversary of John's death. I really miss him and feel very alone with the thought of my imminent death. I don't talk to Kate about it much. I don't want to scare her more than she already is. I decide to go to tonight's cancer support group session.

The group sits on a circle of couches surrounding a coffee table. Brochures about different programs for cancer survivors are stacked at one end of the table, and a bowl of candy is within reach. Members continuously pass it around. Comfort food. If we have a new member, we always introduce ourselves and retell our stories.

"Hi, my name is Bob, and I have non-Hodgkin's indolent lymphoma," says the big, burly FedEx driver. "I was diagnosed last year and was told that I might have long periods of remission, but basically the damn thing always comes back sooner or later. I'm just hoping to hang around long enough for them to find a cure. Otherwise, I'm actually doing pretty well."

Next in the circle, to my right, is a prim, ladylike English teacher. "Hi, my name is Marcy, and I have anal cancer. It was discovered during a routine rectal exam. My doctor put his finger up there and literally said, 'Uh-oh.'" The circle of nine men and women break into laughter. I look at our new member, Elaine, who's forcing a smile.

"I know, I know," Marcy smiles at Elaine. "It gets pretty graphic in here."

"Yeah," chimes in Bill. "There's no taboo topic. We go from bowel movements to erectile difficulties to burials. Sometimes in the same sentence."

Elaine's eyes widen.

"Bill, let's remember that this is Elaine's first time with us," our group leader, Ellen, says gently but firmly. She's good at helping us not go too far with our gallows humor.

"Yes, ma'am," Bill says, with a good-natured smile on his gaunt face. Our IT genius, Bill injects a wry, sharp sense of humor into the group. He has been declared days from death several times, and by now he has outlived his doctors' prediction by a year. He has two little boys, Mikey and Kevin. At eight years old, Kevin gets to play hooky from school to go with Bill to chemo and help the nurse. He wants to be a doctor when he grows up.

My turn. I want to be funny, too, but I don't want to elicit a frown from Ellen. So I say, "Hi, my name's David, and you've probably already figured out that I have cancer, too." I get the group chuckle I was looking for but wonder why in the world I am worrying about being entertaining and well liked, here of all places. The group is supposed to be the place where we let down our hair (what little we have left) and share with each other.

I went to my first session at the end of June, after several rounds of treatment. I was weak and sick and bald as a baby. Without eyebrows and eyelashes, I looked like a dying alien. I listened to their stories and their struggles, and they listened to mine. Many of them were dealing with their second or third recurrence. Rick was on a feeding tube, had a Port-A-Cath and a Hickman for blood draws and food infusions, and a colostomy bag and a catheter. He was in enormous pain from an untreatable fissure in his bowel. Frank announced casually when he introduced himself, "I'm on chemo till death." Others looked fine and were doing well in various stages of treatment and remission. Throughout that first session, I was struck by how courageous and normal they all were. I found humor, tenderness, empathy, fear, and denial there. I was scared and inspired and somehow felt like I truly belonged in this club that no one wanted to be in.

The group isn't just a "share and care" support group that meets once a week. There is enormous emotional commitment. Members e-mail each other between sessions, and when a member is sick, everyone visits him or her in the hospital. When Bill again seems to be dying, many of the group members visit him at home for a last good-bye. I don't, as I only had met him a few times. Everybody assumes he will rally, as he had so many times before. But this time he dies.

Afterward, his wife, Clarisse, invites us to "be" with him as a group during the wake at their home. Everyone is going, even a newer member. I don't want to sit with a dead man, when I might be dead myself in the next six months. I say to Kate petulantly, "Why the hell would I want to use some of the precious time I have left on the planet to go sit with a guy who just left it?"

Kate smiles. She knows I will make myself go, and I do. Bill's body is tucked into bed. He has on a ski cap that makes him look like one of Santa's elves. To me, he looks the same as when I met him, just quietly lying there as if he might wake at any moment and give one of his wry little grins and say something like, "Fooled ya."

The group squeezes in around the bed. There is a lot of animated conversation, mostly affectionate Bill stories. He had been the heart and soul of the group, and his defiance of death and doctors had given each of us tremendous hope and inspiration.

I am still forcing myself to go to the group meetings, even though they are an unforgiving mirror, reflecting parts of myself I don't like. I like to think of myself as a compassionate and caring person. As a therapist, I have spent my whole life as a caretaker. And what I don't give at the office, I try to give to Kate and the boys, and my shattered siblings, and my aging father, and even my friends. But I don't want to care about this group. I don't want to nurture them. My heart feels like a shrunken, dried prune.

◇◇◇

Another methotrexate weekend is about to begin. The regular chemo, CHOP-R, doesn't penetrate the brain lining. Because back at the beginning I had cancer in the dura layer of tissue surrounding my brain and along my trigeminal nerve, which goes into my brain, this treatment is supposedly necessary to prevent central nervous system lymphoma, which is untreatable and rapidly terminal. The methotrexate is supposed to kill off any stray cancer cells that might have migrated into my brain. They have tapped my spine three times and my fluid was clear, but they don't want to take any chances. My unusual trigeminal nerve inflammation and involvement of the dura led to lengthy discussions about how to address my extremely high risk. Effi proposed to continue these treatments prophylactically for a year. It has never been done before. I am an experiment, a lab rat.

Thank God for Kate. Many of the people in my support group are studying their disease on the Internet and wondering whether they have the right doctor or hospital. I feel utterly cradled by Kate's competence and knowledge, her confidence in Effi and my team, and the fact that she is beloved in her hospital. Everyone is anxious to give me the best care possible. It is like being the spouse of a VIP.

So this is going to be a long weekend. They will load me up with saline for a few hours and then put in a highly toxic chemical brew, which they then will thoroughly flush out of my system after it has done its dirty work. The fluid intake is so intense that I have to pee every twenty minutes around the clock. Since I am attached to bags on the portable metal pump, I don't try to maneuver myself to the bathroom. I just fill up the urine bottles, which the nurses continually check to make sure I have the right pH levels. Most of the nurses are young and sweet and encouraging. One even held up the urine bottle in her gloved hand and said, "My, you're putting out a lot of volume. Good boy." I felt like a toddler having successfully made a bowel movement in the toilet.

This weekend, I have a window bed. Outside in the brilliant summer sunshine, the Charles River is dotted with sailboats. The green esplanade next to the river is filled with joggers, bikers, roller bladers, and lovers strolling hand in hand, homeless lying on benches, solitary people feeding pigeons, bare-torsoed sunbathers, and tourists snapping pictures. From the fourteenth floor, they look like ants. I remember when Sam was three, and we took him on a ferry. He looked down at the people on the dock from the high, upper deck and said, "Look at all the little people. I'd like to put them in a pot and eat them." We all laughed. It became a family story, and inevitably one of us always repeats that line when we're looking down at people from a height like this.

Kate, Michael, and Sam visit me in the afternoon. They gather around my bed and we play cards, make jokes, and playfully trash-talk each other. We don't waste a lot of time talking about my illness. And we try not to bother my roommate. I talk about getting up to our boat for at least one sail this summer. I don't want to talk about my PET scan, which will happen sometime this weekend and that will reveal how effective the treatment has been. Kate's been very anxious about it. But I am still quite disengaged, bordering on blasé. Even if the chemo is working, it doesn't mean that my cancer won't come screaming back the moment I've finished treatment. But at least we'll know something. Kate and I know that if I am not in complete remission then the chemo didn't work and it will just be a matter of time. We don't tell the boys that.

◇◇◇

I'm down in the waiting room waiting for my PET scan. I am dressed in my absurd hospital johnny and attached to an IV pole. Across from me in the same garb is a scowling hulk of a man. He looks like he's a North End mobster whose just been hauled into jail; he seems sullen and wary, like a snake coiled and ready to strike. We aren't making small talk, and somehow I am afraid he will be annoyed that the nurse calls me in first. As I shuffle out, I say as pleasantly as I can, "Have a good day."

He looks up at me and flashes a mix of grimace and smile. In a low growl, he says, "Any day above ground is a good day."

I suddenly can see the frightened tough man behind the grim visage. I smile back at him, "Well, makes sense to me."

Michael

SATURDAY. I WAKE UP AT TEN AND MEANDER DOWNSTAIRS WITH THE HOPE that there is still coffee left. I feel tired, having gone to bed only five hours ago. Not that I was out late. I just couldn't sleep. That's been happening a lot.

Before I reach for the coffee I stop at one of the Purell stations that have been set up in various rooms of our house. This is done because Dad's chemo treatment leaves him immunosuppressed—meaning that he has no natural immune system. Even a mild infection that would not exhibit any symptoms in me could be enough to make him dangerously ill. None of us wants to make Dad sick. Consequently, each of us uses Purell constantly. I usually feel better afterward. I can't tell if I like the cool, soft liquid or the simple fact that it's something I can do.

"Michael," my dad calls from his office. As usual, he looks tired. He had his second round of outpatient chemo yesterday.

"Yeah, Pops?" My dad used to call his grandfather "Pops," and he always likes it when I use the name on him, which is why I do it.

"Could you mow the lawn today?" He asks without raising his voice at the end as one typically does when forming a question.

"Sure, Pops."

"And we need some groceries. Eggs, butter, milk . . ." he trails off. He isn't interested in groceries.

"No problem."

"Great." He returns to a letter on his desk.

It's been a few weeks since my dad's workshop in Pennsylvania. Now, he has lost all his hair; his skin has adopted a permanent green hue, the color that makes you anticipate a sour smell. The swollen bump in his skull has receded, and he just has a big dent there. His overall weakened state makes him appear wizened, as if he were preparing to fold in on himself. Miraculously, he seems to have retained his spirits. He still works, and he still makes time for each of us. I wonder whether I will be able to handle it so well when my own time comes.

I walk out the back door to grab the lawnmower. In the back of my parents' gray colonial house is a deck, with a trellis covered in wisteria; along the edge are flowerbeds leading to our beautiful, spacious lawn.

On the far side of the lawn stand several large trees, including a towering pine, easily rising fifty or sixty feet into the air. I have always loved our backyard. It was my stomping ground as a young boy

I give the lawnmower cord a pull. And another. When the engine starts, I begin to make circles around the lawn, starting on the outside. Mowing the lawn was one of my chores growing up, and it used to feel like an interminable task. Since I have come back home, doing errands for my parents is one of my primary jobs. Both continue to work, although my father has cut back his schedule to fifteen hours a week. So far, the process of finding a research job has been slow. Normally, this would make me worry about not getting into graduate school, about being a failure. But for some reason, simply being home with my dad this summer has been enough to hold those thoughts at bay. Nothing on my resume is as important as what I'm doing right now.

I bring the mower around another curve in the lawn and catch a glimpse of a rusted wheel peeking out behind one of the pines. It's my old go-cart. (Or "the car," as we used to call it.) Dad and I built it when I was eight. It was not your typical go-cart; as a child I never wanted typical, as my parents would frequently lament.

When I was young, I routinely dreamed up projects that were far outside my reach. I was anxious most of the time at school and painfully shy. When I would come home, I would often go to the swing set in the backyard and swing for hours, fantasizing about ways to impress the kids in my class. For several years, I would always imagine the same scene. All the kids would be lined up waiting for the school buses to take us home. And then, shattering every preconception anyone had about me, my amazing go-cart would arrive. The kids would look up at me in silent wonder, their stunned expressions confirming to me what I wanted so much to believe: that I was important, that I was a star.

Dad had been skeptical about my go-cart ambitions, but I begged him until he eventually relented. Growing up, both my parents always had an intuitive sense as to when something was really important to Sam or me. I described to him what I wanted (although he drew the line when I said I wanted to build the go-cart so that it could fly), and we compromised on a simpler design that would include a steering wheel (instead of two pieces of string) and an engine in back (instead of the friends that were supposed to push me). Though a far cry from the fantasy car from my daydreams, it was significantly more ambitious than anything we had attempted before. Initially I was enthusiastic, particularly when we were buying the parts. But over time my attention waned; the more progress we made on the actual car, the further it went from the car in my imagination.

All in all, it took almost two and a half years to complete. When it was finally finished, my dad was excited. I was not. By then I was almost eleven, and my fantasies about magic cars had begun to morph into a fascination with girls. We took "the car" to the high school parking lot, where I drove several victory laps as my parents watched with grins on their faces. I was a little shy of its acceleration; especially given how rickety the thing felt, but on the whole, I had to admit that it worked surprisingly well.

I never drove it again. I had already moved on, and an unsteady, homemade go-cart was hardly the way to impress anyone in middle school. But my desire to be admired by my peers never waned. By the time I had left college and was working in finance, I had upgraded from my fantasy go-cart to a BMW, but the idea was essentially the same. I still wanted to drive up to my elementary school and impress everyone.

I think my intense desire for recognition confused my parents as much as it did me. After all, they had always emphasized how meaningful it was to work in professions that were dedicated to helping other people. My dad, ever the psychologist, has suggested that it must date back to my earliest days. For the first six months of my life, my mother had taken time off between medical school and her internship to stay home with me. We were inseparable. But then we moved to Cambridge. Dad couldn't join us for the first month or so, and Mom immediately started her internship. She was plunged into thirty-six-hour shifts, weekends on call, and only two weeks off a year. For the next several years, while Mom completed her residency, I was taken care of by a nanny. Mom was away most weekends, so I spent them with my dad. It was an endless parade of games, visits to the park, long walks, and exploring our small neighborhood in Cambridge. Because my parents could not afford any extra child care, I would occasionally have to sit on my dad's lap while he conducted a therapy session, if one of dad's clients had to meet over the weekend.

My dad has argued that the sudden absence of my mom as well as his working really hard was traumatizing for me. Both my parents tell the story of the time, at age three, I casually announced to my mother that I believed that she went to work because I was bad. She was crushed. She describes crying so hard on her drive to the hospital that she had to pull over. She was dumbfounded by how I could have concocted such a sad and terrible logic and had no idea what to do next. Salvation came from my preschool principal, who suggested that my mom present me with a color-coded calendar of her schedule for the entire year. That way I could see for myself that mom's work was completely separate from my behavior.

Although the calendar worked, my father has always taken that story as evidence that sometime in those early years I got the idea that I was responsible for my parents' behavior. That I internalized the sometimes chaotic nature of their marriage and careers as something I needed to fix. I have always found this hard to believe. It didn't feel like such a relatively benign event could have led to such unrelenting insecurity.

I make one final lap around the house and then tuck the mower back into the woodshed in the back of our house. The other explanation my dad likes to speculate on is that I was influenced by his temper when I was young. Though he mellowed somewhat after Sam was born, I remember him yelling a lot. He was never very angry at *me*, but he was often wound up and it frightened me. And I would freeze and then try to be nonchalant, as if it didn't bother me. I think that's why he always assumed it didn't. It wasn't until I was at least six or seven, when my father asked me what it was like for me when he yelled, that I was able to say that it made me scared.

I walk into the kitchen, with its wraparound wooden cabinets with white countertops. I start to Purell my hands. My mother is at the kitchen table, which stands at the end of the room by the doors onto the back porch. She gives me a warm smile.

"Thanks for doing that, sweetie," She reaches her arm out to give me a quick hug. "It's good to have you here."

I smile; it is good to be here. Living at home and helping out around the house has in many ways been the most meaningful job I've ever had. Sam is in the living room, and I go in and sit next to him

"Dumb," he says, without looking away from the TV.

I chuckle. "Dumb" is Sam's all-purpose word, said in response to just about anything said by another person:

Other: "Hi, Sam!" Sam: "Dumb."

Other: "Sam, do you know why we're leaving for the restaurant so early?" Sam: "No, but I do why you're so dumb . . . because you're dumb."

Other: "Whoa, that last shot was pretty amazing."

Sam: "And you're pretty dumb."

Through sheer force of repetition, Sam has taken a gimmick that is not very funny and made it hilarious. Sam can always make us laugh. When the four of us are together, we all use it constantly.

I am feeling especially close to Sam since we've been back home. I haven't always. And I haven't always been the best older brother. I was extremely competitive with Sam when we were growing up, which was hard on him. Despite being almost seven years older, I had trouble allowing him to enjoy any successes, as if somehow his ability to ride a bike or read one of the Berenstain Bears books would have undermined my place in the family. Whenever Sam did anything, I felt compelled to remind him that I could do it better.

I was six when Sam was born and was used to being an only child. I viewed most other children with fear and anxiety, whereas I felt very comfortable with adults and liked having their attention. When my mother told me that I was going to have a baby brother, I marched upstairs and locked myself in my room. I hated changes of any kind. I even protested the most mundane changes to my daily routine, like a new shampoo my parents used to wash my hair. Having a brother sounded like a much bigger change than that.

I decided to make a counteroffer. (I suppose most six-year olds don't view their mother's pregnancy as an opportunity for negotiation, but I did.) "All right, mother," I said to her, trying to sound grown-up. "You may have this child, but you may not love it." I felt confident she'd agree. I'd accept a sibling provided he did not impinge upon the attention my parents gave me. My mother was taken aback. I had always surprised my parents with my curious ability to talk like an adult when I was very young. Usually, this formality was just a way for me to hide my feelings. My mother saw through this and put her arms around me. She asked if I was afraid that having a brother would change how she felt about me, and I said yes. She assured me that she could love both of us equally, just like she loved me and my dad equally. That made sense.

◊◊◊

I run a few errands, come home, and take a nap. When I wake up it's already evening.

"Michael!" my mom calls from the kitchen. "Didn't you say you were going to pick up Dad from his cancer group? It's already seven-thirty."

"What?" I yell back without getting up. "Did I say I would do that? I'm not sure that that's what—" Then I remember. Shit. I did agree to do it. He asked me last night on his way up to bed.

Mom is already explaining the reasons. "Sam can't because he's going out, and I had asked not to because I have to get up at five-thirty tomorrow for a board meeting."

"Crap. Yes. Got it. What time is it? I'm going." I begin a frantic search for the keys. I will be late, probably at least by twenty minutes, and I know Dad will be pissed. He usually comes out of his cancer group meetings feeling irritable. I find the keys and run out, letting the screen door slam behind me.

As I race down I-95, I start coming up with excuses—such as that I got caught up in a conversation with Sam, who wanted to talk about Dad's cancer. Dad would be delighted that Sam was opening up and expressing his feelings. Dad is always delighted when things are opening up and being expressed. He would forget about his anger. I imagine how the conversation would unfold:

ME: "Dad, I'm really sorry I'm late."

DAD: "Goddamn it, Michael! I've been out here thirty-five goddamn minutes!"

ME: "I know, Dad, I'm so sorry. I just got into a heavy conversation with Sam."

DAD: "What do you mean?" (anger had not yet subsided but is suddenly put on hold)

ME: "Well, he just really wanted to talk. I think he finally wanted to open up a bit and start expressing some of the things he's been in denial about."

DAD: "Oh!" (surprise morphing into relief) "What did he say?"

ME: "Well, he was kind of cagey about it; you know how he gets. He asked that I really not speak about it."

Dad is very big into its being okay for people not to speak about things; he is constantly reading the family our Miranda rights. Ironically, in the process, he usually gets us to spill whatever beans are in question, if only to avoid having to listen to yet another speech about why it is important for us to know that we don't have to.

> **DAD:** "Well, I totally understand that. And I think it's important that Sam knows that he can talk to you without feeling that it will get back to me or your mother."
>
> **ME:** "Yeah, well, I just want to say I'm sorry I'm late, again."
>
> **DAD:** "Ah, it's no big deal. I'm just glad that you were able to be there for Sam. That's much more important."

It would work, and I am tempted, but I resist the urge. It has been a long time since I've lied to my parents to avoid their getting mad at me. Both my parents used to have pretty big tempers that often scared me. By the time I was old enough to lie, I usually did. Not that I got in a lot of trouble; I was an extremely well-behaved kid. But I still lied to my parents, even about small stuff. I wanted to turn that A– into an A, or tell them I had done all my homework when in fact I was only half done. At the time, it just seemed like a good idea to play it safe.

Dad is outside when I drive up. He raises both his arms in a "What the hell?" kind of motion and approaches the car, slowly shaking his head. He gets in.

"I'm sorry." I say quietly.

As if on cue, he yells, "I have been out there for thirty-five fucking minutes!"

"I know, I'm—"

"I mean, what were you doing?" He looks at me with wide eyes. "I'm serious. What. Were. You. Doing?"

"Dad, I, just lost track of time. I'm—"

"Do know what kind of shitty day I've had?"

I repeat my "I'm sorry" mantra whenever he runs out of breath, but otherwise I am quiet. I feel like I am five again, afraid of what will happen next, even though I know perfectly well there is nothing to be afraid of. Dad is just angry, and it will pass. I look over at him. He looks gaunt and haggard. I notice the dent in his forehead. It looks like something you'd see on furniture; it's surprising that human flesh can take on such signs of wear and tear. Even in his anger, he is frail and weak.

Dad calms down and stares out the window. It is dark by the time we arrive home. I follow him into the house, not saying anything.

Kate

LIFE HAS BEGUN TO FALL INTO SOME TYPE OF PATTERN. DAVID AND I are both working. We take time in the early morning to have coffee together and briefly read the paper. I administer David's Arixtra injection, an anticoagulant he needs because during his first hospitalization, he developed a blood clot in his leg. Then we talk, which usually consists of my cross-examining David about how he is feeling. He puts up with my morning interrogation, sighing and answering each of my questions carefully. It is not a great way for him to start the day, but I can't help myself. I can't leave for work unless I can reassure myself that for the next twelve hours, he will probably be all right. Part of me knows this is ridiculous.

I drag myself to work. I find it impossible to keep my mind quiet. I go over and over how David looks, how he feels, what I have read yet again about lymphoma; the knot in my stomach twists even tighter. I usually spend the thirty-minute car ride sobbing.

At work, I am constantly surprised by how hard it is to make decisions, which in the normal course of a day, I do dozens of times. When a patient has a straightforward problem to take care of, I do fine. But when a patient has a complex or difficult problem, I feel overwhelmed. It makes me realize what an emotional cost my normal work life extracts; one to which I am usually oblivious. Paperwork is agony. Sometimes I just stare at lab results for what seems like hours without being able to make any decisions about what to do. Administrative meetings are in some ways worse, since I find it nearly impossible to pay attention to anything and sit mostly lost in my own worries. I cannot see my normal load of patients, so some of my colleagues volunteer to squeeze some of my patients into their own packed schedules. It is yet another gift of inestimable value. I do not think I adequately convey how much it means to me. To do so would mean talking directly about how tenuous I feel, and I cannot do that.

For both of us, it takes almost all our energy to get through the days. What makes it all bearable is that both boys are home. Except for holidays and brief vacations, this has not happened since Michael graduated from Columbia in 2000. Both of them pitch in to do anything that needs doing: shopping, dishes, picking up, taking the car in—all the tasks that now seem completely unmanageable.

After looking for a month, Michael found a job working in a lab at the MGH Charlestown campus. Often in the evening, he takes a shuttle to the main hospital and I give him a ride home. Every time I see him, I feel a deep soul comfort. It is the same when I see Sam. Even in these dark days, his infectious smile can lift my spirits. He has not gotten a job, and we do not push. He is the master of errands, except for weeding. This is a standing joke, because both boys have always hated weeding. Anyway, Sam has been spared that job because one of my good friends has taken care of it. Everything else he does with his usual good cheer and humor. It is a huge relief.

In the evenings, we usually play bridge. None of us could remotely be termed serious bridge players. Two years ago, on a family skiing trip to Colorado, we started playing bridge in the late afternoons. It was really just a way for the four of us to hang out and talk and for the boys to fall into their ever-changing comedic riffs: a takeoff of a movie scene, or a *Saturday Night Live* skit, or something from Monty Python. Sam can recite verbatim long passages from *Monty Python and the Holy Grail* that, no matter how many times I hear them, never fail to make me laugh.

Playing bridge provides a time to be together, to laugh together, and mostly to totally avoid having to discuss why we are together. I had felt a deep, aching need to have the family reunited, and remarkably now they are here. We are all home, all together. It almost feels normal.

After the first terrible reaction, David is tolerating his CHOP-Rituxan incredibly well. I usually go to the outpatient infusion center with him, staying while the nurses get him settled and give him Ativan and Benadryl to help prevent side effects during the infusion. I wait until he gets sleepy and then I go to work. On these days I feel safe. He is in the hospital. He is getting treatment. He seems to be responding.

We will know soon enough. David's first PET scan since starting treatment was over the weekend. It is a very big deal because, if it is clean—meaning there's no evidence of the cancer—David will have cleared the first big hurdle. If it isn't clean, we know we are in trouble: the treatment is not working, and he will be unlikely to survive for more than a year.

I have had many patients go through a test to find out if their cancer has recurred, and I have known it is hard. But as I am finding over and over, knowing in the abstract is not the same as experiencing it. David is feeling well, but that is not much consolation since he felt good before all this happened, too. We will see Effi the day after tomorrow. It seems like an interminable wait.

"You know, I can look up the results," I tell David. The thought fills me with dread. I remember how awful it was to be alone in the hall reading David's MRI. I do not want to do that again.

"If you do, you have to tell me immediately. I do not want you knowing something I don't." David is adamant. I do not want to be in that position. If it is bad news, I will need to be David's support, not the person delivering the news. I also know that Effi will not want to discuss bad news by phone. We decide I will not look.

As I wait for the results, I am in a panic. I have an image of a tiny sailboat on a huge, flat sea. One half of the sky is filled with brilliant sunshine, bathing the boat in golden light. But just beyond, the sky is black and ominous with an approaching storm. We are sailing just on the edge.

Since PET scans can take a few days to read, I do not expect the call I get from Effi the day after the scan. "Hi, Kate. It's Effi."

I am instantly scared. "Hi, Effi." Why is he calling me? But his voice sounds excited.

"Kate, I just had to call. The PET scan is clean. There's no sign of disease." He is obviously elated. We both know how important this is, although it is only one step of many that must go well. I am deeply grateful, grateful that he called and grateful for the caring it conveys. I put down the phone, weak with relief. Effi said he will call David, so I wait a few minutes before calling home. I look out the window of my office. The sun is shining; the leaves are fluttering in a light breeze. My initial elation is short-lived. I am surprised that I can't sustain the sense of relief. I feel like a giant tanker on the ocean trying to suddenly shift direction. It will take time for the news to sink in. I also know that this is only one of many scans to come, and, as I have been told several times, given the advanced and aggressive nature of this disease, it will be only after the two-year mark that we can really begin to believe this might be curable.

Once the clean PET scan results are in, David insists that I still go on the hiking trip to Norway that was planned long before his cancer. He said it was his gift to me. Although I worry every day during the trip to Norway, it is a much needed break from the constant tension. Although I do feel guilty because I know David's having no such interlude. As is so often the case this summer, David is thinking of me even though he's the person who is so sick.

It is a good trip, but once home again, I become consumed with the unresolved issue of David's brain. When David was diagnosed, there was tremendous concern about the high risk of recurrence of lymphoma in his brain, his central nervous system. CNS disease is essentially incurable. If he developed CNS lymphoma, his prognosis would be a matter of months.

David had every risk factor for recurrence in his brain: his extensive bone marrow involvement, his kidney involvement, the aggressiveness of his tumor. But more disturbing was the episode of numbness and severe pain in his face along the course of his trigeminal nerve. An MRI showed nodular deposits on the dura, the tough outer layer of the brain. He had three spinal taps during his first admission to see if the leptomeninges were involved, which would be considered CNS disease. While the first showed an abnormal number of lymphocytes, the cells themselves did not appear to be abnormal. The second two taps were normal. I still worry about what his initial symptoms meant. Even though the MRI and spinal taps did not show CNS disease, his facial numbness has not been explained. In addition, I want to know whether involvement of the dura has implications for his treatment. It is clear that no one really knows. I am obsessed with this problem and spend hours in the medical library at Harvard searching for information. There is a paucity of litera ture on the significance of dural involvement or mechanisms to explain his facial symptoms.

David knows I am worried about this but does not want to know the details, nor do I want to share them. We agree that I will talk to Effi, and he makes me promise I will report to him everything Effi says. This has become our pattern. I take care of thinking about the medical details, and he just shows up. It makes sense, but even so, sometimes he seems almost too detached from the process, as though this were happening to someone else. I have become dependent on Effi almost as though I were the patient, because I am the one pursuing the questions. In some ways, David depends on him through me.

With David's consent, I ask Effi if I can meet with him to go over my questions. I carefully outline the literature I have found and review my concerns. Effi listens intently to my questions and patiently reviews the literature I have brought. He agrees that David's initial facial numbness was likely due to dural involvement compressing the trigeminal nerve, though we both know that this is only one of several possibilities. He also agrees that even though all the tests indicate that David does not have CNS disease, given his dural involvement, his risk is very high. "Kate, I would have to say that David is as close as anyone could be to having CNS lymphoma without actually having it."

It is clear that there is no experience to decide how to handle David's very high risk. Many doctors would have been annoyed or impatient with me, taking all my research as a criticism. I can remember my own irritation, at times, when faced with what seemed to be an overly anxious family member. Whatever Effi's real feelings, he is remarkably patient with me, not defensive or annoyed or dismissive. In the end, he decides to extend the methotrexate therapy over the course of a year, when David's risk of CNS recurrence is highest. As Effi describes it, we are definitely "in the weeds." There are risks of toxicity, but it seems worth it, given the risk of a CNS recurrence and what that would mean.

Every three weeks, David is given methotrexate over a weekend. We definitely would rather be sailing. The methotrexate weekends are tough for both of us. David hates the nausea it causes and the intense fluid load given to wash out the drug after it is administered. I hate coming back to the hospital on the weekend, having been there all week, but I cannot imagine not being with David. We often just sit together, finding comfort in each other's presence. I lie next to him on his hospital bed for a while each night before I leave. I close my eyes, feeling his body next to me, willing him to be well. An inexplicable calm washes over me. It helps when later I lie in my bed alone at home.

Sam

"MOM, YOU CAN REACH ME AT 1-800-I-DOMIN-8," MY BROTHER SAYS when he wins the game for us. Playing bridge has been the main event each night this summer. Some families bond over sports, others bond over dinner. Others don't bond at all. Over the past couple of years, our family has bonded over bridge. When I was younger, my grandfather taught me the basics of the classic card game. Then, a few years back, with the help of my parents, I convinced Michael to learn the game so that the four of us could play together. Turns out, it just clicked for all of us, because it's challenging, fun, and leaves time for talking and joking around.

Six months ago, I happened to mention to my father that Mike and I were better at bridge than he and my mother. I didn't think I was announcing any big news. My dad's competitive side got the best of him and since then, Michael and I have been partnered in a heated battle against Mom and Dad. Every score is carefully written down in a hard-covered journal that we to refer to as our "little black book." Other people have black books full of phone numbers of hot women; we have a black book of bridge rivalry.

While some families might have serious yelling matches, we do our "battles" over bridge. Outside that, we don't often have real fights. We rarely even raise our voices because, thanks to my dad the shrink, we have a history of talking things through. And when we do argue and shout, everyone is quick to apologize. So by "battle," I mean we joke around while playing cards almost every night. We even play online when I'm off at school. (And all online games are recorded in the black book.) So far my brother and I are showing our dominance, but the end is not in sight. We've decided that to be declared the better players, a team has to be ahead by more than 10,000 points. A game is won by reaching 100 points. You can see how this competition might take a while.

We play in our living room, which is also Dad's waiting room. This multipurpose room was frustrating for me growing up, because my dad's clients would routinely interrupt a TV show or video game. Now that its main purpose is a bridge room, I'm feeling better about it.

Whenever Dad's not at the hospital, and sometimes when he is, our family is probably playing bridge. The days we do have to be in the hospital, it is amazing that my dad is willing to play bridge. He's doing it for us. Even with the chemo making him sick and tired, he hangs in there so we can play bridge and have some normalcy. It's almost pathetic how much we play, but at least we're all together. Not that we keep our composure.

"Damn it!" My mom pouts as she starts to shuffle the cards. "Just one good hand. One hand. That's all I want. I've been getting crummy cards."

"Some would argue that bridge is a game of skill, not a game of dumb," I cut in, "and if you guys want us to share the wealth, you just have to concede that we're better. Then we can rotate the teams."

"Come on, you've got to take it easy on the chemo boy," Dad pipes up, trying to diffuse the situation with humor. "I'm not up to my usual snuff. I'd be whoopin' you boys if it wasn't for my brain feeling like cotton."

"Yeah, you better be careful." Mom picks up the humor. "Your father might not be around all that long. Do you really want to beat him at bridge now?"

Her attempt at lightness falls flat.

"Buzz kill," my brother mumbles, taking a sip of wine.

"Yeah, Mom, you don't have to be such a downer," I agree.

"I didn't mean for it to come out like that. I'm sorry," she says, as she starts dealing. And we're back at it again.

◇◇◇

It's late. I'm in bed, sweating, although it's not hot out. My eyes are wide open, looking out the window, watching the cars go by on the always busy Route 20. My thoughts fight back and forth in my head as if it were the tenth round of a bare-knuckle boxing match.

Dad might die?

No, he's fine. He's just really sick. But he will be okay.

Mom said he might not be around—

She was being melodramatic. She was making a not-funny joke.

What if his chance of dying is like fifty percent?

Why am I refusing to hear the facts from my mom?

What if everyone knows he's going to die but me?

They would have told me if it were that serious. Right?

I don't know. I just don't know.

*I don't want my dad to die, I don't want my dad to die, I don't want
my dad to die, I don't want my dad to die . . .*

I start to cry. A few tears at first, while this impromptu mantra plays
in my head. Then full-on sobs as I start to mumble it out loud. I roll over
and hide my face in my pillow. I want to call out to someone. I want to
go to my parents. I want to call Sarah. But I can't. It's too late. I'm alone.
I'm alone without my father.

The next morning I tell Dad about my night. He thinks its really
touching, naturally. He says we're all going through times like that, and
that for everyone else, it's been more often. This isn't encouraging.

Everyone in the family is aware of my very vocal opinion that
worrying isn't going to help anything. My first week home, I adamantly
told my mother I didn't want to hear any of the details of my dad's
illness. Especially nothing about his poor chances of surviving. Since
Dad's going to make it, worrying about his chances doesn't help. After
my meltdown last night, I'm convinced that my way is the best way to
handle things. Mom doesn't have that luxury. She's a doctor: she knows
all the angles, and she has to live a dual life of sorts. She's the key holder
to all the information. She has a doctor's knowledge with a spouse's fear.
Me? I can just be loving toward my dad without having to be worried
about his mortality.

I'm the only one in the family who seems to be using the denial
strategy for coping. My mom and dad can't escape it. For Michael, it
almost seems like therapy for him to immerse himself in depression
about the illness. I, on the other hand, spend as much time as possible
not thinking about the whole situation. Deep down, in a secret vault of
thoughts, I know that there is a chance that he might die. But if I keep

it all locked up, I won't think about it except when it seeps through the cracks occasionally, like last night.

My mom has told me it's fine not to worry but that I need to work on my relationship with my dad, just in case. I know she's right. I've wanted to reconcile our issues for a while. Our difficulties are irrational and mostly my fault. The man just agitates me. The way he eats, the way he carries himself, the way he talks to other people. Everything he does seems inappropriate; it doesn't follow my internal code of what's right and wrong. Like the other day, when he globbed pat after pat of butter onto his toast. It was disgusting, so I chided him for it. The man is horribly sick; if he wants to have extra butter on his toast, so be it. But my response is so instinctual I couldn't stop myself. He got defensive and we argued. Of course, I know it is ridiculous for me to be so anal and sensitive. I can't even live by my own moral code, so why should I expect him to adhere to my strict standards? The logical side of me knows that I really shouldn't get so mad, so I have been trying my best not to get upset by him. I have a heightened sense of duty to support him and the family.

I have plenty of free time to help out around the house. Every day I try to wake up before noon and then spend the afternoon running errands and doing chores around the house. I have dinner with the family, and of course play bridge. After that I have time to go out with friends and party until two or three in the morning.

Since my friends are all home from college, we just change the parties from one house to the next around town. Weston was a great place to grow up as a kid. A safe small town with lots of woods for adventuring. It was always nice to bike from house to house amongst my friends. But now that we're older, there is nothing to do. First of all Weston is a dry town, and besides a tiny shopping center there is nothing else in it besides a bunch of expensive houses. I hold on to my youthful, romanticized view of the town, and merely tolerate the reality of it being a wealthy, precious suburb. Sometimes I forget how lucky our family is. Even though I know we aren't rich, we are pretty well off. It's nice that my parents can support me all summer.

Sarah called me out on the fact that I'm using my dad's cancer as an excuse for not looking for a job. At least I'm not as bad as Michael. He tells anyone who will listen that our father has cancer. He even used it with a police officer to avoid a ticket. When asked what he was doing in

Massachusetts (he has a New York driver's license), he said "I just came home to be with my dad, who just got diagnosed with cancer." I couldn't believe it!

◇◇◇

"Have you gotten a chance to look at your dad's birthday present yet?" my mom asks, pulling out the green leather-bound photo album. I immediately close up. It's a physical reaction, like the way you feel when a mean dog starts barking at you. I force myself to look interested. She sees me failing at this.

"Come on, Sam. I took a lot of time to make this. A bunch of different people wrote some really nice things for your dad." She tries to coax me, but all I hear is an unsaid "and you're not one of those people who wrote something worthwhile." She shows me what people wrote. My uncle Stephen wrote three pages, and my dad's friend Jay Lappin had a long section, too. Both had poignant stories about their times on the boat with Dad. My mom wasn't lying. They were really nice things that people had written. And she added all sorts of photos of my dad and the family and the people he loves.

She says nothing about my contribution, but that's all I can think of. She was right. My stupid poem isn't in the same ballpark as these letters. Hell, we're not even playing the same sport. I feel guilty and ashamed about my poem. Dad must have read all of these touching letters, and then he had gotten to mine. My poem, summing up our relationship in twenty-eight rhyming lines, must have been a sucker punch of crudeness. At the same time, I feel defensive. Mostly because I'm a male, and men are stupid when it comes to feelings and trying to express them. Unless, of course, you're my father, and then that's what you love to do.

". . . And here is what your brother wrote," my mom goes on. He decided to stick with the boat theme. Par for the course, it's loving and sentimental. His maturity comes shining through. He spent more than a half hour on his.

She turns the page, and there it is. A big, fat blemish. I'm a pimple in my dad's special birthday book. I reread what I wrote for the first time since I threw it together:

Dear Dad,

I'm sure while you've been reading
You haven't been thinking about the weeding
Well it just has to get done
And I know it's not fun
But just think about what Mom would say
If we didn't keep those dandelions at bay
She'd puff and pout and then do it herself
She wouldn't be happy being the weeding elf
Even with everything she does, she makes time
For our family and even weeding the vine
We're lucky to have her in our lives
She's the best of the best of wives
And she's one great mom
One might say "she's the bomb"

I'm telling you how great your wife is
To let you know how great life is
In this turbulent time when nothing seems right
We should remember that life doesn't bite
There's love everywhere
And you can love too if you dare
This summer will be a time for family
A time to enjoy stability
When everything seems shaky
And when God's pulling a fakey

So we'll all chip in
So keep up your chin
We'll all get through this
With a smile a hug and a kiss

Happy 60th Birthday, Dad

Embarrassment floods past my defensiveness. It is shockingly bad. It had nothing to do with Dad. I just wrote about how great my mom was, and, oh yeah, my dad has cancer. Wow, I've never been more inappropriate. Tears pop up, but I force them back. I shakily say to my mom, "Can I change this?"

◇◇◇

Later that night, I'm on the phone with Sarah, who is in Northfield. It's been tough keeping up the long distance relationship. I'm having fun at home with friends and not working, while she's stuck in Minnesota with a job she hates and no friends. We've only seen each other once since I left, when she flew out to see an O.A.R. concert with me.

"Okay, sweetheart," I tell her, "I'll talk to you tomorrow or maybe Thursday. And remember, I'll be up sailing with my folks next weekend, so I won't be able to call. But I'll talk to you before that. I love you." Sarah says that she loves me, too, and we wish each other goodnight.

We talk almost every night, mostly about day-to-day things. This or that happened at her job, or so and so said this to me last night while we were drunk. Since the decision was made that she would stay in Northfield, I've been trying to get back to a normal relationship with her. Having someone to talk to is a nice crutch to lean on. Though it's been hard since I'm home and she's stuck there. And my home life is dominated by my dad's sickness. I only mention my dad to Sarah after visits to see him in the hospital. I sometimes feel awkward sharing my feelings about my dad's cancer. She is so great at supporting me through this, but it doesn't actually make me feel much better. I don't know why.

I get off the bed, still fully clothed, because 11 p.m. is early on my clock. Maybe Michael wants to stay up and watch TV. I find him in our joint bathroom, which, ever since it was built, he has claimed for himself, sending me to use our parents' bathroom. He's never been a mean older brother, but he is a little territorial. Like how he didn't want me to learn to play the piano because that was his instrument.

He's brushing his teeth.

"Dumb. Let's go watch *Family Guy*. It just started on Cartoon Network," I say as if it's a done deal that we're going to watch TV.

"Uhhh . . . Shhuurrrrd," he mumbles with toothpaste froth all around his mouth.

I go downstairs to the living room, plop down on the couch, and turn on *Family Guy*. A minute later, my brother steps into the doorway.

"Nope. Not going to happen. My couch," he says. I'm on the only comfortable couch in the room.

"Duuummb," I groan as I get up and go to the chair. Not much is said as we laugh along with the Griffins.

During the commercials, we talk about our day, and I ask if he needs me to do any errands tomorrow. More toilet paper for "his" bathroom. We joke about which one of us was using so much toilet paper.

After the show, I protest when he says he needs to go to bed. I'm in a funky mood and don't want him to leave. Channel surfing is so much better with my brother. Watching crap on TV has been a good, albeit pointless, ritual for the last few years with Michael. But now he has a job and has to wake up in the morning. He goes to bed. After wasting a few more hours in front of the TV, I finally trudge up to my room at 4 a.m. and nosedive into bed. If you stay awake until you can't keep your eyes open, then you can't have bad dreams.

AUGUST
David

Traffic is crawling on the Maine Turnpike. Saturday is rental turnaround day for the two-week folks. We picked the wrong day to go up to the boat for a short two-day sail. The surrounding cars are stuffed with suitcases and children. Many of them have kayaks on top, bicycles on the back, and trailers pulling boats—all suggesting each family's yearning for fun, closeness, escape, and good memories. In my office, I frequently hear a litany of complaints about much anticipated and profoundly disappointing summer vacations. The weather was bad, the kids were bored, it was too expensive, no time for sex, same work just in a different place, etc. One exasperated mom summed it up when she said, "Once you have kids, going away is never a vacation. It's just a trip."

We live in a culture that seems to assume that happiness is a birthright rather than an ephemeral, glorious moment we can't manufacture or preserve. Many of my clients feel that if they aren't happy most of the time, it's a failing of theirs or someone else's. One of the most simple and profound insights the Buddha had is called the first Noble truth: that all life involves suffering; part of it is created by our endless wish to hold onto our good feelings and to avoid harsh experiences and feelings.

Before the cancer I was diligently working in my Buddhist practice to embrace my life and live more authentically, being true to myself without self-judgment or fear or my compulsive need to please other people. This is bumper-sticker level wisdom but nonetheless very hard to live by. Since the cancer, I am definitely living in the moment, because in truth that's all there is. This notion of staying in the present is much easier to swallow when your Buddhist teacher is reminding you of it during a meditation session. It's very challenging when any moment may be the beginning of your imminent demise. None of my spiritual practice prepared me for this, when having nothing but the present moment became a literal fact of my life.

I've tried to act brave and strong, but Buddhism doesn't mean being numb, uncaring, disengaged. I sometimes speak glibly about the transformational power of illness, the gift of cancer. In reality, I've been quite dissociative. I have stopped caring about my life. Like many trauma survivors, I've become a spectator of it, a dead man walking. I've been the opposite of Lance Armstrong, who exemplified the "I'm going to beat this thing" approach. I've been practicing "Surrender and prepare to die."

This rush of depressing thoughts makes me wish I had just stayed home. I close my eyes and try to center on my breath as Michael speeds along. Normally, I'm the typical dad hunched behind the wheel muttering profanities at my fellow sufferers, but not today. Michael is driving, I'm riding shotgun, and Kate and Sam are in the back. I've been looking forward to getting up to the boat all summer, but I've been too sick to go for the last two months. I was hoping it would evoke our years together as a family adventuring on the *Crow* and give us all a little break. I wish I were well enough for us to go for a real cruise.

I know Kate and the boys are expecting me to be true to form and say something shrinky, like, "Hey, guys, why don't we have a little check-in? You know, family meeting. See how everyone is doing." For years, on the drive up to the boat, I always initiated family meetings, which invariably was met with moans and groans. Even Kate would join with the boys and tease me. "Can't we just go on vacation like normal people? Do you think any of the other families in any of these cars is having a family meeting?" Sam, in particular, hates my efforts to get everyone to talk about their underlying feelings. He has said vehemently and often, "I talk about my feelings more than any of my friends, and in this family it's never enough. This is the talkingest family on the planet!"

I always persisted. I grew up in a family where politeness, teasing, artificial amiability, and frequent thick silences were how we communicated while my parents and siblings slowly descended into mental illness and addiction. I have been anxious about my kids being vulnerable to mental illness ever since they were born. So everyone has put up with my need for family meetings and intimate conversations, both at home and inevitably somewhere along the Maine Turnpike on the way to the boat for our summer vacation.

I remember one time when Sam volunteered to start. Michael asked him how he was feeling about his tennis; a sport he had worked hard at for years without much pleasure or success. "Hmmm, tennis. Yes, good topic, Mike," he started, with a slight hint of sarcasm. "I'd have to say, tennis blows major goats."

We all laughed.

"Sam, where in the world does that come from?" Kate asked with a smile.

"It's just what tennis is," was Sam's curt response, and the phrase was immediately incorporated into our family lexicon. While we were playing bridge earlier in the summer, Sam asked me how I felt about the chemo, and almost in unison, Kate, Michael, and I said, "It blows major goats!"

They're waiting for me to break the silence, but I'm not going there. My vile mood has lifted, and I don't want to slip back into it. This is one year when a break from sharing our feelings might be a relief for all of us, even me.

When we get to the marina, I hold the dinghy next to the *Crow*, and Kate, Michael, and Sam clamber up over the lifelines into the cockpit. As I stand up to follow them, I realize I don't have the strength to pull myself up. Michael leans over and extends a hand, without saying a word. He gives me a strong tug aboard. I am sure that nobody else noticed.

The sky is that deep royal blue that almost mimics the ocean. There's not a cloud, and the sun is warm without being too humid or hot. The breeze is light, but I can tell the afternoon southwesterly will be brisk. It's a perfect Maine day in our little home port of Robinhood, where I have kept the boat for the past ten or eleven years. I have had *Crow* for thirty years and have sailed it all over the North Atlantic. Prior to finding Robinhood, I had wintered the boat everywhere from Canada to the Virgin Islands, from the Bermuda to Scotland.

Sailing the oceans was my life's dream. Every day during the summers when I was a child I would escape the tensions in my family and head out on my bike for the Sandy Bay yacht club. My sail bag and my PB & J lunch were tucked in the basket on the handlebars. Having the day to myself was heavenly. Even at that age, I had already crafted a persona that appeared relaxed, affable, and basically good, but in reality I have been deeply anxious and insecure throughout my successful life. Being out on my boat alone has been an enormous relief from my relentless sense of performing.

My grandfather, aptly nicknamed Skipper, introduced me to sailing when I was three. By the time I was nine and had my own little boat, I thought I was a pretty seasoned seaman. I would set out in my nine-and-half-foot, lime green tub of a boat called, incongruously, *Typhoon*. Once past the harbor breakwater, I was at sea and steered my bow through the swells toward the endless horizon. I would spend the day sailing out of sight of land and luxuriating in the simple feel of wind, sail, and boat— the gurgle of the bow wave, the gentle rocking motion. For countless hours, I'd imagine brave voyages and high adventures to all the distant ports that lay beyond. My future possibilities seemed as boundless and infinite as the sea itself. Thinking of them soothed me like a mother's lullaby.

My dream happened. After years of crewing on major ocean passages to and from the Virgin Islands and chartering boats, I finally convinced Kate to let me beg, borrow, and steal enough money to buy our own boat. I had supported her through medical school, and she agreed to support my dream.

In 1981, I fulfilled my childhood ambition of sailing solo across the Atlantic, from the Azores to Rockport, Massachusetts. Nineteen days on the ocean alone. I expected it to be life transforming. What I found instead was the same old me. I was surprised with my preoccupations about exactly where I was (celestial navigation is not a precise science), the weather vicissitudes, and what to eat for the next meal. Man alone at sea turned out to be kind of like regular life intensified by being utterly alone, at the mercy of the elements, and focused literally on only one day at a time. Yet, life was so much more vivid out there, just like the shocking pinks and baby blues of the sunrises and sunsets. Living with cancer is different. I am again living a day at a time, but it's not vivid; it's dull and lifeless. I am shuffling through the hours as best I can. The irony is that most people say I seem so calm and brave.

The other part of our deal when I bought the boat was that Kate would let me sail to faraway places as long as she didn't have to go. Then she and the kids would join me once I got to my destination for some less adventurous coastal sailing for a couple of weeks. It didn't always work as planned. One time, I convinced Kate to sail with me and the boys from Nova Scotia to Prince Edward Island and on to the Magdalens, the French islands in the middle of the Gulf of St. Lawrence. We pulled out of the harbor on a gray, threatening day with the wind rising. We had sailed about a half mile off the beach when suddenly the boat shuddered to a stop. We had run aground.

We had to move quickly: first, we had to get the sails down, then, we tried to back off the bar under power. The boat wouldn't budge.

I sent Kate, Sam, and Michael up on the bow to shift all the weight forward. We powered up in reverse again. Nothing. We pumped up and launched the dinghy and then dug the anchor out of the cockpit locker with eighty feet of line. Rowed the dinghy directly astern of where we went aground. Dropped the anchor. Then back to the boat. We wrapped the line around the winch. Pulled hard on that line until it was bar taut. I sent everybody up forward again. Powered up the engine. Nothing. Meanwhile, the wind had come up and the tide was dropping. We could have gotten into very serious trouble with a rising wind and a falling tide leaving the boat to be wrecked and us stranded on a deserted sand spit. I didn't want to panic the crew, but we were close to having to radio the Coast Guard and declare "Mayday." They might not have been able to get to us in time.

Now desperate, we tried one last thing: heeling the boat way over on its side. I left Michael on the tiller with the engine controls. We put the boom out at right angles to the boat. Kate and Sam leaned way out, and I took the dinghy to the far end of the boom. I wrapped my arms around the boom as if I were going to do a chin-up, heeling the boat as far over as possible. The dinghy slid out from under me and I was suddenly a 175 lb. weight dangling from the end of the boom. The boat heeled over and began to slide backward off the bar. As the boat slipped astern, Kate pulled the boom back in and retrieved her thankful husband. "I hate sailing," Kate said, with a smile and a hug.

I looked at the three of them. They were chattering about how silly I looked when the dinghy slipped out from underneath me. They had no idea how dangerous our situation really had been. It didn't matter; we made it.

That was fifteen years ago. Now it's the cancer. Here we are again, aground on a rising wind and falling tide; engine in reverse, anchor rode taut, boom out to the side, and me dangling off the end of it.

"Dad, ready to cast off?" Michael calls out from the bow, interrupting my reverie.

"Let her go." I back the boat down gently to make sure we don't get tangled on the mooring line. As soon as we get going, Sam goes forward to hoist the mainsail, and Kate passes up the cushions and suntan lotion. Like I said, we're a team.

That's the real reason Kate's put up with this craziness all these years. From the moment the kids were born, we discovered what a sanctuary the boat could be. With both Kate and me working like maniacs and with the kids passed off to school, child care, and play groups, our time together was severely limited. Plus, Michael and Sam are six years apart, so they were more like two only children than playmates. Our annual two weeks on the boat was when we became a foursome. We were away from phones, TVs, work, friends, shopping, and housework. We were more often than not on faraway shores, frequently in deserted harbors or the only boat tucked in among a group of islands.

We always got off to a rough start, bickering, bumping into hard objects, and complaining about too much or too little wind or sun and too little space and too much stuff. Sailboats the size of the *Crow* are not set up like summer rental cottages. Every summer, it took some getting used to. I tried to please everyone, because I was painfully aware that this was "Dad's thing." Then I felt unappreciated. Kate sometimes complained that it was just like housekeeping except in a confined, lurching space. Michael and Sam were prone to pronouncing the onset of terminal boredom after the first fifteen minutes. Sometimes Michael would be annoyed about having to wear a life vest, or Sam fussed about being hungry, having eaten an hour earlier. It was no surprise that our sailing cruises became known as "forced family fun."

Today, as the boat eases out of the harbor, I simply enjoy watching Sam hoisting the mainsail, Michael trimming the sheets. I had wanted my sons to enjoy sailing like I did and to teach them all the skills my grandfather taught me. But when you're little, it's difficult to get much of a feel for sailing on a big, heavy boat. I had learned on my own little boat. My boys were trying to learn on Dad's big boat.

Teaching is one of my strengths, but I wasn't a patient teacher as a parent. I expected them to know too much, I didn't let them learn by mistakes, and I couldn't articulate what I wanted them to do. And of course, nautical language is incomprehensible to anyone who hasn't grown up with it. Once, when Michael was six, I was teaching him how to sail close to the wind—not too close to be "pinching," but not too "far off" to be giving up "ground to windward." In other words, trying to find that magical groove when the boat is going as fast as possible as close to the wind as possible. Michael had no feel for what I was talking about, and he repeatedly let the boat "luff" or wander into a "reach" in the wrong direction. We tried over and over again. The kid was a gamer but the dad got impatient. "Michael, can't you see when the tell tails are flying straight?" I practically spat. "Can't you feel when the boat's in a groove, for God's sake?!"

He looked at me anxiously, both hands clutching the tiller, his little knuckles white and lip quivering. "I'm just not very good at this, Dad. I'm sorry."

I looked at my little boy. I had frightened him with my anger. I felt awful. I had lost my temper, again. The tension and anxiety that lurked below my mellow, easygoing façade had been exposed once we had children. Kate and I were both startled at how vulnerable I was as a parent and how quick to lose my temper. Since he was very little, Michael bore the brunt of my anxiety, which would flip into anger in a nanosecond. These outbursts at him finally pushed me into therapy back in the late eighties to deal with the underlying volcano of feelings I had been running away from since my own childhood. Therapist, heal thyself.

◇◇◇

Despite the difficult starts to our sailing vacations, somewhere on the second or third day, the magic began to happen. The boys would get Kate to read out loud, from *Winnie-the-Pooh* when they were young or one of Dave Barry's humor books these days. She would get caught up in the humor and start laughing so hard she couldn't keep reading and almost wet herself. The three of us would get swept into gales of laughter, even though she hadn't gotten to part that set her off in the first place. Sam once admitted that he never knew what was so funny about Dave Barry, but his mom's sidesplitting guffawing made him laugh just as hard as the rest of us.

When the boys were younger, Kate and I took turns entertaining them with endless games. After dinner we all would play board games and card games. We would laugh and tease, be silly and un-self-conscious. And sometimes we even had good talks without my pushing for them. Every summer we left our struggles and anxieties behind, like bubbles in the wake.

In 1994, we circumnavigated Newfoundland. I remember roaring into a little harbor with a strong breeze behind us—we were on the lookout for a "sunker," a group of unmarked rocks just below the surface of the water in the middle of the harbor entrance. On the chart, it was called Mad Moll Rock. Kate and Michael were at the bow looking off to port and starboard. I had the helm, my eyes glued on our GPS position, and Sam was calling out the depths on our fathometer. We really had become a team.

My long desire for the boys to learn sailing is finally being fulfilled. After he finished college, Michael said to me, "I think I am ready to really learn how to sail the boat on my own." That summer, we took the boat out together for a week by ourselves. He took in everything like a sponge. Somehow, after twenty-five years of being on the boat, it was as if he had learned everything by osmosis. And he loved it. Just this past year, Sam, who was enthralled by the movie *Pirates of the Caribbean*, announced that he wanted to help me take the boat to New Zealand: a lifelong dream of mine. Both boys seem ready to embrace my passion. But that was before the lymphoma.

"Dad, do you want to lie down for a bit? I can take the helm," offers Michael. I am a little tired and, to my surprise, nauseous. I never have been seasick before; must be the chemo. "Sure, Mike." I go below. I lie in the bunk and listen to the light banter in the cockpit. I wonder what Kate and the boys will do with the *Crow*.

Sam

My dad usually does the early morning driving when we head to the boat, more than three hours away, but today my brother has taken over the job. Today Dad's tired and is just watching the cars go by, rather than engaging us in talking about our feelings as he usually does. I don't know which dad I like better, cheerful and annoying or quiet and scary. Scary because I know it isn't normal. I see the reflection of his face in the window. Beneath his blue shirt, the one he always wears when sailing, little foreign cells are trying to make a comeback despite the chemo. His immune system is being fried by the drugs the doctors administer every few weeks. Mom explained that the chemotherapy is a good thing despite the fact that it wipes out everything in the body and leaves you so weak. Today he is weak. It's a bad day to start a sailing trip.

On most sailing trips, we leave early in the morning and get to the boat around nine or ten This Saturday morning we didn't leave until after nine. By the time we arrive at the boat yard, its twelve-fifteen. My dad silently grimaces at his watch and grabs the smallest bag he can while my brother and I grab three each. Things just aren't quite the same. Deep in my gut, I briefly wonder if they'll ever be the same.

The team is definitely not at full strength. My mom has been frazzled lately with trying to plan her course, see patients, and still be a loving wife and mother to her sick husband and her two grown sons. Michael is stressed out about the process of applying to grad schools. And my dad has cancer. I think I'm the only one happy to go sailing. I'm feeling pretty solid, actually. I am confident that things will get back to normal once we get to the boat.

Once in the dinghy, we motor out to our sailboat, the *Crow*. According to my dad, our boat is more beautiful than others even though it's small and thirty years old. He says it's the "shear line" of the boat that matters. Kind of like the curves of a woman, I guess. As soon as we're all on the boat, Dad starts his usual orders. "Michael, tie up the dinghy; Kate, get below and I'll hand you the groceries; Sam, get that sail cover off."

I've already started my designated task. I'm a good deckhand, but I don't like steering or doing any nitpicky stuff, like adjusting the sails in infinitesimally small increments. With the sail cover off and folded into its compartment, my dad starts up the motor and Michael casts off. Mom sets up the cabin belowdecks. Dad takes the helm, and I raise the main sail and then carefully coil the lines. (Ropes are not called ropes on a boat; they're called "lines." I can understand the port and starboard lingo, so that you can have universal left and right, but the other boat terminology doesn't make sense to me.)

Mom and Mike join me in the cockpit, and we make small talk while Dad stands holding the tiller. He is quiet, his green eyes soaking up the sea from behind his wire-framed glasses that haven't been popular for two decades. His *Crow* hat sits lightly atop his bald head. For a moment I see almost a grim determination. I'm sure he feels like shit, but on *his* boat, with *his* family, he is the captain. He draws strength from the sea, from the salt air, from the wind in his face. My dad, the sailor.

Sailing is the one part of his life where my dad is unquestionably manly. The rest of the time he is a therapist, all touchy-feely and sensitive. He plays tennis, wearing preppy white. He can't fix anything in the house. But on the boat, he switches from Dr. Treadway to Cap'n Dave. The boat is old, and nothing can be done easily. My dad is usually the only one who knows how to do anything. He's capable when he's on his boat. Can't light the stove? Dad can do it. Don't know where that line goes? Dad knows. Engine won't start? Dad will fix it. Or he'll work on it for hours, then yell obscenities, and just sail without the damn engine. Engines are for pansies anyway.

Seeing my dad now, standing proud, defying all of the pain and weakness, makes me smile. He radiates sureness. It's good to see. After a moment I join in the small talk. "Yeah, I'm glad, too, that the weather is good. Lord knows we would still be dumb and headed out even if it were raining and storming."

"Well, maybe not these days, with your dad feeling how he is," my mom corrects.

"It's true. Even without cancer, just getting older, I've gotten a little wiser, a little less risky and crazy." My dad smiles, but as he looks out over the bow I see a tinge of regret flash across his face.

"All I'm saying is the Cap'n Dave I know would laugh at a hurricane and beckon the tumbling seas. He would reef the main sail, strap himself in, and get out in it," I say with dramatic flare.

"Well, that would be true of my younger self," my dad chuckles.

"I mean, come on, what about the gale we were in when I was, like, seven?" We all know the story. My mom likes to tell it when describing the harder aspects of having a sailor for a husband. I'm sure it backfires when she tells it to some of my dad's salty sailor buddies up in Maine. They probably like the image of the rough and tough sailor battling the sea and yelling down to his family to stay down below while he rides the beast out. But that's truly what happened. Dad was up on deck in full foul-weather gear. I was down below vomiting up both kidneys and trying to get my lungs out as well. Mom was sitting next to me, splitting her attention between comforting me and glaring at the closed door to the cockpit, beyond which my father stood in the rain, slogging away on the rolling sea.

My brother had been asleep for the entire morning, despite the gale. Right above his berth is the forward hatch that opens onto the deck. As the boat was heaving up and down, the lock on the hatch suddenly broke, letting in a deluge of water. Michael woke up screaming, soaked in icy water. Mom tried to fix the lock, but with the boat heaving she couldn't lock it before the water crashed in again. Water was every-where. Eventually she must have convinced Dad to stop sailing and get to safety.

"Why had we started out, and where did we end up anchoring?" I ask. Dad looks abashed, but Mom is quick to respond.

"Oh, we had somewhere really important to get to," she starts off, sarcastically. "Yeah, we had to go to port so-and-so because that was just part of the plan. And we can't mess with the plan. That would ruin the whole vacation!" She emphasizes the last word, highlighting the irony of battling a storm as part of a vacation.

"Easy, Kate," my dad chimes in. "I didn't know how bad it was going to be, and I wanted to have some miles behind us and get to a safer harbor if it ended up getting worse. To answer your question, Sam, we stopped at as good a place as I could find on the charts. And I started looking for it as soon as the weather turned ugly. But once you're stuck in it, there is only one way out." There it was again. The smile and strength. A hint of Mr. Macho. Mom rolls her eyes, but she sees it, too. And likes it.

My dad has always been gung-ho, passionate about sailing. My mom reluctantly comes along and enjoys it occasionally. My brother and I are indifferent. It is what it is. Sailing has brought us together as a family through the years. Just being forced to stay, for weeks at a time, in close quarters with your family every summer helps bind you together. It's so different than being at a resort, where people can go off and do their own thing. The best you can do to get away is put on headphones and sit ten feet away from the rest of the family, which, of course, is what I did through most of my teenage years, as my brother did before me.

I pull out *The Lord of Chaos*, by Robert Jordan (the sixth book in an especially long fantasy series), while the others continue the chit-chat. One of the first books I ever read was a fantasy novel, and I've been reading them ever since. They suck me into amazing other worlds, keeping reality at bay. Which comes in handy when you're stuck on a thirty-three-foot boat for two weeks.

My mom lies back, trying to make the most of the warmth. The problem on a sailboat is that there is always a huge sail to cast a shadow over you, so Mom is constantly moving to different spots on the boat to find the sun. (She usually blames my dad for conspiring against her and purposely avoiding the sun, or at least making sure the sail shades her.)

Dad turns off the engine and the sails begin to fill. Within moments, the *Crow* finds its groove, just as each of us settles in. I'm reading, my mom's enjoying the sun, and my dad and brother are talking. Their conversation has turned to Michael's career choices. The only other sound is the soft gurgle and splash of the water along the edges of the boat. We may do slightly separate things while on the boat, but we all stick together, all in the same groove.

Kate

We head out of Robinhood into a beautiful day with light winds. David takes a turn at the tiller but not for long. Looks pass between me and the boys when he says he needs to lie down. Michael takes the helm and steers for Seguin, a rocky island lying in the slipstream of the Kennebec River with a lighthouse that rises 180 feet above the ocean. I stare out at the water as I have done so many times before, trying to find the calm that I have so often felt in the gentle motion of the boat and the beauty of the sea and land around me, but I remain tense. I am surprised that even though David looks ill all the time these days—thin, tired, and hairless—it is still a jolt to see him unable to do the things he has always done. It was distressing to watch Michael pull David onto the boat, and now to have him go lie down below. These seemingly small shifts from normal are deeply disturbing. They are perhaps a more immediate measure of how much our lives have changed.

Once ashore, we climb to the lighthouse, pretending halfway up to look at the view so David can catch his breath. At the base of the lighthouse, David rests while we climb to the top. We walk up the ornate spiral staircase to the huge lens of the light and step out onto the small balcony at the top. The ocean shimmers in the sun and we can see for miles in all directions. As I do so often, I send a prayer into the ether that David will be well.

In the early days of our relationship, as David and I slowly moved into each other's hearts, we talked of the things we cherished. David talked of sailing. It was obvious how much he loved the sea and being on a boat. For him, sailing was a refuge from the emotional complexity of his family. He had sailed from the age of five. I, on the other hand, had been on a sailboat only once before I met David.

Soon after we were married, while we were visiting his father and stepmother in Massachusetts, he arranged to charter a nineteen-foot open sailboat for a day trip up the coast. We sailed out through the fog from Manchester Harbor bound for Rockport, his childhood summer home. Shortly beyond the harbor, the fog lifted and it became a warm, sunny day. The wind was light, and there was only an easy rocking motion as we sailed north. When we got to Rockport, we walked around the town—a classic New England village with neat, white clapboard houses. He took me to his old summer house. It felt as though I was being allowed to peer into his most precious memories. We had a lobster lunch and sailed home. It was a wonderful day.

Nothing about that day prepared me for the sailing trips that began soon thereafter. While there were plenty of days like that first one, there were also moments of sheer terror; the next year found us taking off in thirty-five-knot winds in a small chartered boat, with me clinging to the mast or a winch as the boat heeled, convinced that we'd capsize despite David's reassurance that we wouldn't. The ocean was powerful and unpredictable, and sailing stopped being my idea of fun.

I have always been somewhat fearful of deep water, dark water, and water at night. Drowning is particularly terrifying for me. When I was a child, I witnessed an eight-year-old boy's drowning. I was swimming with my friends when the lifeguards suddenly jumped into their boat and rowed out to a child flailing in the water. They laid him on the sand and tried to push the water out of his lungs. I remember the horror as I watched the water pour out of his mouth. Perhaps worse than anything was seeing the Evanston police car pull up to the beach and the child's mother get out of the car. When she saw her son lying on the sand, her knees buckled and the two policemen had to hold her up.

Now, married to David, I found myself rowing in a dinghy at night to get onto the boat or lying in my berth at night knowing I was below the waterline or hearing the deep groan of chain moving on the bottom as we shifted positions in the tide. All of these evoked scary images of dark water and things unseen grabbing at my ankles and pulling me down into the deep. Eventually I came to love these things, but in the early days of our sailing together, I spent most of my time either terrified or simply cold, wet and miserable, a phrase that was often repeated most summers when we went sailing.

We tended to sail north, where fog, rain, and cold were common. While part of me longed to lie on a sunny beach in a resort, increasingly another part of me loved the coast of Maine, the massive granite rock and the pines—to cherish those days of working our way together through pea-soup fog, navigating between the large steel buoys that marked rocks and ledges. I would be below with the chart, dividers, and parallels calling our courses, David was at the helm, adjusting the course to the current and wind. Then there was the glorious reward of days of sun and wind, tearing down a bay at the end of an afternoon to end up in a deserted harbor, listening to the loons and watching the sun set. From time to time we ventured further north, to Nova Scotia and Newfoundland—cold, wet, and miserable often but also enthralled by the wonder of the northern lights at 1 a.m. or a sky literally thick with stars on a moonless night or the magic of a group of porpoises playing in our bow wave.

Our summer vacations were spent at sea. These trips to remote places bound us together. Our normal lives were filled with the usual struggles of trying to patch together family time between school, home-work, sports, and work. Family dinners became increasingly rare once Michael was in high school and our schedules grew more complex. Because of their age difference, Michael and Sam moved in completely different worlds. But on the boat, with all the distractions of the outside world gone, we became a unit. There were no electronics, no TV, and no radio except the weather and emergency stations.

On good days, the sun was out and the wind fair. The boys and I would sit along the windward rail gazing out at the sea, watching for whales or seals, mesmerized by the endless procession of swells. On bad days, when it was rainy or cold, we all sat on deck, huddled under the dodger, the canvas windbreak covering part of the cockpit, trying to stay dry, longing for warmth. Sam was easily seasick, so sitting below was not an option. No matter how wet, how windy, how cold, David was at the helm, in control and always the source of calm when things got rough. He was genuinely happy at sea in all conditions. Despite the fact that each of us could take the helm and handle the boat up to a point, David was always the one on whom we relied to tell us if we were a bit high on the wind or too far off. David allowed us all to feel secure.

Those summers, we moved from one deserted anchorage to the next, savoring being alone in some beautiful cove surrounded by towering pines and granite. We would climb into the dinghy and go ashore to explore the rocks and tidal pools. David rarely joined us for these land forays. He always felt he should stay on the boat in case anything happened. We went off, carefree, knowing David was keeping watch. Evenings were spent playing endless card games and reading aloud. Once the anchor was down, we were snug and secure. We were together.

◇◇◇

Back at the boat, David and Sam pull out the chessboard and start setting up the pieces. Sam will be returning to school soon; I am desperate to have him stay. Somehow when we are all together, things feel safer. Sam has provided a constant flow of humor and has conveyed his love and concern by cheerfully doing numerous chores that would have been overwhelming for me to accomplish on my own. I will miss him dreadfully. While Sam and David start to play, Michael heads out in the dinghy to collect the mussels he had seen earlier. We will have them for dinner.

Michael

A FULL MOON SHINES ON THE INKY BLACK WATERS OFF OF SEGUIN ISLAND. The halyards rap against the mast in a light northeasterly breeze. With each strike of the rope, the hollow aluminum mast gives off an almost shrill tone. In gusts of wind, the clattering tempo increases, creating a sense of urgency, like the yelp of a mother seal calling to her pups. I'm glad for the wind. Not so strong as to be unpleasant, but strong enough to ensure that no one below will catch a whiff of my cigarette.

This is the end of our first day of sailing, and the family has gone to bed. I snuck up to the deck through the boat's forward hatch to treat myself to a cigarette. I've never been a regular smoker, but I enjoy cigarettes. Since Dad got cancer, I find myself smoking more, usually at night, out by the far side of the house from my parent's bedroom. They have always been opposed to my smoking, especially my mother. Smoking claimed the lives of both her parents, and now her husband may be dying of cancer. My smoking is too much for her now.

Since coming home because of Dad's illness, I seem unable to deny myself anything. I take another drag and recall the course of the evening. As usual on the boat, we ended the night with several rounds of bridge. Given the amount of time we spend playing bridge, one might expect us to be good. We're not. But that's because card games are mostly a vehicle for us to make jokes. Sometimes our kidding can become rough, particularly Sam's teasing of Dad. Sam and Dad have struggled to get along ever since Sam was in high school. As Dad has started to feel better, Sam has been less careful about showing his frustration with him, and it bubbles out in the form of taunts and jibes. I find myself feeling uncomfortable even as I laugh. It's no secret that beneath his comic delivery, Sam's anger toward Dad is ever-brewing. Nor is Dad's pain and regret ever far from the surface. It's hard to watch these two people that I love so much and who, underneath it all, love each other so much.

The worst of it is Sam's apparent unwillingness to ever really try to work out his anger with Dad. Despite his growing awareness that the anger exists, Sam seems almost resigned to having a bad father-son relationship. Sam's tensions with Dad cause tension between him and me, too. I get annoyed at Sam's refusal to work on himself.

I have been in therapy for years trying to figure out who I am and what I wanted to do with my life, and I am still struggling to find answers. I've lumbered from one career to the other, working hard and trying to do well. Sam always seemed to just coast along. By the time Sam was born, Mom had completed her residency and was no longer working insane hours. Dad had learned to control his temper. Sam seemed to have had it easy.

Now, anytime he and Mom and I are alone together and want to talk about how we will get by if Dad dies, Sam simply refuses to talk about it. I've tried a half-dozen times to start conversations with him about it, but they don't go anywhere. Sam just shrugs and says it will be okay, which I find infuriating.

I take another drag and start to cough, quickly burying my face in my elbow so no one can hear me. I think of the coughing spell Dad had earlier in the day, at the docks.

With his sailing cap covering his bald head, he almost looked strong as he dragged the rubber dinghy along the dock to put it in the water. I caught my mother's eyes and she smiled. "You know, I always thought your dad's sailing was so—" she hesitated "—cool."

I winked at her. "I don't think *cool* is the word you'd have used if you weren't talking to your child."

"That is absolutely correct." My parents laughed and exchanged a flirtatious look. But the moment faded quickly. Dad began to cough violently and uncontrollably. His head bobbed up and down, as he gasped for air, and spittle spurted from his mouth. Finally the coughing subsided, but the moment of strength was over.

As a child I used to love the landscape of the boat. All available space was crammed with pulleys, gears, cables, tubes, pipes, ropes, electrical wires, and hidden compartments. It was an ideal backdrop for make-believe. I'd imagine the boat was a battleship, or under attack, or I'd play with GI Joe soldiers and act out tales of heroes and villains navigating the treacherous labyrinth of cleats and winches.

No matter how old I was, the boat was always a place for escape. Sometimes that even meant escape from my family. When I was a surly adolescent, not wanting to talk much to my parents, they learned to leave me alone, even if we were, by necessity, sitting right next to each other. But with practice, we learned to give each other the space we needed and were therefore always able to come back together.

When I was in high school, I used to spend most of my time on the boat perched at midships, watching the water and listening to music. I would find the perfect section of a piece of music to fit whatever fantasy I wanted to create and play it over and over. It was especially easy to do with rock music, but I could use small pieces of classical music, too. I would listen, repeat, listen, repeat, for hours.

In college I had majored in music and musicology. Not exactly the course of study of someone obsessed with becoming a future world leader, but in that choice I had been fortunate enough to settle on something that I loved. My parents had been especially reassuring; even as I grew concerned that my choice might hurt my chances of getting into law school, they insisted that it was more important to study something in which I took genuine interest. It was in college that I learned how to listen to a piece of music in its entirety. I was amazed to discover the intricate ways in which all those moments of loud dramatic sound I used to isolate were related and how the tension and excitement that they inspired was enhanced by all the intervening notes that I had blithely passed over. I realized that I had not been listening to music all those summers on the boat; I was merely using it, like a drug that facilitated an escape.

With Dad's cancer, I once again am using music the way I had as a teenager. I'm using the music to ease my fear and pain, to make the threat of losing my father feel like a grand tragedy. An inner critical voice often rises when I start feeling the sadness well up that shuts me down fast. *So what if you lose your father? People lose their father every day. They get on with it. They keep going. What makes you so special?* But when I listen to music, somehow it's okay to feel, and tears flow freely.

I wish I had brought my iPod up-deck with me so that I could listen to some music while I smoke a few more cigarettes. I consider crawling back down below to retrieve it, but decide against it. I really don't want to be caught smoking.

Our anchorage tonight is one of our usual haunts, only a day's sail from the marina where Dad keeps the boat. For dinner, we had fresh mussels that I gathered from the nearby mud flats. I love mussels. When I was a boy, I used to explore the water's edge of each anchorage we visited, looking for treasure of some kind. I never came across much, but I could always make my parents happy by bringing back a bucketful of mussels. For some reason, I find mussels incredibly funny—something about the shape of their shells, the way they jut out from the sand and rock suggest a certain defiance of the world. As if to say, "I'm a mussel, damn you, and you will not ignore me!" When I harvest them, I imagine them yelling, "Here he comes! Hold your ground, men! Do not move an inch! Do not surrender!"

After we ate our mussels, we washed the dishes, drank some wine, and decided to suspend our regular bridge game for a game of Scrabble. Like virtually every other game our family plays, Scrabble can become a competitive event.

"Okay, I'm putting down *duct*. It's on a double letter and a double word, so that's fifteen points." Sam said authoritatively.

"You took my spot," Mom complained.

"At least you have a spot," I said. "I have nothing but vowels."

"Hey guys, I have an idea . . . ," Dad began.

"Sam," Mom continued to lament, "Why did you take my spot?"

"Why are you so dumb?"

"Guys, listen," Dad continued, "what if we took a break—"

I sense that Dad wants to have a check-in, as he didn't get to have one during the car ride up.

"Could I do *ducttape*?" Mom asked hopefully.

"That's not a word," I said.

"Well it's got to be a word, because it's the only word Dad knows anytime he tries to fix anything," Sam teased.

"—and maybe do a check-in?" Dad continued.

"Oh, God, tell me about it." Mom jumped back in. "Do you know that when your father was preparing for his transatlantic and I asked him if he had packed a safety kit, he pointed to a box containing a roll of duct tape and a can of WD-40."

"That is patently not true," Dad said.

"I know honey. I'm teasing."

"And I'll have you all know that I can fix an ocean liner using nothing but duct tape and WD-40," Dad said with a grin.

"But seriously, *ducttape* is a word."

"So not a word." Sam said, shaking his head.

"Mom, you're running out of time."

"Now come on, gang. I'd like to do a check-in."

"David, it's late, it's cold. We're on the boat. I'm about to have to crawl into a damp, freezing sleeping bag, you have cancer, and Sam just took my spot."

"And you're pretty dumb."

Eventually we broke into the giggles before we could complete the game. Not an uncommon way for us to end an evening.

I finish my cigarette and drop back down below through the forward hatch. I do so quietly to make sure that no one below hears me. I haven't spent much time on this trip wondering if it will be our last. Part of that is doubtless due to the five glasses of wine I enjoyed with dinner. But it's also a result of the fact that the boat has always been our place of escape, familiar and easy. As sleep settles in on me, I can still hear the halyards rapping against the mast. I used to find it grating when I was trying to fall asleep. Tonight it feels familiar, a welcome distraction.

FALL 2005

David

I'M IN MY OFFICE, WAITING TO SAY GOOD-BYE TO SAM. HE PROCRASTINATED packing for school until the last minute. I'm discreetly hiding out while he and Kate race about the house, tense and irritated.

Sam's been great this summer, despite his irritability with me. He's always been there, willing to do whatever would help. I will miss him, even his sarcastic teasing. I just plain get on his nerves, and we've really not addressed it. Sometime soon we really have to deal with our relationship, because I don't want to wait for deathbed reconciliation.

It's been an enormous comfort to me for all of us to be together this summer. We've had time to adjust together to this new plane of reality we live on: simply not knowing how long I'm going to live. Sometimes all I really care about is that we all have enough time together so we'll be as prepared as possible if things go poorly. So we can face it together.

With Sam going back to Minnesota, I'm worried that reality might hit him hard. He's pretty isolated at school, and he's locked up inside himself. He doesn't like our inevitable questions, so I don't think he'll stay connected with us. Besides, I hate trying to engage him over the phone. He gets very annoyed when I ask him the standard dad questions, like, "Sam, how are you?"

"Fine."

Back when he was a little boy, "Fine" would be his cheerful answer to my questions. It took a long time before I realized that it was his way of not answering. When he became an adolescent, it became obvious that he found our interest invasive and his "Fine" was clearly evasive.

There's so much I wanted to talk to Sam about this summer that we just never got around to. I have a lot of concerns about how he avoids dealing with difficult issues in his life, like school, the future, and his relationship with Sarah, and his difficulty accepting help. But he can't stand my efforts to mentor him. He sees my offers of support and advice as a vote of no confidence, and no matter how I say it, I manage to push him away. Being a father has been much more difficult than being a therapist, and there are ways in which I have harmed both sons, which makes me heartsick.

"David, Sam's ready," calls out Kate. "He's got to get going. Get Michael up." I know Kate's going to cry when he leaves; I feel like crying. I am sure Sam doesn't want a lugubrious send-off , but it might be unavoidable. I drag Michael out of bed and we go out to the porch. Sam's forcing down the lid of the trunk. Kate's crying.

Sam comes back and gives Kate a big hug. "Don't go crying on me"

"It's been really good to have you here, buddy," says Michael, as he gives Sam a quick, manly-man kind of hug.

My eyes are filled with the tears I am holding back. "Come here, Sam. Let the old man give you a hug."

"Okay, Daddo, just don't pull a 'Mom' on me. One of you is enough."

I hug him a little longer than I think he would like. I just don't want to let him go. Then he's off in his baby blue Volkswagen Jetta. He honks the horn as he pulls out of the driveway. Kate reaches for me. She's doing the crying for both of us.

Sam

My fifth day of work at the Tavern of Northfield drags on and on. I look at the bowl of pretzels, mini breadsticks and, my favorite, the rye crisps. I decide to put them out of reach because the owner doesn't like bartenders eating the snacks. My customers are all outside enjoying the patio, so I have nothing to do and no one to talk to. It's five in the afternoon; I have eight more hours of work. Neither college has started the fall term yet, and the town is still empty. It's going to be a long night.

I came back to Northfield early, ostensibly because Sarah was lonely. In reality, I just needed to get away from the family's crisis. I hate to admit it, but it's a relief. I've only been back for six days, but I appreciate every single mile that separates me and the cancer. It's nice to be able to use Sarah as an excuse to be here.

I don't understand why Sarah's living here after graduating. She hates her job, hates her tiny apartment, and hates having no friends. Some days I wake up next to her happy that she's here and that we're together. Other days, I feel smothered and resent her. (Wow, do I sound like the son of a shrink or what?)

Since being back I've worked every day. The Tavern is a little restaurant tucked underneath the Archer House Hotel, the nicest of the five hotels in Northfield. This is my second year bartending. It's not so bad. We have a lot of regulars from around town. One's Benny, the body-piercing guy who works at the tattoo parlor across the street. His face looks like the bottom of a handyman's toolbox. Stan works in the Twin Cities but always comes in for a beer on his way home. Sophia, a hot, middle-aged woman, works at another pub but likes to do her drinking at the Tavern. My favorite is a professor of geology at Carleton. He comes in every Thursday afternoon during the school year to have two beers. He says he'll just have one, but we get to talking and he always stays for a second. He is an encyclopedia of knowledge and wisdom. I wish I could have him as a professor, but geology holds no interest for me.

When I walk out to the patio, the blinding sunlight and the last of the summer's heat hit me. I chat with Chris, another regular, about the youth group he runs. I look out at the Cannon River rushing by and daydream about getting off at one in the morning.

The next day, after running errands, I show up triumphantly at Sarah's apartment. "I just spent seven dollars and fifty cents in quarters trying to get matching rings for us out of that toy vending machine at the drugstore. But I finally got them! Here you go. I also got us fake tattoos, an armband, a couple Pokémon plastic toys, and a blow pop."

"Awww, you shouldn't have," she says, as she slips on the sparkling pink plastic ring. I put on a matching one that's blue.

"Aren't we cute?" I grin and realize that I still love to make Sarah smile. I still love Sarah.

"So, check out these photos I picked up." I jump onto the bed with her. It's her day off, so she's watching movies. "They are from that weekend with my friends in New Hampshire I told you about."

"Yeah, let me just pause this."

I start flipping through the photos, slowly. I don't recognize anyone in the photos. I quickly flip through a few more, not seeing anyone I know at all.

"Your film got switched with someone else's," Sarah says, reaching the realization of what happened before I do.

I look at the photo in my hand. The girl who has been the star of the last few pictures is flashing a brilliant smile. She's gorgeous. Blonde hair, blue eyes, perfect teeth. Her smile looks so genuine, so pure. A guy stands to her left and slightly behind, staring intensely at her. Maybe a boyfriend? Or someone who wants to be the boyfriend?

"That's too bad. You can bring it back tomorrow and get it sorted out," Sarah says brightly. "Do you want to watch the rest of Notting Hill with me?"

"Sure," I agree absentmindedly. I flip to the next photo. Again the same girl, this time not so happy. She's still smiling for the camera, but I can tell something is wrong. Her eyes seem distant, as if she's distracted. There is something on her mind, troubling her. What happened? She's not wearing the same shirt, so it's a different day, maybe a different week or month. Did she break up with that boyfriend? Or something worse? "Sarah, look at these two photos. See how different her smile is? What do you think happened?" I drag her attention away from Hugh Grant being awkwardly charming.

"Yeah, I see it, I guess. Wasn't a Kodak moment for her?"

"No, I think it's more than that. There is something eating at her. She's lost something, or someone. Maybe a family member died, like her grandmother probably," I say with confidence.

"Geez, that's morbid. She probably was just having a bad day. Someone told her to smile for the camera and she did the best she could. People have bad days all the time. Why would you jump to the conclusion that her grandmother died?"

"I don't know." I sit back. The TV's glow washes over me. This was probably a roll of film from someone at St. Olaf, the college where beautiful Minnesotans go to be Lutheran and sing in a choir. I think about why that photo affects me so powerfully. Sarah is right, why did I jump to that conclusion?

I look at the two photos in my hand again. She's stunning in both, but something is distinctly off in the second picture. The first seems to be a party scene, because there is a plastic red cup in the "boyfriend's" hand. In the second she's holding up a piece of paper, but I can't make out what it reads. She's proud of something. An A+ on a paper? A love note? But then why do her eyes tell me she's sad? What's upsetting her? Why am I so intrigued by this stranger? Is that how I look? I know my father's going to be fine, but he has cancer. He's sick and weak. Subconsciously, am I a worrying mess? Do my eyes tell a different story than my smile?

I flip through the rest of the photos. In all the others, her beaming face doesn't betray any dark secrets. Sarah is probably right again: she was just having a bad day. Even with this assurance, I tuck the "bad day" photo away. I'll exchange the rest in the package tomorrow.

David

It's two o'clock in the morning and Kate is snoring away gently, and no doubt happily, beside me. She's happy because I got another clean PET scan today. No detectable cancer. The chemo's worked. I am not happy. I just can't even believe it. I was braced for the worst, and now I feel vaguely let down. I've been prepping for my imminent demise, and they tricked me. What difference does another clean scan mean, anyway?

My mind is racing, a middle-of-the-night rush of roaring energy, fear, and loathing, clear and hard like a mountain stream tumbling headlong beneath the snow on a late March day. Sleeping meds didn't calm me down a bit. Maybe, I think, this is the beginning of the end. I'm going out of my mind. Or maybe it's just a bad night. Maybe the PET was right and the cancer will never come back and I'll die of heart disease or maybe, if I'm lucky, a gentle pneumonia when I'm in my nineties, my dad's age.

I'd like to feel grateful for my good test results. Instead, I'm lying here, convinced the other shoe is going to drop. I belong to a vast fraternity of fear and waiting. All over the world, millions of us are tossing and turning in our beds, waiting and worrying, filled with dread about cancer recurrences, our bills, our marriages, hair loss, pimples, getting asked to the prom, whether we are good enough moms or dads. And what about those who lie awake with the cold fear that they might not be able to find food for their children in the morning, or that their neighborhood might be bombed?

If ever there was a time to meditate, this would be it, but just the thought annoys me.

The cat lies on its back, beside me, purring. Her soft steady breath calms me a little. Maybe it's okay that I am freaked out rather than happy with my good news. This fear has been relentless all summer. Most of the time, in front of everyone, even Kate sometimes, I've maintained a faux equanimity and placid acceptance of my dire situation. But when I am by myself, I have times of sheer panic. I'm doing the best I can, but I'm glad I have a session with my therapist, Nancy, coming up. She's as steady as a heartbeat when I am flailing about.

My eyes leak water like a drippy old faucet. Just below the noise of the snap, crackle, and pop of agitation, I can feel myself in a river of sadness meandering slowly down to the sea. I am sinking. I am rising again. Bobbing along past meadows, stands of trees, white farm houses in the distance. No one sees my head above the water. No one knows I am passing by.

Maybe I am more afraid of dying than I think I am.

Soon there will be another day and the only price paid for this midnight ramble will be a tired, worn-down, slow feeling. Maybe there will be time for a nap. I should try taking a nap right now. Maybe now I can spend a little time focusing on my breath.

Michael

WE ARE PUTTING DOWN ANNIE, OUR BLACK LAB MIX, TONIGHT. WE BOUGHT her as a birthday present for Mom when I was sixteen. Upon her initial arrival into our home, my mom was the only family member who particularly liked Annie. This was not due to any lack of effort on Annie's part, more *because* of her efforts. She would bark enthusiastically any time anyone so much as moved a muscle. If you got up from your spot in the living room, she would start barking, jumping, and drooling. Annie was never mean and she never bit; she was just very, very excitable. Sam referred to Annie as a "dumb dog" almost any time she came up in conversation. (Indeed, Sam's eventual catholic use of the word dumb can be traced back to his descriptions of Annie.) My mother speculated that Annie had some border collie in her lineage, to which Sam would respond that she had some dumb in her lineage.

Although Sam's appraisal of Annie might strike the casual observer as a tad harsh, there was no denying that he was right. No matter how many times Mom argued otherwise, it was clear to everyone that Annie was possessed of a dim intelligence. Even the squirrels in our yard seemed to regard Annie as something of an intellectual lightweight. They would not even look up when Annie barked at them as they stole seed from our bird feeder. She'd bark like a rabid animal but never make the slightest movement toward the culprit. For all her bluster, Annie was a pacifist at heart.

And, for all *our* bluster, we all loved Annie. Her enthusiasm was infectious. When I came home for the holidays, Annie was always the most excited to see me. She was always willing to accompany you to the store, or keep you company while you shoveled snow off the walkway, or stay by your side when you went for a run. Whether person or pet, no one seemed to take such unbridled pleasure in your company as Annie did in ours. Thus had she won us over. Even Sam, though he would never admit it.

When I got the call about Annie from Dad, I was driving home from work. When I heard the sound of his voice, I immediately thought it was about his PET scan. Something had changed; it wasn't a clean scan after all. Ever since we had gotten the news last week, I had been feeling slightly less scared. Then all the fear snapped back. This is it. This must be it. This is what I get for daring to believe he might be getting better. Instead, he told me that Annie had been hit by a car, and we were going to have to put her down. I was instantly relieved. Then I burst into tears.

We wait for Mom to get home from the hospital. She walks through the front door and with her ritual sigh, she puts her briefcase down by the coat rack. As soon as she sees me, tears well up. Dad and I have our coats on and are ready to go. It's probably a good thing that Sam has gone back to college; this would've been hard for him. We don't say much as we drive the short distance to the vet.

The waiting room smells of animal fur and formaldehyde and vaguely reminds me of my high school biology classroom. It's mid-September and unseasonably cold. The several "pet doors" are open to the outside, so we sit in the waiting room with our coats and scarves on.

Before we can see Annie, we meet with the vet to go over all the options one more time. Our decision has already been made; we are going to put her down.

The vet tech is young and pretty and wears an expression of gentle concern.

"Annie is ready for you," she says quietly. Her anthropomorphism seems so natural that I half expect to find Annie lying prone in a hospital gurney with an IV and an EKG. Instead, she is lying on a blanket in the middle of the floor in a small, windowless room. Her hind legs are wrapped in a hospital-blue tourniquet to keep them from moving. Although she is heavily sedated, and her hips and pelvis are shattered, she still manages to wag her tail slightly when she sees us. Even now, she wants to make sure we know how much she loves us. The vet asks if we want some time to say good-bye. We say we do, but we don't really. No one wants to say good-bye. Not right now; not to anyone.

Mom and I sit on the floor and pet Annie's face. Dad sits in a chair near her side and pets her head. Annie seems to relax a little. We tell her that we love her; we tell her that it will be okay; we tell her that she's a good girl. We tell her that we'll miss her. I watch my father. He must be thinking what we all are thinking. After a few minutes, the pretty vet tech returns with a syringe and small brown bottle. She briefly describes the procedure. It will only take thirty seconds, and Annie won't feel anything. She sticks the needle into the bottle and draws back the plunger. My overcoat suddenly feels incredibly heavy. I don't feel ready for this. I don't want this to happen. The vet tech asks my mom if we're ready. Mom nods.

The needle goes in. Annie stirs slightly.

"It's okay," the vet tech whispers to her. My parents quietly gaze down at Annie. I'm sweating under my coat, and my scarf feels like a noose.

"Shh . . ." the vet tech whispers to Annie, but I feel like she's really speaking to me. "It's okay."

It's not okay! I'm not ready! I want to scream. *We're not ready. We need Annie right now. Annie needs us. We need more time. We NEED MORE*—

"All right," the vet says, drawing out the needle. "She's gone."

And that's it. I look first at my mom and then at my dad. No one says anything. We need more time.

Kate

I MISS ANNIE. WALKS ALWAYS SEEMED SO MUCH MORE ENJOYABLE WITH her exuberance. It was hard not to feel better, even during these last few months, when out walking in the woods, watching Annie joyously run from one exciting smell to the next. When David was in the hospital for his methotrexate weekends, her presence was a particular comfort—hearing her turn in circles on her bed at the foot of mine, finally finding the perfect spot, landing with a thump and a low woof of contentment.

David has now finished his CHOP-R chemotherapy. Nothing will be preventing a recurrence except for his continued methotrexate every three months for his brain. Over the years, my patients have talked to me about how hard it is to come to the end of chemo. That has always made sense to me. On the one hand, who could be sorry to end the nausea and fatigue, but on the other it means that nothing active is being done

◇◇◇

As the weeks go by, despite a second clean PET scan, I find myself increasingly anxious. When he was in treatment, I was focused on the effects of his chemo and what might go wrong. Now I begin to focus on what might lie ahead. I watch David intently for any sign that something is wrong. I am obsessed with wanting to know what is going to happen to him. I reread the survival statistics for lymphoma. I comb the Internet for new prognosis data, looking for something that will give me an answer. I develop the totally irrational sense that if I ask Effi, he will have the answer, as though he actually knows the outcome. I know perfectly well this is not the case, and yet my impulse is to call him hourly to ask what he thinks.

It is this constant fear that drives me to look for signs everywhere. Walking through the halls of the hospital gives me too much time to think, so I develop the habit of counting out the syllables of my question with each step: "Will-Da-vid-have-a-re-cur-rence-of-his-high-ly-aggres-sive-stage- 4-B-dif-fuse-large-B-cell-lymph-om-a-in-two-thou-sand-and-five-yes-no-yes-no-yes-no" until my foot crosses the bottom step or the change in linoleum color or the end of the corridor. It never really matters whether my foot crosses the line at yes or no, because I just start again. Besides, at least it is an answer.

I finally talk to Effi and ask him what he thinks will happen. We talk in the vague ways medicine has of answering and not answering these questions—the problem of statistics being about a group and not about the person, that the data I have is all before Rituxan started being used, since the five-year survival data with Rituxan has not been published yet. He assures me that David's prognosis is better than the old data suggest, despite all of the factors that put David in the worst prognostic category. I realize I do not want this discussion. I have read everything I can get my hands on. I know all this.

"Effi, I guess what I really want to know is what *you* think. Are you worried about David?" By this time we had moved from standing in the hall to sitting in an empty exam room. Effi is sitting across from me. He looks at me for a moment and then leans forward, his elbows on his knees, his hands together, his eyes looking at the floor. Part of me knows he has no idea what will happen, because we all learn in medicine that predicting outcome is a very uncertain business. He looks up at me, his face full of concern.

"I guess I would say, cherish this time." he says softly.

My stomach knots, but at the same time, in an odd way it is a relief to me to know that things are as grim as I have supposed. Knowing this does not change my belief that there is a chance we will get through this. It simply means I am not making things worse than they are. In many ways, my being a doctor is a tremendous relief to David. He does not feel compelled to comb the Internet or go from doctor to doctor to find the "right" answer. He has left that up to me. But he has also paid a price, because he knows what I know and what it means.

David has told me many times over the last few months that he wants to know everything I know. It is a way of keeping me close, of not letting the special knowledge I have as a doctor separate us. Even though at his insistence, I have promised not to hold back anything, I do not tell him about this conversation with Effi immediately. Reporting something Effi said might give it more weight, and I wonder if I should repeat a conversation that was perhaps more direct than if David had been there. But I find that keeping this to myself creates a slight distance between us. In other circumstances, I doubt either of us would have noticed, but in the hyperaware state in which we live, any change in the connection between us is magnified. I am torn about what to do. I know I will tell him, just not now.

David and I frequently watch old movies at night. It is a way to be together, snuggled up but not talking, not going over the same territory of fear and worry and questions. Tonight we watch *Volcano,* a late '90s thriller with Tommy Lee Jones about a lava flow under Los Angeles. Through most of the movie, everyone in L.A. is going about their daily lives, blissfully unaware of the danger growing beneath them. At the end, of course, the lava erupts, causing death and mayhem. The analogy is far more disturbing than it might have been under other circumstances. The image of unseen danger growing larger, coming ever nearer, haunts me. It seems to perfectly echo my constant vigil, waiting for the lava to erupt.

David

NOW I AM FINALLY DONE WITH ONE OF MY TWO CHEMO REGIMENS, THE CHOP-R. I'm feeling healthier, and am even playing tennis a little. Badly, but who cares? Michael's away for the weekend, and Kate and I have been looking forward to some alone time. It seems very strange not to have Annie here. Actually, very sad.

We are ensconced on the sofa in front of the fire, with a platter of cheese and crackers on the coffee table. I am hoping we'll watch *Shakespeare in Love* again, share a bottle of cabernet, and maybe, just maybe, light a little romantic fire between us. At least that's my plan.

Lately, we have been ships passing in the night. She's been working incredibly hard, and we haven't been making time for our talks. She still grills me about how I am, but that's not connecting. And I am definitely not telling her how often I feel a twinge, an ache, numbness, tingling, and assorted other bodily sensations that loom large in my mind. I bring my more paranoid thoughts to my therapist and do my best to spare Dr. Kate. She has enough on her plate. But not talking separates us.

Kate says she doesn't want to watch the Shakespeare movie and begins flipping through the movie channels. "There's nothing ever on," she complains. "And I hate having to choose between hundreds of movies." She's in a bad mood; my vision of the evening fades and my disappointment morphs into irritability. Maybe we should talk.

"Listen, before we pick a movie, let's do the talking thing and check in with each other. We haven't done it for a while," I propose, as cheerfully as I can. Silence.

She keeps clicking the clicker. "I really don't know if I'm in the mood to talk about things. I'm just exhausted, and I don't want to deal with anything."

"So, you really aren't in the mood to open up about the tough stuff, and you're feeling pretty tired, and—"

"Please don't do the active listening gimmick. That sounds so contrived, and it drives me crazy," she says with a smile that is dead serious.

"So, I hear you saying you really don't want me to do the talk/listen tech—" I continue trying to get a laugh out of her.

"Stop." she says sharply.

"All right. Seriously, can I talk then?"

She sighs. "Sure."

"I've been feeling like ever since Sam's gone back and Michael has been away a lot more, you and I haven't really been connecting. It's been feeling really distant."

Kate stares at the fire and doesn't say anything for a long time. Then she starts to cry. "There is something that I haven't talked to you about."

"What?"

"About three weeks ago, I had a conversation with Effi that was upsetting to me, and I didn't want to tell you about it because I was pretty sure it would upset you and—"

"Hold on, Kate. You made a promise never to hold back any information. You fucking promised!"

"Please don't be mad. Please." She's crying hard. "It wasn't really different information. It's just—"

"Listen," I say, trying hard to calm down and control my tone of voice. "I don't want to get angry. I just need you to tell me everything. It's so not like you to break a promise."

"I know. It's been making me feel terrible."

"So tell me."

"Ever since you got the clean PET scan, I've continued to feel really scared about your cancer and I began to feel like I was just overreacting. You know, being melodramatic about it all. So I called up Effi and asked him if I was being too anxious about your chances being bad. He said, very softly and kindly, 'No, Kate, you're not overreacting.' I couldn't stand the idea of telling you. I didn't know what to do."

She'd been trying to protect me. I felt a surge of love for her and understanding of the extraordinary bind she'd been in. Of course she didn't want to tell me. And, as is so often true, the truth was less harsh than the silence. I reach out to her.

OCTOBER

Michael

TRAFFIC IS MOVING SLOWLY ALONG STORROW DRIVE IN BOSTON. I AM listening to Brahms's fourth and final symphony. The first movement, which opens with a sad, sloping chain of thirds, tells the story of a profound loss weathered many years ago. As I listen to it, I see an image of myself years from now, sitting in a symphony hall next to a future wife and young child, both of whom never had a chance to meet my father. The finale, with its thirty-two repetitions of the same defiantly ascending melody, creates a swell of tension that resolves in a renewed defeat at the end of each variation.

This has been my morning ritual for weeks, and as usual, I am crying. It's one time when I can reliably get myself to cry. The tears bring relief, and every day I find myself wanting to cry, craving the sharp release that gushes alongside the tears. I may now better understand the point of crying, which I often used to wonder about. The sadness I feel about losing my father feels less overwhelming, closer to a sad nostalgia than harsh grief. Through it, I feel a sense of connection and closeness with all the other people I imagine are suffering. I make up stories about the other drivers. That one is working in a dead-end job, desperately trying to find a sense of meaning in the world. Two years ago, she lost her husband to a car accident. The world blurs behind the tears. Everyone's struggles can be shared.

I arrive at work at 8:45, grab a cup of coffee from the cafeteria downstairs in the atrium, and make my way to my office on the second floor. It's my second month as a research assistant at Massachusetts General Hospital, my first job in my new career path. The office is cramped. Within the strict hierarchy of academic medicine, the head of the lab, Joanne, has not yet earned the right to her own office, so three of us share an office the size of a small sedan. It's a lot different from the large office I had when I worked in venture capital. But I do not mind, because now I'm actually doing something that I enjoy. And as an added bonus, my desk has me facing out to the hallway, which affords me the best part of my day: the time when Anna walks by in the morning.

She is the first woman my age I've known for whom the best adjective is *distinguished*. She is unfalteringly graceful and poised. I do not know much about her, just that she is a graduate student on some kind of research fellowship. We have not been formally introduced. All the same, every morning at 10 a.m., Anna glides down the hallway, holding a hot cup of tea with both hands and smiling when she passes my door. Her eyes sparkle, and somehow their color always matches perfectly whatever scarf she is wearing that day. I smile back.

Having just come out of a difficult relationship with Kristin, I am not eager to start dating again. Furthermore, I am mortified at the thought of telling a new girlfriend that I live at home and work in the job of a twenty-two-year-old. I used to be important (kind of). Dad insists that this is not an obstacle and that I should stop taking myself so seriously when it comes to how much I've accomplished. He even suggested that women will be attracted to my vulnerability. I find this dubious. Vulnerability is attractive when you're rich and powerful, not when you are actually vulnerable. When I make this observation to Dad, he points out that if I want to be important, I should be spending more time on my grad school applications and less time worrying about Anna's perception of me.

Dad has always been my go-to guy for love advice. Working next door to Anna has made me feel thirteen again, and living at home has also rekindled my old thirteen-year-old reliance on my dad for romantic counsel. When I was thirteen, it wasn't Anna, but a girl named Cathy Patterson who was the target of my romantic interest.

Cathy's chocolate brown hair fell slightly below her shoulders; she had soft doe brown eyes, freckled cheeks, and two dimples when she smiled, and I desperately wanted her to "go out" with me. "Going out" with someone was eighth-grade parlance to describe some vague form of romantic attachment, the details of which were never clear to me then, or now, for that matter. What I did know, however, was that for someone to "go out" with you, you first had to ask them to "go out" with you, and this was what I wanted to do with Cathy.

I got the courage to ask her out at the end of a school dance. It was a Friday night, December 20, 1991. I am not making that date up, nor do I have it written down; I just remember it. Like all our school dances, this one took place in the cafeteria of the Weston Middle School. It was a large room, with a wall of windows on one side, and was covered completely in brick red hexagonal tiling. All the tables and chairs had been pushed aside to make plenty of room for the students to huddle together in small, awkward groups and take turns looking around the room, which is how we spent our time at dances. All of us affected a casual, confident look as we gazed around, as if to suggest that we couldn't care less about each other but were scanning the room because we were each expecting a *very important person* who had *nothing to do with* being in eighth grade to walk onto the dance floor at any moment.

Because I was planning to ask Cathy out at the end of the dance, I spent most of the dance studiously avoiding any contact with her. Now, instead of imagining sailing away in a magic go-cart in front of all my classmates, I dreamed of Cathy giving me a kiss in front of everyone, proving to all that I was special enough to win her love. And that I wasn't a loser.

At the end of the dance, the lights went up, and I made a beeline to Cathy. We were both still on the dance floor. I don't remember what I said, but I remember Cathy's response. Her eyes grew wide and she looked utterly panicked, as if I had told her that I was holding her family hostage. After a moment, she regained her composure and quite gently explained that she liked me just as a friend. She concluded by asking me to give her a hug, which felt really nice. All in all, I think Cathy gave me an honest, warm, and thoughtful explanation for why she didn't want to go out with me; pretty good for a thirteen-year-old. Unfortunately for us both, I took her kindness as an invitation to keep trying. And the next time I would bring in my secret weapon: my dad.

My dad, whom we were told was a ladies' man in his youth, would surely give me the right tips and tactics to win Cathy over. I assumed Cathy *wanted* to go out with me but that she just didn't *know* it yet. So, I enlisted my dad in helping her along in the process of self-discovery. Dad was happy to oblige, and over five excruciating months, he and I schemed, cajoled, and practically begged Cathy in our varied attempts to convince her to go out with me. Of the many hypotheses tested, the most obvious, that she simply didn't want to go out with me, was never given much consideration. It wasn't until we came up with a plan for me to write Cathy a letter explaining my feelings (Dad's idea), and in response she burst into tears and said she didn't want to talk to me again, that we began to reevaluate our strategy.

◇◇◇

It's 9:51 and my coffee is finished. I want a second cup, but even more, I don't want to miss out on Anna's walk-by. I decide to chance it. She usually arrives on the later side of ten anyway. I reach the atrium and see Anna coming toward me. She is wearing a green skirt with a blue-jean blazer and black stockings. She slows, tilts her head, and gives me an alluring smile. She juts out her hand and says, "Hi, I'm Anna."

Her introduction is confident and direct, and I find myself having a hard time remembering my name. "Hi. I'm Michael."

"It's nice to meet you. I figure, since we work so close to each other, we should be introduced." I nod, still impressed that I remembered my name. We are standing close to one another. She wears a knowing smile. "So you work for Joanne?"

"Yes." I focus on the surprisingly small distance between our faces.

"I work for Marcus." She answers the question that I was too flustered to ask.

"Great," I manage to say. "The molecular genetics guy, right?

She nods. With the same abruptness with which it began, the encounter ends. Anna starts to walk away. "Nice to meet you," she says over her shoulder. The warmth of her smile stays with me for the rest of the day. On the ride home, I decide to take a break from Brahms.

David

It's a warm Monday afternoon in mid-October, five-plus months since I got sick. The docs didn't let me out of the hospital yesterday because the methotrexate didn't clear from my body completely. I became agitated and impatient with the poor nurses, and when Kate scolded me for being irritable with them, I got irritated with her, too. I whispered harshly at her as we walked out: "Listen, you try living on death row and let's see how gracious you are to the guards!"

She rolled her eyes at me.

The leaves on our trees are all brilliant red, gold, and orange. Many already litter the ground. The scene is an obvious metaphor for my circumstances. I still feel utterly querulous and can't settle down to work, so I go out to get the mail. There's a package for me from Northfield; obviously from Sam. I haven't heard much from him this fall. I take the package into the kitchen and open it with a knife.

Inside, there's a white coffee cup. I hold it up and turn it around. In bold, black letters it reads, **fuck cancer**. It is so Sam. I laugh out loud. The kid's got a way with words. Thank you, Sammy.

I begin to relax, remembering that both my sons are doing fine. Sam's finishing college, and, Michael? Well, Michael's "twitterpated," as Kate calls it, referring to the intensity of having a crush like the rabbit, Thumper, in *Bambi*. He's interested in a graduate student in the lab cubicle next to him, and he's so excited by her he can't even see straight. It's as if he's back in middle school, when he used to analyze the tiniest gesture, toss of head, inflection of voice, to figure out whether the current girl of his dreams liked him.

I went to all-boys schools from the fourth grade on, and the discovery of girls was liberating; I liked them so much better than boys. Although I managed the competitive male culture of a boys' boarding school, it was a relief to relate to girls, who seemed to want to talk about things like feelings and vulnerabilities and relationships that I would never have talked to one of my guy friends about. Being with girls romantically and socially was the best and easiest part of my adolescence.

So, like many of the parents I treat, I projected my experience onto Michael. After all, he was a handsome, sweet, emotionally present, articulate boy, so I assumed that connecting with girls would come easily for him. It didn't. Michael was shy and awkward. Of course, I wanted to help him. Being the anxious and somewhat over-functioning parent I was, I usually rushed in to help Michael manage his own feelings. He was responsive, so I was often able to comfort him. Once Michael stepped into the fraught drama of engaging the opposite sex, we engaged in endless conversations obsessing about this girl or that. Despite my attempts to help him relax and enjoy the courtship game, our nightly chats and my continuously dispensed wisdom actually intensified his anxiety. I continued being his confidante straight through his recent relationship with Kristin.

Moving home has given Michael a fresh start. He is working at a great lab, is taking courses, and is starting to apply for PhD programs around the country. He has been reinventing himself and has come home to what Kate and I are so deeply committed to—a life's calling based on service to others. Michael's clinical neuroscience studies put his new career right down the middle between my psychology and Kate's medicine.

Most people, myself included, blithely tell our children we just want them to be happy, do what they want, marry whomever they love, and live where they please. This is almost total baloney. We have thousands of years of hardwired programming to want our kids to follow in our footsteps, stay close, marry someone of our ilk, and take care of us as we age. In our heart of hearts, we don't want the apple to fall far from the tree.

The phone rings. "Hey, Dad," Michael whispers into the phone.

"Hi, Mike," I whisper back. "Why are we whispering?"

"Because the walls are paper thin and she's at her desk."

"Okay. What's up?"

"Do you think it would be pushing things too fast if I asked her out to dinner again, even though she said she couldn't do it last week?"

I feel myself slipping into my old role. The truth is I like Michael using me as a mentor. Being his "love" advisor is frankly fun, despite my serious reservations about whether I offer any more wisdom than the daily horoscope. "So, Michael, it kind of depends on how she turned you down last week. Did she seem disappointed not to be able to go out? Did she say anything, about maybe another time? I mean, if you think you're rushing things, maybe you could just ask her out for a cup of coffee in the middle of the day—"

"Dad, I can't really talk about it right now. Don't worry, I'll figure it out. I gotta go."

I was just warming up. I take a deep breath. I know he's got to work through this stuff on his own. And I know I have to let him. I feel suddenly superfluous. That actually could be a good thing.

Later that day, I plop down on my therapist's white leather sofa in her softly lit office. I launch right in. "Michael's applications are due and he's way behind on his essays and I am trying really hard not to be on his case but I am really getting agitated about how self-defeating he's being. He's twenty-seven years old, and I feel like he's acting like a teenager." I take a breath. "So, Nancy, don't tell me the obvious, that I need to let go, blah, blah, blah. I've got to figure out some way of helping Michael without pushing him. The more stressed I get, the more stubborn and resistant he gets. I am completely tied up in knots."

"How about we just sit for a moment," she says, "and take a few centering breaths."

"Damn it, you're always trying to get me to do that when I am really stressed. I hate that!"

She smiles and with a twinkle in her eyes, says, "You could take a moment just to sound off a bit more if that would help. We have plenty of time."

I smile, in spite of myself. I am having a snit fit and don't want it to be interrupted by anything helpful. Sometimes I wonder what she really thinks of me as a client. I am older than she and more senior in our field, and I can be very controlling about our therapy work. She manages me by simply conveying compassion and understanding, faith in my journey, and my need to work on things my way. Most important, she's unshakeable in the face of my mercurial propensities to be a drama queen. Manic-depression runs in my family, and I sometimes worry about the intensity of my mood swings.

I went back into therapy long before the cancer because I was still struggling with the sense of being "bad to the bone" that I have had ever since I was a child. Despite my professional success, loving wife, great kids, and wonderful friends, I have never been able to accept myself or the love that's been showered on me. Years ago I had worked with another therapist trying to accept my failings as a child and as a man and even forgive myself for having turned my back on my mother before she killed herself. But Barbara, my wonderful therapist, got terminal ovarian cancer and eventually died.

Nancy and I had almost completed our therapy last spring. I had worked hard to exorcise my remaining childhood demons, grieve the loss of Barbara, and break through the thick Plexiglas walls that had separated me from those I loved. Then came the cancer. Nancy's borne with me with love, encouragement, and a no-bullshit acceptance of how badly the story might end. She and I have discussed how my tendency to disconnect from my emotions helps me handle the likelihood of my death.

One day I asked her if she thought I was brave or just in denial. She answered, "Sometimes, denial is part of bravery. Soldiers in combat situations are often extraordinarily courageous but completely out of touch with themselves and their vulnerability at the same time." She paused, "I think you are being brave, honestly, but I also feel like now is the time to be even more fully in your life, more attuned to yourself—even your feelings of terror and sadness."

"I don't have any problem being afraid of the pain, thank you very much. But it is hard to feel sorry for myself. I mean really, I can't stand people who think they don't 'deserve' to die young or some such shit. I just want Kate and the kids to be okay."

Nancy stared into my eyes for a long time. "David, maybe the time will come when you can bring the same compassion you have for your boys and Kate to yourself."

Throughout my illness, Nancy's office has been a sanctuary for me. And I count on her bringing her steadfast care to my deathbed, if the need arises. After bitching and moaning about Michael for a while longer, I look at Nancy, who seems to be waiting patiently for me to notice her presence, and I say, "Okay, I suppose since I am the client, I should listen to what you have to say."

"Thought you would never ask," she teases. She pauses to gather her thoughts. "You might consider that Michael's really conflicted about how dependent he still feels and how difficult that conflict must be for him, given your illness and that he might lose you. And, he's living at home. No wonder he's acting like a teenager!"

Of course Michael is struggling with not only the possibility of losing me but also being at home in his childhood space. No wonder he was irritable and defensive in response to my nagging him about the applications. I feel relieved, ready to go home and offer my help calmly, so he feels nurtured instead of criticized.

Michael isn't there. He's not answering his cell phone.

Finally I hear him walk through the door. And I pounce on him demanding to know where he's been. He's been out with Anna

"Goddamn it, Michael, the stuff's got to be mailed by Thursday and you're telling me that Anna and you went out to lunch, and then to the movies and then walked around for hours. What the hell were you thinking?" Michael looks embarrassed and mad. I can see the little boy side of him afraid of my anger struggling with his grown-up self who is furious about being treated like a teenager. And I can see that he is ashamed that he hadn't gotten his priorities straight. I'm not sure which side will win out.

With a sharp edge in his voice, he says, "Dad, I'm not fifteen. Besides, I thought you already went to graduate school. These aren't your applications. It just so happens that I had a really, really great day. Excuse me if that is such a crime." He turns on his heels, stomps out of my office, slams the door, gets in his car, and peels out of the driveway.

So much for insight and understanding. I collapse on the sofa. My history of parenting has been about my overwhelming anxiety about the boys being okay. I tried so hard to make sure they always felt good about themselves and when they were struggling I felt horrible about myself. My friend Al Rossiter once said, "You're only as happy as your least happy child." That's been painfully true for me.

My parents were so self-involved that it sometimes seemed like they didn't know they had kids. When my brother Jim was eight and I was ten, we sailed my little nine-and-a-half-foot boat from Rockport to Marblehead across eighteen miles of open ocean. They didn't blink an eye. Then, early on, they shipped us off to boarding schools. When Jim was a senior at St. Paul's they moved temporarily to San Francisco and forgot to tell him they wouldn't be home for Thanksgiving. He arrived home to an empty house.

I vowed I would be a different kind of parent—no nannies, no boarding schools, no endless rounds of cocktail parties and charity events. Instead, I truly wanted to be there for my kids. This determination to make up for my own childhood spawned its own form of narcissism. Despite appearing to be an easygoing parent I was intensely anxious and insecure about my kids' well-being and my own parenting. When Michael was nineteen he told me about some difficult and hurtful thing I had said or done when he was younger that I didn't remember. I instantly began to explain to Michael about how bad I felt about it, what a shitty parent I had been, how sorry I was. He finally interrupted me and said with some force, "Ah, Dad, this isn't about you."

Anxious, overinvolved, self-centered parents trying to raise perfect Renaissance children are a staple of my clinical practice. It's hard to acknowledge how much I still fit the description. I wonder if my concern for how my boys will make it after I'm gone is just more of the same.

Just as I am about to go up to bed, there's a soft knock on my door. It's Michael.

"Dad, I'm so sorry. I shouldn't have been yelling at you, and I know—" He starts to sob. I jump out of my chair and put my arms around him. He hugs me tight and cries.

"Well, I shouldn't have been so pissy with you, either."

"It's not about that. It's, ah, I don't want anything to happen. I mean, you know what I mean."

"I'm really scared, too." Tears run down my cheeks.

"I just don't want to lose my dad."

The next day, I cancel all my clients. Sometimes my family has to come before others. Michael and I work on the applications all day and all evening. He gets them mailed by midnight, the deadline. He did almost all the work himself. I was just there.

David

It's a cold, raw, Saturday morning. The leaves are gone, leaving the trees looking exposed and vulnerable. I have to call my younger brother, Jim, and my older sister, Lauris, to invite them and their families to Thanksgiving. I haven't fully let them in on how bad the cancer really is because in my relationships with my siblings I tend to be the caretaker rather than the care receiver. I don't offer much of myself to them and don't get back much in return. They're excited about coming to Boston. We don't get together that often.

But it does seem wildly premature to be doing a big holiday shindig, as if I'm tempting the gods' wrath to be "celebrating" Thanksgiving. The odds of my getting a recurrence are still extremely high, and given the incredibly rapid development of my type of cancer, I could be in trouble in a hurry. Effi told us I would immediately get a highly intensive chemo protocol called ICE and then, if I responded, I would have a stem cell transplant. And if that happens, even the best I can hope for is less than a 50-50 chance, which is still much better than where I started. Some people don't even survive the stem cell transplant. For all I know I could already have a recurrence right now as I am sitting here thinking about Thanksgiving.

But we have to make plans anyway, as if we own our future. It's the everyday denial in life. However, I certainly hope that an optimistic, positive attitude is not actually a key element in surviving cancer, as some have claimed. The research is quite sketchy. I think being encouraged to "fight" cancer carries a subtle message of responsibility for the outcome. If I die of this damn thing, does that mean I didn't fight it "hard" enough? That implication really pisses me off. I have been trying to live with the likely reality of dying as graciously and courageously as I know how. I have been braced for the worst. Is that negative thinking? Does it breed cancer cells?

I feel generally pissy. Sam hardly calls at all. Michael and Anna are utterly preoccupied with each other. Kate's thrown herself back into work and seems distant and distracted. And I am tired of telling my friends how I am doing and them always telling me, "You look great." Lately, I haven't even been able to respond positively to Nancy's steadfast care.

I feel suddenly very alone. This has been building. Kate and I haven't done our check-in talks for several weeks. I've noticed myself eating and drinking with abandon and even stealing the occasional Percocet from my emergency supply for nothing but mind-numbing purposes. I should be grateful to be alive. I should be on my hands and knees, repeating Annie Lamott's favorite prayers—"Thank you, thank, you, thank you" and "Help me, help me, help me." I should be getting to my office work, e-mails, and bills. I should be calling Jim and Lauris.

Instead, I'm going to get in the car and go to Bruegger's for a six-pack of bagels and a couple of tubs of cream cheese. Now that's a plan. As I get up, I glance over at my blue sofa, where my clients usually sit. I am actually quite good at helping people struggle with anxiety and depression, and that's what I have right now, a goodly measure of both, with a little terror and despair thrown in. What would I say to myself?

I sit back in my therapist's chair and imagine my own calm and caring voice and my professionally kind, compassionate eyes turned toward me. "David, I actually think you're expecting too much of yourself. You've been dreadfully sick and convinced you're going to die. It's been a relentless round of chemo and tests and soldiering on. Honestly, I think you're only just beginning to come out of a state of shock and numbness. You're actually beginning to feel the enormity of what's happened, how totally your life and Kate's and the boys' have been completely turned upside down. So be gentle with yourself. You're still getting chemo, after all. You're not out of the woods yet, by any means. Let's start with a few small positive steps. Okay?"

I mentally switch chairs and sit on the client sofa. With a cold glare back at the therapist's chair, I say, "Screw you and screw your small steps." I put on my coat and head for the bagels. I'm glad I don't have Nancy's job.

<><><>

Thanksgiving with Jim, his wife, Jan, and his two daughters and Lauris is going surprisingly well. Lots of banter and teasing, mostly Kate being on Jim's case for his relentless, adolescent jokes. (E.g., "What do they call the Clinton administration these days?" Pause. "Sex between the

Bushes." Kate fits easily in the role of scolding mother, and Jim loves the attention. The rest of us just relax and enjoy the show.

General Kate is barking orders and basting the turkey. Everyone is scurrying about in "help" mode, setting up the hors d'oeuvres, the bar, the table, the fireplace. Jim has taken over the bartending and is doling out libations. Just as Kate, with some exasperation, reviews one more time the preparation and timing of every course in the elaborate spread, Jim innocently asks her, "So, Kate would you like to use Clamato in the Bloody Marys?"

"I *hate* Clamato!!" she replies with a vehemence that startles us all. The whole group stops dead in their tracks. It's as if the whole six months of tension exploded out of her mouth like a shotgun blast. I freeze.

But Jim, with exquisite comedic timing, waits for a full ten count. Then he says, very sweetly and with tongue firmly in cheek, "Oh, Kate, I'm sorry. I didn't know you had such strong negative feelings about Clamato."

Kate bursts out laughing. "Well, I guess I didn't know that I felt that strongly, either. Maybe I've been feeling slightly tense lately."

"Well, I promise never to mention it again," says Jim with an impish smile.

In less than five minutes, he innocently turns to Kate and asks her "Kate, how do you really feel about Clamato?" I suspect he'll continue this track for the rest of their visit. I smile at Jim. Easing tension by teasing and humor is how he and I got by as kids. He's a pro. It's good to laugh.

WINTER 2005

Kate

CHRISTMAS HAS ALWAYS BEEN A MAGICAL TIME FOR ME. AS A CHILD, IT was filled with excitement and surprise. It rapidly changed from a focus on Santa Claus to one of religious awe. I was utterly thrilled when, at the age of eight, I was considered grown-up enough to go to the midnight mass. We went to a beautiful stone church, with extraordinary music and a lot of incense, all of which made it a magical experience. When we got home, we would light the fire in the library and open our presents in the middle of the night, sometimes until four or five in the morning. I felt so happy and content with my family. I learned that presents were to be given with great thought and care, so early on I was as excited to give presents and see people be pleased with what I had picked as I was getting presents. After my father died, Christmas was pretty awful for a while, with Mother, Stephen, and I putting on a brave front while each of us struggled alone with our grief.

After David and I married, I took over creating Christmases with the same sense of family and giving that I grew up with. Now my children love Christmas, too, and love spending the holidays together. Even David has slowly thawed. But every Christmas still contains, for me, a kernel of that early loss, which has always charged the present with a sense of poignancy that these times are so special and that they might end. So here we are, approaching Christmas with the thought that it might be the last together, and I am overwhelmed.

Sam and I are driving to the mall for last-minute shopping. It is a gray day. Piles of dirty snow line the road. We are alone and can talk— the car is always a good place for that—but I am completely incapable of saying anything about the emotions that I am feeling so intensely. Sam has made it clear that he does not really want to know too much. I certainly don't want to terrify him or make him too pessimistic. On the other hand, I know what it is like to lose a parent at a young age—that in a single moment your life changes forever and that you carry the loss into every part of your life; that every achievement, every one of life's milestones, every family gathering carries a bittersweet reminder of loss. I know what it feels like to never be able to have another conversation, to never be able to be together again. It's simply unimaginable until it happens. I remember worrying intensely for years about whether my father knew how much I loved him. It was not until fifteen years later, when I became a parent, that I realized that he would have known, and I stopped worrying about it. I do not want Sam to have his father die and never have said the things he needs to say. I know how much that would help afterward, but I don't want to imply that David is going to die, even though it is hard for me to believe otherwise.

As I maneuver through the Christmas-rush traffic, I try to gently say to Sam that he might want to think about the things he thinks are important for his father to know and to talk about them, just in case. Sam grunts some reply that tells me we aren't going any further with this conversation. I am quiet. I know there are feelings Sam cannot share. I do not assume he doesn't care, as I might have done earlier in my life. I learned that lesson with Michael. When my mother was dying, I was upset that Michael, at the age of nine, did not seem to care. I am sure he felt that anger. Of course, I realized later that he did care, that her death had been very sad and scary for him, but at the age of nine he could not express those feelings.

Shortly after she died, I remember watching him walk carefully around the rooms we had added onto our house for Mother to live in, filled with her furniture, softly touching her things and saying, "This is so rememberful," with a sad wistfulness. A few months later, he began telling me several times a day, "I love you, Mom," until finally, one after-noon in his bedroom, I said to him, "Michael, it's wonderful that you feel that way, but why are you saying this so much?" He answered, "I just want to be sure that the last thing I say to you is something nice, in case something happens to you." I sat down on his bed, hugged him and told him that I knew that he loved me. I explained that no matter what he said—even if he told me he hated me as I was going to work and then I was killed in a car accident—I would always know he loved me and that he should never feel bad about what he had said to me. He must have been reassured, because he stopped telling me he loved me quite so often. I realized the impact my mother's death had had on him even though he didn't talk about it directly.

So I am gentler with Sam. I know that, in his own way, Sam is trying very hard. His unfailing cheerful willingness to help whenever asked suggests that he is more aware than perhaps he consciously knows. That evening, I talk to David about my worries about Sam and he, as usual, brings clarity to the problem. He reminds me that Sam will likely have time after he knows his father is dying to confront this more directly. Then David smiles at me, his eyes soft with love, not communicating any of his own fear, as though he can simply step outside himself and hold me.

Sam

I DON'T KNOW WHO SAID IT FIRST, BUT THE IDEA OF THIS CHRISTMAS being my dad's last has settled on the family. It's been too much to handle for all of us. Mom looks haggard and tired as we enter the Natick Mall for last-minute shopping. I worry about her almost as much as I do about Dad. This has been so hard for her; I don't know how she does it. I've kept to my game plan of ignoring reality and being the family cheerleader, but it was way easier to be detached when I was at school.

This past term I had to give my Senior Comprehensive Talk, which was on fractals and chaotic dynamics—not exactly a light topic, but amazingly interesting. That was difficult enough, but a few weeks ago, I broke up with Sarah and she moved home. It just wasn't working. I wanted to be a college student and she, understandably, was done with college life. She demanded too much of my time and constantly complained about her life and job in Northfield. She was in a holding pattern to be with me, while I was struggling to stay afloat with my schoolwork, working at the bar, and trips home to see my family. We began to resent one another, when neither of us was doing anything wrong. Things got to the boiling point and finally I had to end it. No screaming match, nothing ugly. She packed up and moved out a few days later. That left me studying for finals and hoping that I hadn't made a huge mistake. I really love her; maybe things would have gotten better next term.

Carleton has a trimester system, which means my time off, from Thanksgiving to New Year's Day, doesn't coincide with the winter breaks of my high school friends. Since I've been home, I've been to UMass twice, keeping my friends from studying for finals. Mostly I was visiting Lisa. This is the first time that both of us are unattached since I met her sophomore year of high school. Since the breakup, I've been thinking a lot about Lisa. I think it's her smile that gets me the most; I love making her laugh. I recognize that it's a crazy infatuation, but until I explore the potential with her, I'll never fully understand my feelings. That's why I'm so excited about New Year's this year. She invited me to her family's Caribbean house for the holidays as a kind of stand-in boyfriend because her sister and brother are bringing significant others, too. This will be the best New Year's ever!

"So what are you looking for today?" My mom asks me.

"Jeans for Michael." I hope that if I'm focused and efficient, I can zip in and out of the dreaded mall. "What about you?"

"Thankfully, I'm finishing up. That means stocking stuffers and anything that catches my eye. Good thought on the jeans; he said he wanted you to pick them out. Well, you can grab those while I look for things for you. Then call me and we'll keep looking for things for other people."

I realize that, as always, a "quick run to the mall" will not be quick at all. I leave my mom and head into Express for Men. Ripped, stained, patched, and even gaping holes. That's what I have to choose from. Why is it that all jeans these days come purposefully "pre-distressed"? You throw jeans out when they have huge holes, not buy them like that. Of course, I'm thinking all this while wearing a pair of jeans from Express with all sorts of extra stitching to make them look like repaired tears. Sarah said I looked hot in them.

I'm amazed that Michael trusts me enough to pick out jeans for him. That means he actually likes my style. Granted it's a style that has been guided by past girlfriends, especially Sarah, but it's *my* style all the same. His style (also created by girlfriends) had him, at one point, wearing odd, hippy-looking dress shirts with flower designs that should have been wallpaper in a day-care center. Thankfully, he has moved past that stage and wants a little help from the fashionista. Little does he know that I have no idea what I'm doing.

Nadia to the rescue. She's my girly-girl friend at college. She keeps me up-to-date on all sorts of pop culture, which I could do without, and the latest fashion trends. "Hey, Nadia," I say, phone pinched between shoulder and ear, leaving my hands free to grab different pairs of jeans. "I've got a fun job for you. It's going to be a little tough over the phone, but I think we can do it. I'm shopping for jeans for my brother for Christmas, and I've narrowed it down to a couple different ones, but I need your help. I'll try describing them to you."

"Whoa, Sam, hold on. I'm kind of busy. Just take pictures with your phone, send them to me, and I'll text you back with which ones you should go with. This is the brother with sandy blonde hair, shorter than you, well-built, blue eyes, and a dimpled smile?"

"I only have one, and, wow, you have a good memory."

"Only a memory for the cute ones. Bye!"

Thanks to Nadia, after just a couple of electronic exchanges I'm confident about the $50 pair of jeans I'm buying. Amazingly, those are the cheap ones. I leave the store feeling good, only to remember that I need to find my mom and trudge around this damn place for what I'm sure will feel like eternity.

Michael

THE DAYS BEFORE CHRISTMAS ARE OFTEN TENSE, AND THIS YEAR IS NO exception. But for all the various kerfluffles that seem to surround the lead-up, Christmas day itself is always wonderful.

My mother was always able to inspire a spirit of giving in Sam and me. She taught us to be thoughtful about the presents we gave and always encouraged giving a gift that was personal rather than a gift that was expensive or flashy. This manifested, when I was young, in her assurance that Dad would most appreciate any art I created, which led to an outpouring of Magic Marker drawings, virtually all of which I deemed to be suitable gift material for my father. To make my drawings seem like official gifts, my mother would even frame them, as if she had given birth to a budding Picasso. Re-gifting was not a common event in our household.

It's Christmas Eve, and the house is fully regaled in our traditional Christmas decorations. Fresh-cut evergreen boughs are draped over the various fireplace mantels, ropes of dried berries hang from the banister, wreathes are placed on the doors and over the great bay window that overlooks the yard. The house smells of wood and pine and good things to eat. Tables are covered with gift boxes filled with fresh oranges and grapefruits from my parents' patients and colleagues, along with boxes of chocolates, homemade desserts, toasted almonds, rare cheeses, and the occasional bottle of wine, each gift a small sign of the difference my parents make in other people's lives. There's even a hand-crafted white chocolate sleigh made each year by one of my mother's close friends. Mom insists that we not touch the sleigh until Christmas day, but somehow it has always magically disappeared by then.

I walk through the living room to take another look at all the gifts under our Christmas tree. When we were little, my mom was so good at creating excitement around Santa Claus that I believed he was real until I was ten years old. At that point, my parents were not really sure what to do with me. I'm not sure how they managed to break the news to me, but I imagine them discussing it with furrowed brows, trying to decide what to do. "Why don't we just let his friends tell him?" My mom would worry. "I mean, his friends all have to know, right?"

"But what if they don't? What if they're too embarrassed?" My dad would predictably respond. "What if he turns fifteen and still believes in Santa Claus? He'll never get a date."

"But it means so much to him," my mom would protest. "Girls will still date him even if he believes in Santa Claus. They'll think it's cute."

Whatever actually took place, somehow they decided that Santa would give only one gift that year. Additionally, Santa would write a card explaining that I was now "too old" to receive any more gifts from him. Just because they couldn't resist, they made sure to disguise their handwriting on the card. I had noticed before that Santa's writing looked increasingly like Mom's—probably a subtle attempt on her part to spur some insight on my part—but I had always managed to ignore this rather glaring evidence.

When I opened the gift from Santa, I was so thrilled by it that I completely forgot that it was to be Santa's last. It was a present I had begun asking for almost four years prior: a small robot toy, called the space dragon, which was featured in one my favorite childhood cartoons. By the time I was ten, I had almost outgrown it. I had of course been told by my friends that Santa wasn't real, but I had refused to believe them. Or maybe I did believe them but just didn't want to let go. At any rate, real or not, I finally recognized that this gift was Santa's way of saying good-bye; that was enough.

Christmas also taught me about getting gifts from real people in addition to jolly old elves. When I was eight, my dad bought me a little science kit for exploring the natural environment. I was interested in science and had loved the chemistry sets my parents had given me previously. But that year the present just failed to grab me; I put it away in one of my toy cabinets and promptly forgot about it. A year and a half later, my dad was helping me clean out the cabinet when we stumbled across the science kit. He slowly pulled it out, the unopened plastic wrap crinkling in his hands.

"You never even opened this," he said, more to himself than to me.

I was horrified. I wanted to tell him I didn't mean anything by it, that I loved the gift; it was my favorite. I had just forgotten it was there. I would go play with it right now; with it and nothing else. I wanted to hug him and tell him it was okay; to make him feel better. It was the first time that I really recognized that the presents my dad gave me were as important to him as they were to me.

I hear Dad in the kitchen, so I join him there. He is unpacking last-minute groceries for tomorrow's Christmas dinner. He looks better these days; his weight has come back and his skin no longer looks so pale. I come behind him and put my arms around him. He turns and smiles at me warmly.

For the last several weeks, I've found myself imagining, often against my will, what Christmas would be like without my dad. It's not a helpful thing to do. Maybe Sam's denial strategy isn't so bad after all.

The best way I've found to ignore these thoughts is to get completely fixated on Anna. Not that I am making much progress on the wooing front. We went out on a non-date, had a wonderful time, and ended up making out in her kitchen. Then she told me that she really wasn't interested in dating anyone. This has only increased my desire for her, and two months later I find myself able to think of little else. I can't tell if I think this obsession is successful coping or just really messed up. Either way, I have found myself helpless to stop it.

David

The post-Thanksgiving buildup to Christmas has been as frantic as always, despite my entreaties to Kate to cut back. That's like standing in front of the Acela train coming at you at 120 mph. Now it's Christmas Eve, and Sam, Michael, Kate, and I are sitting down to one of our favorite meals that I cook: chicken in mustard cream sauce with green beans and french fries. We're taking a break from rushing about wrapping, food shopping, prepping for the big feast with Kate's family tomorrow, and our ongoing bridge game.

The mood is heavy. We eat in silence. We still haven't resolved the annual Christmas Eve church service question. "Is there more chicken?" asks Sam, who, like me, uses food to modulate tension.

"Before you get up, Sam, can we just decide about church?" asks Kate with some irritability. This is a sore topic in our family. Kate grew up with a wonderfully rich and deep relationship to God, the church, and all of the traditions. I grew up with a cynical attitude toward religion. Underneath my intellectualized agnosticism was bitterness stemming from how unsuccessfully my mother reached for solace and help from God and her minister in the last years of her life.

Throughout Michael and Sam's childhood, we tried to find a workable compromise around participating in church. I dutifully dragged the boys off to church and Sunday school while Kate sang in the choir. But my negative attitude rubbed off on them, and as adolescents, they stopped going to church except for the midnight mass on Christmas Eve and Easter. In the last couple of years, one or both of them has even bowed out of the midnight mass, which hurt Kate's feelings. Celebrating Christ's birth and the renewal of hope and singing the traditional carols is the one service that means the most to her.

"If nobody minds, I'd just as soon skip this year," Michael says carefully.

"Count me in on that vote," chimes in Sam, a little too quickly, a little too loudly.

Kate looks at me from across the table. There are tears in her eyes.

"Look, honey," I say, "if it were just up to me, I would probably really prefer to skip it, too, but if you really want to go, I'll go."

"Dad, you shouldn't have to go if you don't want to." Sam looks pointedly at Kate. "That's not fair. You of all of us should get to do what you want."

Kate says softly, beginning to tear up, "I am sorry. I just thought that, given everything, maybe this would be a particularly good year for all of us to go to church."

"I don't get why, just because church might be a good thing for you, you think it would be good for the rest of us," Sam argues.

"Sam," I say, raising my voice.

We drop into dead silence; no sound except the scrapping of knives and forks on plates, the tinkle of ice in raised glasses, the grandfather clock ticking. That loud silence, the silence I grew up with. I think back to the last Christmas with my mother, in 1966. Lauris, Jim, and I drove up from New York on Christmas Eve afternoon. None of us having called to say we would get there much later than expected. We all dreaded going home and facing the rising tension in the family as my mother became progressively more depressed and bedridden. My older brother, Jon, had already arrived from Florida. I was twenty and would have preferred not to go home at all. My father greeted us at the door with a hushed whisper, "I am so glad you're here. Your mother was getting worried."

We apologized and trooped into the living room. Mom was on the floor in her bathrobe, surrounded by our Christmas tradition: a black ship model, a collection of tiny animals, some Scrabble pieces, and tissue paper. Every year, she piled the ship high with tiny white packages and put it on the mantel, and a menagerie of animals following behind. It was a rather odd crèche.

"Hi, Mom," Lauris said. "Where are the already wrapped little pieces from last year?"

"Someone must have thrown them out." Mom didn't look up. "I decided to wrap a new pile of them while I was waiting."

Jon, Jim, and I made a beeline for the liquor cabinet. We all sat and watched my mother try to wrap. Her hands were shaking too hard to accomplish much. Lauris got down on the floor to help. Soon Jon and Jim slipped downstairs to watch TV. I felt trapped. I wanted to be downstairs, too, but I felt like the proverbial rat deserting the sinking ship. Suddenly Mom stopped and said in a distracted way, "Well, this will have to do. The Santa boat just won't be so full this year. I must be off to bed." My father, my sister, and I watched in resigned silence as she wafted out of the room.

A month later, my mother broke into the carefully locked medicine box, took more than thirty seconal tablets, and died.

My attention returns to my own family. The silence is unbearable. Each of us is painfully aware of the subtext of this "church" conversation. "Listen, I can't just sit here like this," I say. "This is the way it was growing up in my family. Nobody ever said anything. Obviously, all of us are having our own version of last-Christmas thoughts. Let's just say it: this sucks and we don't know if we'll even all be here next year." I begin to choke up.

"Dad, don't." Michael reaches out and takes my hand.

"Honestly, nobody has to go to church," says Kate quickly.

"It's not about church. It's not even about the cancer. I just can't take sweeping it all under the rug."

"Well, I've been thinking about this 'last time' issue," offers Michael, "and frankly, I think we've been doing pretty well. I don't think anyone's sweeping anything under the rug. We're just trying to have as good a Christmas as we can."

"That's true," Sam adds. "And Michael and I are seriously beating you guys in bridge, and that's what matters the most."

"It's just because we've had crummy cards," retorts Kate.

I smile in spite of myself. "Tell you what, guys. We'll clean up the kitchen and play another rubber of bridge. Whoever wins gets to decide about church." I'm back. Back in my family, our foursome. No matter what happens, we are going through this together.

Kate

I WAKE UP CHRISTMAS MORNING FEELING SURPRISINGLY RELAXED. THE house is quiet. Everyone else is still asleep. David is curled up next to me. I reach over and gently touch the top of his head. All of the strain of the last few days seems to have disappeared. I am aware of how weighted down I have felt by my own gloom over the possibility of these holidays being David's last. But right now, I feel only gratitude. The harsh words of last night seem unimportant. I carefully edge out of bed and put on my robe and slippers to go down and get the coffee and the paper to bring back to David so we can read awhile in bed. The boys will not wake up for at least another hour.

After our quiet time together, I head to the kitchen to start breakfast. David wakes the boys. After breakfast we light the fire and gather in the living room. As we start to open our stockings Sam realizes that for the first time ever, we did not read *The Littlest Angel* on Christmas Eve. Everyone agrees it must be read, and so we read, soothed by the comfortable familiarity of the words. We smile at each other. We open presents. Somehow we have all managed to find presents that we are pleased about. Sam and Michael fall into their familiar banter, teasing each other with affection. I love to watch them together, to see their faces as they give each other presents, the anticipation and hope that the other will like the gift. We all seem to have shed the tensions of the night before. It is a good morning. We are happy. Toward the end of the morning, I open a present from Jan, Jim's wife. It is a photograph taken over Thanksgiving. My eyes fill as I look at it. It is a picture of David and me taken from behind, walking together in the barren woods of late November, the ground covered with fallen leaves, his arm around me, and our steps in perfect synchrony. We had often, in our young lives, felt like two children alone in the woods. Now here we were, having lived a life together.

We have a short respite and then everyone helps get things ready for Christmas dinner. My brother and his family will come, as they have for the last twenty-three years. We will have our traditional multiple-course dinner. Invariably dinner will last several hours, but no one seems to mind. There is always plenty of conversation. My nephew Ben and

Michael will provide musical interludes, improvising raucous Christmas duets on the piano. I put the roast and the potatoes in the oven. Everything else is organized. Sam and Michael are playing a game. David is reading one of the books I gave him. I head upstairs. I have just enough time for a hot bath before I change for dinner.

Sam

CHRISTMAS MORNING. I BOUND DOWN THE STAIRS, FULL OF BOYISH excitement. I can smell breakfast and can almost smell the presents, too. It's nice to see the whole family is up and about in the kitchen. All together. We made it with only a few bumps and bruises along the way. Not least of which was last night, during our Christmas Eve dinner. Unfortunately it wasn't the first time I've made Mom cry on Christmas Eve. The problem is that I stopped believing in God at the age of eleven. It just didn't make sense to me. If the story of Santa Claus is a myth, what makes the God story any more believable? My mom had tried to explain that it's just a feeling, something called faith. And that 90 percent of the world believes in one deity or another. That did little to convince me.

Last night I was quick to veto the whole church thing, not just for me, but because I thought that's what Dad would want, and he is the "cancer dude." But everything went from bad to worse in a couple of heartbeats. I kept eating, while my mind raced to save the situation. I have inherited my dad's need to please, so I desperately wanted to defuse the tension. It's never a good sign when you can hear the tick of that old clock when you're eating dinner. But there it was. The seconds ticking away while we each grew increasingly more uncomfortable.

Finally my father broke the silence. He wanted everyone to check in and take a turn talking about how they were feeling. As each of us got our voices heard, we calmed down and agreed to wait till later in the evening to make a decision. I vowed to myself if Mom really wanted, I would go to church. But by our fifth hand of bridge and few glasses of wine, we all agreed that church was a no-go for this year. This morning it all seems forgotten. "So, should we just open presents around the bridge table?" I joke over our classic Christmas breakfast of scrambled eggs, bacon, and homemade scones. I love it, but I try to save room for the main event tonight. As I finish my last bite of bacon, I'm already thinking of roast beef and potatoes au gratin.

"That's actually not a bad idea, Sam. We could totally play bridge," Dad replies.

"No, no, no." Mom's opinion is quite clear, as always. "We are not going to open presents while playing cards! It's just not going to happen."

"I agree with Mom," my brother adds, pouring himself another cup of coffee. "Let's get to it." With cup in hand, he leads the way out of the kitchen and into the formal living room, which only gets used three or four times a year.

We all get settled, with my mom doling out the stockings. Our copy of *The Littlest Angel* is sitting out, and I remember that we didn't read it last night. "Dumb! We didn't read *The Littlest Angel*!" I shout.

"What?" Everyone responds together, a touch of horror in their voices. We always read the story of the Littlest Angel. It's one of our quirky traditions, but a great one. When I was younger, I liked it because it was all about the little boy, just like I was. As I grew older, I appreciated the poignancy and understood why my parents cried and my brother always teared up. Now, having heard it twenty times, I've been known to cry during one or two parts of the recital.

"We were too busy playing bridge. We must have forgotten," my mom says.

"Well, come on! Who's going to read it?" I don't want to jinx Christmas by not sticking to our idiosyncrasies.

◇◇◇

Hours later, just as I'm digging into my second helping of roast beef, Dad has to interrupt the conversation on my behalf. "Sam has something he wants to show people after dinner, especially Stephen and Ben," he says. I concentrate on my food. I know he means well, but I hate it when he artificially tries to involve me in the group.

My whole life it's been a struggle to fit in with my mom's side of the family. They are all opinionated, with a seemingly limitless variety of knowledge. My two cousins are older than me and just way too smart. Now that I'm older, I have a few things I can contribute to the conversation, usually involving math. I told my dad that maybe I should mention my senior project on fractals, but I didn't think that he'd propose that I show it. I don't want it to be a big deal.

"Well, what is it?" My uncle Stephen asks, turning toward me.

I take one last, longing look at the roast beef on my plate and decide I can't ignore my uncle sitting next to me. "I did a presentation on fractals in the fall," I say matter-of-factly.

"This was his big senior-thesis type of thing," my dad adds. "He has a PowerPoint presentation on his computer." Wow, I could just kill him.

"Sounds great," Ben says. "Did you talk about the Mandelbrot set?"

The last thing I need is for him to be familiar with this stuff. "Ah, yes, that was my focus." I just want to eat and to not be the center of attention.

"Well, this is perfect; that will be a nice thing to do between dinner and dessert," Mom says, and blessedly turns the conversation back to politics. I feel a knot in my stomach starting to form. Even though I'm proud of the work I put into this project, and three faculty members thought I did well, I'm still worried about what my uncle and cousin will think. I start mentally looking through the slides, practicing it the way I had practiced every day the week before my formal presentation in October.

Michael

Despite the emotional buildup around my father's potentially last Christmas, Christmas day arrives with all its usual sense of merriment. Much of this is due to my mother, who has always helped our family take a break from our sometimes chaotic lives and simply enjoy each other's company. Although we and her family only get together as a group on Christmas, it is familiar tradition. We spend hours at the dinner table between courses, talking, joking, telling old stories. Growing up, my cousin Ben and I would put on little "plays" for the adults or spend hours writing Christmas cards in the form of poems or riddles, often spoofing high-Victorian style, which we would read aloud to all. As a group, it was easy to get us to laugh. My uncle Stephen, in particular, who at 6'4" cuts an imposing figure, has a booming laugh that reverberates through the halls and always makes me laugh with him.

This year, Sam gives a presentation about fractals to our cousins. I thought it was cool that he had a chance to show his work to them, because Stephen is an economics PhD and my cousin Ben is completing his PhD in math. I am proud of Sam as he talks. My old sense of competition with him has morphed into respect.

One of my gifts from my mother is a pair of symphony tickets to Berlioz's *Symphony Fantastique*. I know she thinks I will ask Anna to go with me, one of many examples of Mom's divine inspiration when it comes to Christmas. I force myself to wait a few days, and then I call Anna and invite her to go to the symphony with me. She says yes! It's a Christmas miracle. If we hit it off, that will be our anniversary.

David

THE RISE AND FALL OF CHEERFUL CHATTER BLENDS WITH THE RUSHING water from the faucet and the clinking of the silverware and china. The Christmas feast is over, and I'm at the sink. I always lose patience with the social patter sooner than the rest and retreat to the kitchen to confront the mess. I am suddenly aware of the pain in my hip. My mind dismisses it as my old pain from too many years of tennis. But it feels ominously different. A client's son had cancer that metastasized to his hip; it was the beginning of the end.

I pause and look at the Christmas detritus. What will they do next year? Maybe they will go south for the warmth and lack of reminders. Lately, I've begun to have intimations of loss; the loss of me. This is new. I've never really allowed myself to care enough about myself, my life, to be afraid of losing it. It's always been a much more dreadful thought to be doomed to be forever me. But now that I am somewhat physically better, oddly, I feel more afraid. I notice every ache in my body, every twitch in my head. I am holding my breath. Waiting.

Gingerly, I walk across the kitchen, testing the rotation of my hip in the joint, the working of every fiber of muscle, tendon, and tissue. I stop and squat down. I straighten up and stand on the balls of my feet. This could be my old hip pain. Or bone necrosis caused by the steroids I've taken. I know I'm searching for alternative possibilities.

I wash carefully the delicate gold leaf fluted wine glasses that were my mother's favorites. There are only five left from the originally twelve. I refill my wine glass and head for the living room, seeking refuge in the soothing sounds of familiar voices and laughter at the same old stories and jokes.

JANUARY
Sam

I CAN'T BELIEVE I'M ALREADY ON MY WAY BACK FROM MY TRIP TO THE Caribbean. I'm on a JetBlue flight from San Juan to Boston. Tomorrow I will quickly pack and then start the drive across the country to snowy Minnesota. I wish I were still in the Virgin Islands.

Although celebrating New Year's Eve in the Caribbean was wonderful and I loved Lisa's fun-loving family, it wasn't quite the trip I had envisioned. I had hoped that I would sweep Lisa off her feet, that she'd finally know my love for her. Instead, we were caught up in family activities the whole time. On the one afternoon we were alone on the beach, I couldn't get the words right and totally flailed at saying what I wanted to say. Mostly because I still don't know exactly what I want to say to her. Even at midnight on New Year's Eve, I only mustered up the courage to kiss her on the cheek.

I'm watching the end of the in-flight movie, *In Her Shoes*, starring Cameron Diaz. The movie is about two estranged sisters who end up reconciling their issues. Maggie—Cameron Diaz—is finally loving toward her sister on her sister's wedding day. It's so damn touching. When Maggie starts to cry while reading a poem to her sister, I choke up. I try to pretend it's a cough, but with tears pouring down my face, I don't think I'm fooling anyone. I especially would like to not be crying in front of the two little girls sitting next to me. This is pathetic—I'm alone, sitting in an airplane crying about the damn in-flight movie. This realization makes me cry even harder.

By the end of movie, all the characters have reconciled their differences. The sisters have reconnected, the grandma and the dad have apologized to each other, and romance is triumphant. I wish I were living in a happy ending. I want my family to come together and for everything to be happy-go-lucky. Instead, my dad has cancer. I don't want my dad to die, but I really don't want him to die without us reconnecting. I want for things to get back to how they were before I became an adolescent asshole. Back then I looked up to my dad. I was glad he did everything with me and was a part of my life. We played tennis together. We skied together. We even built things together, athough this isn't my dad's forte.

The summer after I turned eleven I wanted a tree house. So my dad offered to help build one with me. And boy did we build one hell of a tree house. Five times the necessary amount of wood was jammed in between three tree trunks. It was a large platform with three walls and a roof. It was spectacular. Mostly because my dad and I had built it. It was ours. I spent endless summer days up there as either a pirate captain standing on deck or the commander of some impenetrable fortress lording over all those people five feet below me. Eventually the wood rotted, and nests of hornets invaded. It slowly decomposed out in our backyard. There are still some remnants that have now more or less become part of the trees.

The credits continue to roll past the final wedding scene. Music plays as all the major characters are shown dancing and having fun. Wouldn't it be nice for all of us to be smiling and dancing at my wedding, years from now, maybe an outdoor ceremony in my parents' backyard.

David

I AM DRIVING WITH SAM AT LEAST HALFWAY TO MINNESOTA SO HE doesn't have to do the whole thing alone in winter weather. The roads are clear, the sun shining. Last night an ice storm coated the limbs of the trees in shimmering ice. Beautiful, but the roads may be treacherous. Sam is sound asleep in the passenger seat, his long, lanky body curled up, and his head resting on a pillow against the window. Despite his beard, I still see the little boy in him. All through his childhood, Sam was a sweet, affable, easygoing boy. Much like I was. It took me years to recognize how much I hid behind my smile. Now it's becoming clear that Sam covers up a lot with his likable persona, too.

Maybe on this trip, I can coax Sam out from behind his smile and denial. I really don't want him to be left with all his bottled-up feelings about me after I am gone the way I was after my mother's death. I am going to try to make it more comfortable for Sam to really address some issues without his feeling like I am trying to "therapize" or "fix" him.

When the boys were young, every week I'd take them out for breakfast before school to Ye Old Cottage restaurant. It was a little, hole-in-the-wall diner straight out of the 1950s, with linoleum floors, vinyl stools, Formica counters, and jukeboxes that played songs by Chuck Berry and Elvis Presley. We all ate huge quantities of eggs, bacon, English muffins, and even doughnuts. In our conversations, I was always quick to stand up for Sam, who was six years younger, when they got into sibling battles.

"So, Sam, what do you think about Mrs. Eberhardt?" I say, bringing up his favorite teacher. I usually tried to direct the conversation Sam's way to make him feel included, because Michael was a big talker.

Before Sam could respond, Michael jumped in and teased, "You know she likes me better."

"Michael, give Sam a chance to talk, for God's sake," I'd say sharply.

"I was just kidding, Dad."

"You're always interrupting him."

"Well, you're always on my case.

"That's ridiculous, Michael."

Meanwhile Sam would sit quietly, wolfing down his breakfast and ignoring Michael and me. This merry-go-round of tension went on for years, until the day when ten-year-old Sam told me to stop protecting him, that he could handle his brother on his own.

Old habits are hard to change. I encouraged Sam, who was an excellent tennis player, to become serious about it in high school. I wanted him to have an oasis of success that would support him through the long, forced march of adolescence. It was a disaster. His coach and I gave him unrealistic expectations about his potential, so Sam decided he wanted to be a nationally ranked junior player. Since his high school team was terrible, he was the #1 player on the team, but he wasn't successful on the tournament circuit. It was a huge frustration and disappointment for him. As he said, it blew major goats.

Sam denies that the whole tennis thing bothered him that much, but he had been prone to depression, lack of commitment, and some social anxiety throughout his adolescence. His college years have been a struggle. Right below the surface, I think he's in enormous pain. Naturally my efforts to help him only served to make him feel worse about himself. It's hard to believe I can be so good with other kids and so awkward and inept with Sam.

The sheet of notes is folded in my shirt pocket. He knows I have an agenda for this road trip. We are able to tease each other about it. Sort of.

Sam

WHOEVER DECIDED THAT TEN O'CLOCK AND TWO O'CLOCK ON THE steering wheel are the best positions for a driver's hands had obviously not been driving on a highway for three hours. My thumbs are nicely hooked on the wheel at five and seven. The leather feels good.

My dad sits low in the passenger seat, a couple of pillows stuffed around him to make my VW more comfy. We are halfway through the day. Being a morning person, he gave us an early start while I slept. After making it into Pennsylvania, I took over, and now we're on the long trek across the Keystone State. Given my dad's energy levels, I plan to drive the rest of the trip to Chicago, where late tonight he will catch a flight back to Boston. I'm touched that even with his sickness, he is willing to help me with this drive and take a whole day out of his life solely for me. Although, it does come at a price.

"So, Sam," Dad breaks what had been a pleasant silence. "I have a little bit of an agenda in terms of what I want us to talk about during this trip." I cringe when he pulls a sheet of paper out, with his crazy handwriting scrawled all over it and what look to be bullet points. So far, all we've talked about is how I'm doing with my breakup with Sarah, then my New Year's Eve adventure with Lisa, and facing my winter term of college. That's already left me drained. I don't think I'm ready for an outlined agenda.

"Wow, written notes. You don't even do that for your clients. Do I need to pull out my checkbook for this?"

"Easy there, wiseass. This is near and dear to my heart, so I wanted to think it through and get it right."

"Whatever, fine," I mutter, looking straight ahead. My hands grip the wheel a little tighter.

"The first thing is an overarching issue you seem to have struggled with in the last few years—"

"What, adolescence? I'm pretty sure everyone has trouble there."

"Ha ha." My dad is trying to get into his flow. "No, what I was going to say was your trouble receiving help. It seems that when I try to check in with you, you're often distant. And when I give you advice, you seem to struggle to even listen to me. I know some of the solutions I've offered in the past haven't worked out so well—"

"Like the three therapists who were all idiots? How about the little assortment of antidepressants that one doc had me on that ended in my having a seizure?" I blurt out in a fury. "No wonder I'm not so big on your, or Mom's, or anyone else's help—it never works. Everyone tells me my problems without giving me any real solutions." Snow-covered farmland streaks by as I speed up, clutching the wheel even tighter.

"I said I know that my solutions haven't been the best," Dad says quietly. "But you never even gave those therapists a chance. You only went to one or two sessions with each of them. I just think that if you're honest with yourself, you'll recognize that you often aren't open to help."

Despite the quiet tone, I can see I've already upset him. How do our conversations always get like this so quickly? What is it about him that puts me in such a frenzy? Ever since I was little and getting tutoring from a speech therapist, my parents have always tried to fix me. I never felt like I've really needed the help. I'd rather just sit back and enjoy life. Sure there are difficulties, but you should just accept them instead of always running to the next therapist or the next drug. My dad's overanalyzing of my life has always frustrated me, especially because he doesn't have all his shit together, either. He had a much worse childhood than me, and he's still in therapy for it. He still has anxiety over being a parent, and he blames himself for every problem Michael and I face. His anxiety and attempts to help me get on my nerves instead of comforting me. I know my anger right now is left over from all his failed efforts and really has nothing to do with the here and now. Even as these thoughts float through my consciousness, I'm still stubbornly defending myself. "Oh, I'd love to be helped," I say, unable to contain the sarcasm. "Maybe if there was a therapist out there who actually had something smart to say, maybe then I would be a little more open!"

The idiotic narrow-mindedness of my comment hits me and I realize I've just insulted my dad and his profession. But I just keep at it. "You keep badgering me about how I'm doing with the breakup with Sarah. Look, I don't want to drive with a therapist for the next ten hours to Chicago!" I finish in a final burst, almost pulling the steering wheel right off.

We drive for a few minutes in silence. Dad looks out the window as we pass a pair of McDonald's golden arches brightly resilient against the gray snowy sky. I feel like a complete asshole. I insult my sick father while he's taking time out of his life to keep me company on an otherwise lonely road trip. All he wants is to help me.

"Look, Sam, I just want you to be happy," he says softly. "Given my lifetime of experience and my professional knowledge, I truly think that I can be useful. That's all. And the first step is figuring out how best for you to receive support. Okay?"

"Listen, I'm sorry for exploding like that. I know you have good intentions, but I just struggle with your help sometimes. I don't like to talk about things. And I really don't want to blame you for my issues or mistakes. I know parenting is hard and you get upset when you see me struggle, but that's just the way of the world." My dad nods and I continue. "I think one issue is that we always talk about how many problems I have. It starts to make a guy feel bad. Let's look at the bright side for a change: I'm a healthy twenty-one-year-old with a bright future. I'm going to graduate from a great school, and then I'll be off and away. I don't do drugs, I have a great family and great friends. Sure I'm coming off a hard breakup last term, and, yeah, I struggled with schoolwork in the fall. And of course the whole cancer thing sucks. But I'll always have struggles and obstacles to overcome—"

"Well, I want to help you when you reach those problems in your life." Sensing my sincerity, my dad is animated.

"Let me try to put this a different way," I begin. "I think you live in the delusion that our family is normal. That having weekly or biweekly "check-ins" is normal. No. Normal is when someone asks you how you are, you say, 'Fine, how are you?' and the person says, 'Fine.' And that part of the conversation is over. It is not normal to ask, 'How are you *really* doing Sam?' and expect me to open up about my life and all its trials and tribulations." I accelerated into the passing lane.

"First of all," I continue, "nothing much changes between the times you or Mom asks me about my life; second of all, it's ridiculous to be so exposed. If a friend of mine wants to talk about something, I let him bring it up. I don't go prying. Neither should you. I know you're parents, and it's your job to be nosy, but come on!" I look at Dad and try to smile. "I think we both need to be aware of where the other person is coming from. I need to respect that you're only trying to help. And you need to realize that it's completely abnormal to analyze and talk as much as you do and we all do as a family."

My dad is laughing. A surge of anger rises in me, until he holds up a hand for me to be patient and says, "I'm laughing because I say the same thing when I am teaching therapists. I've been preaching for thirty years that as a group, we're not normal, and we have to recognize, when we are doling out advice, that we're not the normal people. It's one of my biggest hits as a joke when I'm talking to fellow therapists. Wow, not until this moment did I think to turn that on my own life and my own family."

Finally, a comfortable silence engulfs us. Just the sound of the car and the road. No music, because my dad doesn't like listening to music in the car. It takes away from the talking. "So," he throws out there.

"So," I reply.

"I really appreciate your speaking so honestly. How about if we skip all my other agenda items and I only ask you to talk about one thing? And after that, I'll even listen to the radio the rest of the way."

"Deal."

"Good. I think it would be really interesting for me, if you told me a history of yourself, kind of your autobiography."

"A history of myself? You've got to be kidding! That's the 'one thing' you want me to talk about? Weren't you here for my whole history? You probably know it better than I do."

"I want to know about your experience of growing up from your point of view." He's oddly excited about this idea of his. "What events stand out for you? How do you sort through your memories and organize them? Start from the beginning, what is your first memory, and how did it make you feel?"

I shudder. He says he understands that his way isn't normal, but clearly he doesn't. I glance over at him; he's looking straight ahead, unable to suppress a smile. He's trying to give me space to start talking. I wish he didn't always try so hard. "Fine. You know that little cast footprint that I made in preschool that's hung up in yours and Mom's dressing room?"

"Sure."

"Well I have a clear memory of sticking my foot on the cold, gooey plaster."

"Wow, you can remember that far back. You must have been only two years old. So what was that like for you?" My dad is all smiles, nearly bouncing in his seat. Since this is making him happy, I will tolerate stupid questions and just grit my teeth and get through it.

"I was two and I stuck my foot in plaster. All that I was thinking about was that it was gooey and weird."

"Fair enough, so what's next?"

I can't hide a smile. The man actually wants a play-by-play life history of my life. I guess I should be glad that I have a father so interested in me.

David

I LOOK OVER AT THE WOMAN WHO SHARES MY BED. SHE'S SOUND ASLEEP; her face surrounded by a beautiful tangle of thick silver-gray hair. In this fifty-nine-year-old woman with her few extra pounds and wrinkles, I can still see the girl I fell in love with.

Today we're belatedly celebrating the thirty-eighth anniversary of our wedding day.

It was December 30, 1967, and the Little Church Around the Corner on East 29th Street in New York was overflowing with Kate's and my family and friends and important people we didn't know but had to be invited. I was standing with my brother, Jim, near the altar, fidgeting. I gestured at him to show me the ring, and he pointed at the waistband pocket of his tux, the old black tie and tails of a bygone era. There was a hush, then everyone turned and looked toward the back of the church. A princess in shimmering ivory satin appeared. The music swelled. On the arm of her uncle, Kate slowly glided down the aisle. I smiled as she came toward me to cover my rising sense of panic and disbelief. I was completely in love with Kate and entirely unprepared to get married.

When it was my turn to say my vows, I boomed them out so that everyone on the East Side of New York might hear them: "I, David, take thee, Katharine, to be my lawfully wedded wife . . ."

When it was her turn, Kate was crying so hard she could barely whisper the words between the sobs: "I, Katharine, [sob] take thee, David, [sob] to be my lawfully wedded [sob] husband . . ." I had no idea what she was crying about. (Later, I found out she missed her father.) I did know that we were way too young to be doing this.

Kate and I were brought together by three powerful attractions: the intense physical response we had to each other, our sheer enjoyment of each other's company, and our profound connection derived from how utterly alone each of us felt after a parent's death. However, we were both college seniors about as ready to be married as Sam is. Even then, I suspected we were looking to our relationship to make us complete, whole people and to provide a safe hiding place. We got married because we were in love. And we got married because we were afraid. As we marched down the aisle arm in arm, nodding and smiling, it seemed like we were play-acting. I felt about as real as the plastic groom on the wedding cake.

This year, we skipped our anniversary tradition of staying at the Four Seasons for twenty-four hours of luxurious surroundings, fine food, and a reliably good intimate encounter because Sam and Michael were home. But Sam is now safely back at Carleton, so tomorrow we go to Boca Grande, Florida, to visit our best friends. Kate and I can't wait for a week in the sun by the sea. I hope we can actually take a break from the relentless tension we are both feeling.

Today we will celebrate almost four decades together. I've ordered flowers and bought expensive champagne. There's a card with a photo of a little boy holding a bunch of wild flowers behind his back and a little girl up on her tiptoes, giving him a hint of a kiss. Somehow, it captures us. As to whether we get together later in the bedroom, well, who knows? Activity in that department has seemed both more daunting and less important for both of us. Another consequence of cancer, chemo, and fear.

I remember when I first experienced Kate's tenderness, vulnerability, and grief. We were sitting in a bar and I casually mentioned that my mother had committed suicide the year before. Then I added, for dramatic effect I am sure, that both my father and my sister had gone insane and been hospitalized for an extended period of time. Her eyes widened and grew soft. She reached across the table for my hand. The intensity of her gentle, loving gaze was more than I could handle. I felt suddenly exposed. I averted my eyes and said something self-deprecating like, "Sorry for being so melodramatic, just dropping that bomb on you like that."

"No, don't be sorry. I'm so glad you told me. I really understand. I do. After my father died, I just stopped telling people, because nobody knew what to say and it just felt awkward and made me feel worse. I never have actually talked with someone else who lost a parent."

I wasn't able to respond to her tenderness, but I did know how to be responsive. I leaned toward her, took her hand in both of mine, and said gently, "Tell me about it."

Her eyes brimmed over with tears. "I just didn't want it to be true. After the call, I—" (her voice shaking) "—when they said he had been taken to the hospital, I knew I was never going to see him—" (sobbing)

"—again. And I just lay on my bed and said over and over again, 'Please, please, don't let this be so. Please, please, don't let my daddy die.'" She looked at me and said softly, "I still don't believe it's true. I know it's true, but I cannot believe it's true."

So, right from the start, Kate carried the grief for both of us. By nurturing her, comforting her, I could feel profoundly, intimately close without having to deal with my own overwhelming snake pit of feelings about my childhood. Through holding her in her grief, I was also trying to work through my own. In essence, I borrowed her tears. And I still am borrowing them. It's much easier for me to comfort Kate about her incipient widowhood than to connect emotionally to my own death.

Fortunately, we knew enough not to have children right away, because we were so adolescent ourselves. Finishing college, managing an apartment, and supplementing the allowances from our parents by waiting on tables was plenty enough. We were both overwhelmed with the idea of being married. It seemed so dauntingly grown-up.

Without any thought, we fell quickly into 1950s gender roles, which meant that Kate did virtually all the domestic chores. Until one Sunday, in our little apartment at 46th and Spruce, our own personal feminist revolution took place. Kate was vacuuming our tiny living room and asked me to lift my legs so she could vacuum under the coffee table. I sat up and said, "Sure, hon," without looking up from my book. There was a long pause, and then the vacuum was shut off. I looked up. Kate was looking at me with a quizzical expression on her face.

"Tell me something. Since we're both in school and we're both working at the same job, why do you get to be studying while I have to do the vacuuming?"

To which I unthinkingly answered, "Because my work is more important."

"What did you just say?" she exclaimed as she dropped the vacuum on the floor.

It was the shot heard round the world. We had a fairly dramatic renegotiation of domestic duties after that, leading to a complete 50-50 split of all chores.

Being married to Kate, who has a powerful—sometimes overpowering—presence, was sometimes challenging for me. She grew up in a family used to strong opinions and vociferous disagreement, and I grew up in a family that was pathologically conflict averse. The only person who ever expressed any anger in my family was my mother, who could be unpredictably and scathingly demeaning in a cold, calm, and deadly tone of voice.

I was afraid of making Kate angry and therefore generally deferred to her, which often resulted in her getting her way and my inwardly retreating. I would meet Kate's head-on complaints and criticisms with a winsome smile and glib response, as in "I promise to never do that again," and "Sweetie, I completely agree with you."

In the early years, Kate's main ambition seemed to be making our marriage better. This was like having a nuclear power plant hooked up to run a sewing machine. Fortunately, after about four years of trying to "improve" me, she took her fireball-of-energy self off to medical school, and our marriage began to settle into a working partnership.

It took me a while to find my professional calling, too. I became a therapist almost by accident. Originally, I went to graduate school so I could help transform society. I had been imbued with my own version of late-sixties idealism and grandiosity.

However, I really wasn't cut out to be a radical revolutionary. Almost accidentally I answered an ad for a counselor at the Youth Development Center, a euphemism for a jail for kids. It was there that I discovered the joy of truly engaging with one person or family at a time. I was just trying to help Sherman get a fair hearing in court, Maynard arrange a visit with his dad, Henry deal with his guilt about stealing all his mom's money, Jesse control his murderous rages. I was good at it. I had found an authentic way of trying to have a qualitative impact on people's lives, rather than brandishing slogans and demonizing the opposition. For me, becoming a therapist was a calling and a refuge.

In my workshops for other therapists, I often try to capture my passion for being a therapist. "We therapists practice an arcane art, while feeling the weight of expectation that we be scientific and objective. But after all the theories are spoken, and all of the therapeutic techniques applied, the best of what we have to offer our clients is to share our own flawed humanity without shame. What happens in therapy may be a mystery, but I don't believe we therapists are. Most of us are wounded healers with a deep sense of connection to the suffering of others. We believe that being one caring person, in one session, even in one moment, can sometimes be the difference that makes a difference. That's how it feels on the good days. Sometimes we may feel more like a 'rent-a-friend' offering a much less reliable result than your average escort service."

I have had a rich and successful life taking care of others. I have been a good therapist and a good teacher. But being a caregiver to others has also been a way for me to feel intimacy and connection without much emotional risk. It's been a form of "safe intimacy." In working with my clients' grief, I also worked on my own. Much the same way that I did with Dr. Kate. I was borrowing their tears, too. Is it any wonder that having lost a mother to mental illness I became a psychologist? And having lost a father to heart disease that Kate became a doctor? I shudder to consider the legacy of our childhood wounds on Michael and Sam.

In my own therapy, I discovered the extent to which I had been role-playing my life and had been basically in denial about my anxiety, grief, and pain. For years, I had characterized this dissociative quality as relatively harmless and referred to it as my California postcard:

Dear All,
Having a great time. Wish I were here!

I had to work hard in therapy to integrate the anxious, insecure, competitive, and selfish internal parts of me with my kind, happy, mellow, and cheerful persona. My goal was to learn how to simply be who I am rather than creating a self to please others.

Kate was onto this quality in me right from the beginning of our marriage. She kept saying things like, "I don't feel like you are really there." To which I would respond with exasperation, "What do you mean? I'm here." But it was one of the reasons I loved her. She wanted me to be more "real." In the years following therapy, as I have been more direct and open about my fears, vulnerabilities, dependency, etc. I've had often said to her, "Honey, you should have watched what you wished for."

Since the cancer, I've drifted back to my childhood defenses, taking care of others and acting relaxed and cheerful. Back to hiding behind my smile. It looks kind and loving, even brave. In reality, I am not there.

Thinking back on our early days fills me with tenderness. I decide to get my sleeping bride some coffee. Suddenly, I remember the poem that I wrote for Kate when she went off to medical school. Silly as it was, it caught the feeling of pride and connection and even a little anxiety that I felt as she moved on to a new stage of life. Chances of her having to move on again are still high. I decide to find the poem and slip it into the card I bought. Not long after, I say, "Good morning, sweetie. Coffee, paper, and anniversary card, in any order you want."

She reaches for the card, smiles at the boy with flowers, opens it, and reads the old poem out loud:

A Poem Upon the Occasion of Your Starting Medical School
"I Love You Like a Pair of P. F. Flyers"

Yes,
I know, I'm old
And even smell a little.
And yes, there are holes
In my soles.

But don't forget how fast
I could make you go
Rounding second base.
I know the fit
Of your feet

Now's it's time
For training bras and panty hose,
Lipstick and high heels.
But don't leave me behind,
In the back of your closet

I can still make you run faster
Jump higher,
I know the fit
Of your feet.

Kate smiles at me with tears in her eyes. "That was the best poem you ever wrote me."

"Read what I wrote on your card," I say softly.

And wherever your path takes you,
And wherever the path takes me,
Know this, my darling, Kate,
I will always know the fit of your feet.

Kate starts to cry; I take her in my arms. It's a return to our beginning again. Our way of connecting. Except now, I am crying, too.

Kate

For months it seems, our lives have been all about cancer. But now, after the intensity of the holidays, we are taking a break. We are headed to Florida for a short visit with old and dear friends. It is the first time we have allowed ourselves to make a plan, the future being a place we generally avoid.

From the moment we step off the plane into the bright sun, in such contrast to the gray skies of a Boston winter, we feel lighter. Our friends have a house in an old, small town on the Gulf Coast of Florida, where the fast pace of our usual life is nowhere in evidence. People get around by walking, driving golf carts, or riding bicycles. Cars are noticeably scarce. Our friends indulge us. We have deliciously leisurely days, walking on the beach or going to a club where we lie in the steam bath or float in the pool. We all have a massage. We play tennis, we walk, and we talk. Evenings are spent in the comfortable conversation of people who know each other well. We laugh at well-worn jokes, relive our children's childhood adventures, talk about news and mutual friends. Their concern and love is palpable, even though we do not talk much about David's illness. I find myself relaxing in a way that I had forgotten was possible.

A few days into our visit, as David and I are changing out of our bathing suits, he reaches over and gently caresses my cheek. His eyes twinkle; he smiles and says, "You look so relaxed. It seems as though we left the cancer bag at the airport." I laugh. It is true. It is as though we have simply dropped out of illness into health. Things feel almost normal.

When we return from Florida, David reminds me about the photo shoot that afternoon, part of a project he had agreed to participate in last fall. Shortly after David published an article about his cancer, he received a phone call from someone at the Dana-Farber Cancer Institute asking if he would be part of a study on patients with advanced cancer. They wanted to interview and photograph patients and family members. "Sure, why not?" he responded. The woman told him that after the interview, the photographer on the project would be in touch.

David and I are still feeling pretty good after our escape to Florida.

Mid-afternoon, Nick Nixon, a well-known portrait photographer, arrives. We sit and talk for about forty-five minutes. Nick likes to get to know the people he is photographing. We are about the same age and find ourselves rapidly connecting over shared politics and being children of the sixties. We slowly move on to the topic of the project. He explains that we are beginning a process with a commitment to finish if David's disease progresses. "How are patients chosen for this study?" I ask.

"Oh, in general, they are patients who are not expected to live more than a few years," Nick says, matter-of-factly.

He is not saying anything I do not already know, but somehow hearing it so casually spoken by a stranger sends a shock wave through me. My stomach knots up and I feel as though I can't breathe, but, of course, I say nothing. I just sit there smiling as though he had said, "We picked people born in June."

Nick has us sit on a sofa together and sets up his old box camera. He asks us just to interact, and at first we enjoy being together, smiling at each other. It is a lark. But slowly, as the picture taking continues, Nick's words sink in. I realize that if things go "according to plan," these pictures will document David's death. It almost seems inevitable. Each successive shoot will inexorably be closer to a final picture of David. At the end, he will look gaunt and wasted, just like all the patients I have seen shortly before death. The realization feels like a physical blow; I can see that David feels it, too. Our smiles fade. We get through the rest of the shoot somehow, and Nick leaves. David and I are very quiet and gentle with each other the rest of the afternoon.

Because I am a doctor, I have seen many patients die of cancer and numerous other diseases that slowly consumed them. I have no refuge in denial, not unlike cancer patients who have to face chemotherapy again when they thought they had been cured. They have no illusions about what chemo will be like or what the emotional and physical toll will be. It is something all doctors face when a family member is ill. They have seen the possible future over and over again in the faces of their dying patients.

Although I only understand this in retrospect, for most of the twelve years after my father died, the irrational part of my mind held out hope that somehow I would see him again. I used to dream that he was alive and often woke with a sense of profound joy, almost ecstasy, until I remembered he was dead. Then I would come crashing down.

In the first month of medical school, we were told that in addition to our anatomy class we would all see an autopsy. By that time, we were well into the dissection of our cadavers and were learning how to suppress our feelings about cutting up a dead body as we became engrossed in the details of how beautifully human bodies were made. As our group of ten students made our way to the morgue, I was not concerned. This would not be any different from what we were already doing in anatomy. The autopsy room was large and very white. At one end of the room was the body of a twenty-two-year-old young man who had been found dead at home. The autopsy was being done to determine the cause of death. The diener, whose job was to prepare the body, clearly enjoyed his role and made a big production of revving up the saw before slicing straight through this young man's body from his neck to just below his naval and then angling at the end to create an upside-down Y.

I stood there frozen. This was nothing like dissecting our cadaver, most of which was carefully wrapped in formaldehyde-soaked rags. In our anatomy class, we had only actually uncovered the chest and the abdomen; none of us had uncovered the face yet. Here was a whole body, exposed under the harsh light, with blood and fresh tissues. I pulled my eyes away and looked around the room. There were several bodies, laid out on similar metal tables, waiting for their autopsies. At the end of the room was a man who looked to be in his fifties who had the same barrel chest as my father, the same thinning gray hair, the same aquiline nose. From where I stood, it could have been my father. He, too, had had an autopsy.

I felt a physical shock, as though something had exploded next to me, except that the explosion was silent. I stood transfixed, while inside something profound happened. My father's death was no longer an abstract event. In that moment, I knew he was really dead and that I would never see him again. I wanted to scream, to fall to my knees, with the pain of this understanding, but of course I did not. I did not say anything. I was learning the skill I would use over and over as a physician—to suppress the enormity of what I was seeing until I was alone and could think about it. I never dreamt that my father was alive again.

A few weeks after the shoot, Nick sent us copies of the photographs. I looked through the pictures in sequence and could see in my face my slow realization that it was possible we were photographing the beginning of a process that would end in David's death. For a while, I stared at them obsessively, as though they could answer my constant question about the future. Then I put them in a drawer. They were too painful to look at.

Since David's illness, it is often hard to keep my emotions in check at work. When I go to conferences, I can no longer listen dispassionately to a description of a life-threatening illness, the newest treatment, the complications. My heart pounds and my stomach clenches when I imagine what the patients who have this disease are feeling and how the family is coping. I am astonished that I was ever able to separate the disease from the person. How was I ever able to remain objective enough to make diagnostic or treatment decisions in the face of devastating illness? Now I am powerless to stop the waves of emotion that wash over me as I work. Sometimes I am paralyzed by what patients are going through. Sometimes I am paralyzed by fear that I will make a mistake or miss something important.

Work also means that I have to leave David each morning. I hate being apart from him and feel safe only when we are holed up at home together. We need to be near each other. We need to be able to touch. It is as though I am not whole until I am home. I feel a deep appreciation of David in my life. It is as though all the little annoyances that happen in any marriage have become completely irrelevant. Cancer is a lens that filters out all the background noise. What is left is a clear, clean, and almost pure love and gratitude.

Around this time, David and I begin using the phrase "It's not cancer!" when any problem arises. When one of us is upset, the other says, "It's not cancer!" We look at each other and smile. It puts everything in perspective.

Spring 2006

David

My dad was the eldest child in his family and from an early age was groomed to be the family patriarch. He was always highly respected by his peers and adults alike. Unfortunately this special recognition included his being singled out by his Boy Scout master, who molested him. The experience filled my dad with shame, self-loathing, and confusion that haunted him throughout his life.

The summer Dad turned fourteen, his parents sent him to Camp Wallula on Cape Cod. As he told it seventy years later, Camp Wallula was his chance to make a fresh start, to cleanse himself of his shame by being the best, most enthusiastic, most tireless boy in camp. In the closing ceremony, after the "Wahoo Whoop" song was sung for the last time by the chorus of young campers, my dad was brought up on stage in front of all the boys and their parents and presented with the prestigious silver cup, the Camp Wallula Best Camper Award. For the rest of his life, my dad seemed to relentlessly seek recognition and success as a way of redeeming himself.

Now Dad is ninety-two and slowly dying of congestive heart failure and old age in a nursing home. He can't last much longer. His third wife, Peggy, died last spring, and he's trying to adjust to going it alone. Today we're on our regular Sunday morning phone call. He sounds chipper, but after a few minutes, he manages to tangle up the phone cord with the lines of his oxygen tank. A nurse tries to help, but he gets exasperated. He says he'll call me back.

A few minutes later, he's back, short of breath. "Well, I give myself an A for effort," he says, trying to be cheerful. "As long as I have my oxygen tank with me and someone to wheel me around, I'm quite the social butterfly. And between you and me, I'm still pretty good at lighting up some of the old ladies around here. Of course, I don't have a lot of competition."

"Sounds like you're determined to become best camper again, Dad." We have been referring to his camp prize for decades now as Dad soldiered through the suicide of my mom, followed by two difficult marriages, my siblings' mental illness and addictions, and now his rapidly declining health.

"Well, I am working hard at it, that's for sure. Speaking of being the best camper, am I right that when you cleaned out your basement, you accidentally threw out all my old trophies and medals. Do you remember?" he asks. I can hear the sharp edge in his voice.

"Yes, Dad, I do, and I'm really sorry. It was about fifteen years ago." I swallow the rising bile in my throat. Throughout my childhood, my dad was busy being a prominent politician, president of a large hotel chain, and a thoroughly absent father. But when my family fell apart as my mother's alcoholism and depression slowly took her toward her suicide, Dad turned to me as his confidant, advisor, his pal. At the time, it made me feel important to have the great man lean on me.

After my mother's suicide and his nervous breakdown, my role as the family therapist and dad's caregiver became a permanent job. However, to the old man's credit, in his eighties, he acknowledged how self-centered and narcissistic he had been and made a genuine effort to show interest in my life and my kids. He wasn't very good at it, but it was a good-hearted try. I believe in effortful love, so I had pretty much forgiven him his failings and appreciate his efforts. But now with Dad being critical of me for not taking good care of his stuff that he dumped without asking in our house, my old anger surfaces

I take a deep breath. "I really am sorry, Dad. I know how much it meant to you."

"Well, never mind. It certainly doesn't matter now. But I do wish I had that cup."

"I know. I wish you had it, too."

My dad and I don't talk much about mortality, his or mine. As I listen to how he struggles with keeping his spirits up, trying to adjust to his failing body, the bouts of humiliating diarrhea in his bed, the waves of nausea at mealtime, the shortness of breath, I am touched by my old man. He is a fighter and a finally a role model that I can fully appreciate. I wonder how my Michael and Sam really feel about how I've been handling my cancer.

Sam

"SAM, CAN YOU COME IN HERE PLEASE?" MY DAD CALLS FROM HIS OFFICE.

"What do you want?" I yell from the TV room. I just woke up a little while ago and have been relaxing, trying to recover from my long day of traveling yesterday. Each plane I took to come home was one long delay after the other. Spring break senior year is supposed to be an awesome crazy time. Not home in Boston with crummy weather.

"Could you just come in here, please!" My dad says raising his voice. I hate it when he wants me to come in his office. I hate even remotely feeling like one of his clients.

"What?" I say as I enter the room, the sounds from the TV still floating behind me.

"Close the door. I have something to tell you." I close the door and sit down, not liking the tone my dad has.

"I didn't want to tell you last night when you got home late, but I did want to tell you as soon as possible, so I'll just say it. Your grandfather passed away two nights ago."

I don't know what to say. I feel blank. I look into my dad's eyes. They show nothing. Either he's already grieved or it will hit him later. No emotion. Maybe that's a sign in itself. I try to conjure up tears in my own eyes, but I'm not feeling it, either. Granddad's death just doesn't have much effect on me.

At least I found out about his death in a timely fashion, unlike when his wife, Peggy, passed away. Last July my mom was in the kitchen holding a pink blanket, telling my brother that it used to belong to my step-grandmother. "What material is this?" I asked my mom as I felt the blanket.

"It's mohair. Don't you think it's wonderful? It was so nice of her daughters to send it to me."

Peggy had a generous heart. Even though my cousins and I were her step-grandchildren, she remembered all of our birthdays every year. And was always offering us her vacation residences for our use. "How is Peggy doing these days?" I asked. She had been sick for some time, and my mother had been fearing the worst all spring.

"What? Sam, she's dead," Mom replied with so much incredulity it came out almost like a chuckle.

"What? When?"

"She passed away two months ago, didn't—"

"No one told me that!" I yelled at her. Tears popped into my eyes. I was angry and hurt. Why wasn't I told?

"Sam, are you serious?"

"Are you?" I snapped.

"Oh, my God, Sam. I'm so sorry no one told you. I don't know how this could have happened. I guess you were still at school and we were preoccupied with your father. Oh, Sam, come here." She tried to give me a hug, but I backed away from her. I turned and stumbled toward my dad's office, needing to hear it from someone else.

"Dad! Is Peggy dead?" I asked as I barged into his office. He spun in his office chair and saw the tears now streaking down my face.

"Oh, Sam. Yes, she passed away—"

"Two months ago? Yeah, funny how no one seemed to mention that to me!" I shouted.

"Sam, I'm so sorry. I'm so sorry." My dad also tried to give me a hug. I evaded him and slumped onto his couch. My mom and brother came in and they all looked down at me with sympathy. I had never been touched by death. And now it was real. It felt like it was in the room. I hadn't even been close to Peggy. But even so, the sudden news of her death had hit me hard in the gut. I cried and cried sitting on that couch with my family looking over me. A few minutes before, I had thought she was alive, and then I find out she has been dead for months. I remember looking up at my dad, who looked awfully sick that day. It was really the first time I fully understood that he might die, too.

This time, sitting in my dad's office, I am having no response to death, no tears for Granddad. I've known that he was sick. And last week there had been an ominous series of calls where he wanted to talk to all his children and grandchildren. I had talked to him briefly, just reminding him that I was still a senior in college. I told him a white lie, that I still was playing tennis, knowing he'd be happy to hear it. And afterward he was gone, completely out of my mind until this moment. Now he is really gone.

How do you grieve the loss of something you never really had? I didn't have a significant relationship with my grandfather. He was too old. He was already seventy-one when I came into the picture, so I don't remember him before his eighties. The only thing I can say is that I respected him. Even at eighty, I remember him going out for a swim every morning in the cold Nantucket waters. I played tennis with him several times, and he still could hit the ball when he was eighty-eight. He had a great wink and a great smile. He made you feel like you were in his inner circle. But that wink and smile were the closest I got to feeling any love from him. His heart was probably in the right place, he just didn't show it very well. Unlike my family, where emotions reside right on our sleeve. It's hard for me to understand how my dad is even related to Granddad.

Looking at my dad's dry eyes and knowing the complexity of his relationship with his father, I feel sorrier for him than for Granddad. Had Dad been ready for this? Did he know that Granddad would die soon? Is he now worrying over his own mortality even more? I just hope he's going to be okay and that I won't have to deal with his death for a long time. My parents keep pushing me to talk more about my relationship to Dad and my supposed anger at him. But aside from the little stuff, I don't really feel that mad. Honestly, he really should know how much I love him.

Michael

"YOUR GRANDFATHER DIED LAST NIGHT," MY MOM SAYS SOFTLY. I AM sitting at the kitchen table sipping a cup of coffee, trying to wake up before heading into the lab.

There is a way my mom always has about her when she's talking about death. Something so calm and sure that has a way of being comforting without minimizing or masking. I remember, as a nine-year old, playing in our backyard with a friend from school, when my mom appeared at the back door and called me over. She looked sad and told me my grandmother—her mother—had just died. My grandmother had been the only grandparent I had ever really gotten to know, at least as well as a nine-year-old can be said to know anybody. She was seventy-five when she died after a long battle with cancer brought on by years of smoking. Neither she nor my mother had wanted her to die alone in a hospital bed, so in her final weeks she lived with us.

My mom had asked me if I wanted to see her body, and I said yes. I remember my mother's hand resting gently on my shoulders as we walked to my grandmother's room. My uncle Stephen and my father were at her bedside when I went in. Her head was tilted slightly, her mouth was slack, and her eyes were looking up into the far corner of the room. I leaned in to my mom's hand. It was the only time I had ever seen a dead person, and it was an image I often used as a template when imaging my father's death.

My last grandparent is gone. I did not know my paternal grandfather well, and I knew my father's relationship with him was always tense. I have been mostly focused on my dad. He is almost sixty-one now. It seemed like a good age if you have to lose a parent. By the time you're sixty, your parents have had a full life and chance to see the person you've become. For all the pain and difficulties my dad and his father experienced, by the time my grandfather died, I don't think either of them felt there was anything unresolved or unsaid.

My mother's father died when she was only fifteen, and yet I often felt that I knew her father better than Dad's. When I was a child, my mother would talk about her father as if he were an important diplomat coming to dinner anytime now, and she wanted me to be well-prepared when he arrived. For my part, I was an eager student. I memorized things she'd told me he had said so well that I felt like I'd heard them myself.

My mother described her father as the source of her strong sense of moral obligation, her call to service, her honesty, her belief in sacrifice for others. When she and her two older brothers get together, stories about their father come out so fast it's hard to tell what is true and what is myth. Like the time he invented a system of card counting to see if he could get the math to work but never bothered to go to Vegas or Atlantic City; or the time that he developed a statistical algorithm to predict the outcomes of horse races but never used it to make money. I got the sense that he did things out of a genuine love for problem solving rather than out of such base motivations as making money. In many ways he could not have been more opposite than my paternal grandfather. He did not seem to care if the world viewed him as successful or brilliant; to him it mattered only that he was kind and that he did the right thing.

I often felt as if I were the only person with whom my mother talked about her father. She read me letters he had written her and showed me old photographs. By the time I was a teenager, my mother's father seemed like a legend, but a private one. He was the man that only my mother had known and only I had heard about. At times I felt like I must have known my grandfather better than even my mother's brothers, because only I had been told all of my mother's secrets. Through these stories, I developed a sense that my grandfather hadn't been able to reach his full potential; his life had been cut short by an untimely death. I often wanted to do the things that he had been unable to do, to fulfill the work that he had started. To provide my mother with solace, a sense of completion, which, despite being divided over several generations, would give her a sense of closure around her father's life.

When I reached high school and began racing track and cross-country, my mother reveled in retelling a story her father had shared with her about his own cross-country days. He had been late to school one morning and was running from his house when he crossed paths with one of the stars of the track team, a boy who was a few grades ahead, who was out for a morning run. Despite being adorned in his school clothes and weighed down with all his books, my grandfather kept up with him for the entire run to school, at the end of which the boy insisted he join the track team. My mother often pointed out that I showed a natural talent for track and cross-country at the same age that her father had, and I knew how much my high school racing career pleased her. She took pleasure watching me race. On a quarter-mile track, the third lap is always the hardest, because your adrenaline from the opening quarter has long since faded and you must simply dig in and hold on. During those laps, I would look for my mother in the stands, and I always felt a surge of confidence when I found her watching me. My limbs would relax, my stride would feel more like a continuous groove. It would feel like my promise being realized.

Later that day, I have lunch with Anna. "My grandfather died last night," I say nonchalantly. We have been dating for several months now and have fallen completely in love. I have practically moved in to her apartment in Somerville. I'd told Anna that my grandfather was very ill and that we expected him to die. She knows that he and I have not been close. She looks at me searchingly, her flickering eyes trying to find the right response.

"I'm sorry," she says tenderly. "How are you doing?"

"I'm okay," I say truthfully. I didn't bring it up to talk about my grandfather, or my feelings about him. And yet I know I want something from Anna. Some kind of response. "Yeah," I say with a tone of sadness, an attempt to elicit comfort. Anna moves closer to me on the bench and puts her arms around me. She lays her head on my shoulder.

"Do you want to have kids?" I ask abruptly.

Anna looks up at me with surprise. "Yeah, I guess," she says as she shifts her weight away from me slightly, searching for words. "I think I want children in the abstract. But when I actually think about having them, I don't feel ready. I need more time. Why do you ask?"

Hers is a completely reasonable response. After all, she is only twenty-six, and she is trying to establish her career. Many women in her position wouldn't begin thinking about having children for another ten years. Still, it is not the answer I wanted, though I can't explain why. It's not like I am hoping to start a family anytime soon. I want to get through graduate school. So what am I disappointed about? Maybe I am just looking for some sort of reassurance about the two of us. That we are in it for the long haul. That we want the same thing, even if only in the abstract. If that's what I want, then didn't she tell me just what I wanted to hear? What is missing? I can't put my finger on it.

"I don't know," I say, finally addressing her question. "I guess my granddad dying has just made me feel a sense of urgency about . . . I don't know . . . family stuff."

"I'm sure your dad's cancer also plays into that," Anna adds.

"Yeah." I raise my eyebrows as I nod in agreement. "I'm sure that's right."

David

It's another Sunday morning. Time for my call with my father, but Dad died two weeks ago. I still can't believe he's gone. I got to see him the month before he died, at my stepmother's hurricane-delayed memorial service. He looked like he was on his last legs, curled up in a wheelchair with his oxygen lines in his nostrils, his face wizened and pale. But at the luncheon after the service, we helped him out of the chair at his insistence and, with his stepdaughters holding him up on each side and me propping him up from behind, he sang "In the Good Old Summertime," a favorite song of his and Peggy's. We all sang with him, tears streaming down our faces. He finished with a flourish—a couple of shuffling dance steps and a wave.

He later put on a similar show to entertain the crowd at the nursing home on St Patrick's Day. Afterward, he called us up and said, "Well, I'm ready to go now. What do I have to do?" He was addressing Dr. Kate. We both knew what he meant.

"It's really not that simple, Dick," Kate answered. "I'll have to talk with your doctors and get a sense of what your choices might be. Maybe it is time to consider bringing hospice in, but nobody can just give you drugs to hasten you on your way. That's not allowed."

I was listening to the conversation. Dad talked to Kate as if she were a travel agent and he were planning a trip. They talked about cutting out all his medications, stopping eating, and other alternatives. She asked if he was considering suicide, and he promised not to commit suicide because of the harm already done to all of us by my mother's suicide forty years ago. He ended by reiterating that it was "time to go." He gave the rest of the family the same message and insisted that we needn't worry about coming down to Florida because "I know how busy you are." I didn't protest much.

That Thursday, he got hospice to come in, and on Saturday, while planning a bridge game with his lady pals, he said that he was getting a headache and needed to take a nap. He lay down and never woke up.

A week later, we all gathered at the Oak Harbor Club for Dad's memorial service. Each of us found a way of celebrating his life. His granddaughter played a tape recording of his singing "Tur-a-lur-a-lura."

The service went on and on. Most of the people there were very old, and I was afraid we might kill a few of them off. I spoke last and cut my remarks in half. I told the story of Camp Wallula, because his striving to be the best camper to overcome his feelings of inadequacy was the story of his whole life. My heart softened as I spoke about that anxious, striving boy from long ago. I sat down and they played "Amazing Grace." When the line "and saved a wretch like me" came, sobs welled up inside me and spilled over. A lifetime's worth of tension and ambivalence broke loose like an iceberg calving. Suddenly I felt toward my father the way I always wanted to feel toward him. Suddenly I was just a son crying for his dad.

As I wept, the very real possibility that the next time all my family gathered would be for my services assaulted me. I thought of Sam and Michael trying to speak about me. I thought of Kate unable to talk through her tears. Then I was flushed again with a sense of my dad's courage and grace as he faced his failing body and his diminishing days. He was the best camper to the end. I will be grateful if I can face my future as well as he faced his. Thanks, Dad.

David

"THE WALLS ARE THREE FEET THICK AND SLANTED SO THAT PROJECTILES wouldn't penetrate," says Nino, our host, in his musical Italian accent. He is leading us up the winding staircase to our guest suite at the top of Castello di Loretto, in Umbria, Italy, far off the beaten track. "And that's not all. You see, as you go up these winding stairs, there is no way to swing your sword, only coming down. And at intervals," he says, pointing, "there's these holes where they were pouring hot oil or shooting arrows. See, each thing thought out for the defense. That's why they call this the castle's keep. When all is lost, the lord retreats to here and with all the food stores and the protection he waits out the, you know, what's that word, the, ah, siege. Yes, that's it, the siege, by the enemy."

Umbria is still almost entirely rural and mostly forested. "That's why it's called the green heart of Italia," Nino tells us. It is May 1, exactly one year since my cancer announced its presence in my shoulder. We are, quite inadvertently, celebrating my one-year anniversary with this trip to Italy, which had been planned two years ago. I have been ignoring as best I can the intermittent pain in my right side. We've decided it is due to my weight gain of the last few months. Years ago, when I had put on weight quickly, I was so uncomfortable that I asked Kate if I could have liver cancer. We found out that the pain was caused by wearing pants that had become too tight. Now we agree to believe my pain is again tight-pants disease, not the dreaded recurrence. Not now, not on our trip.

Earlier, in Rome, we walked with a mob of tourists along the Appian Way, through the ruins of the ancient Roman forum down to the Coliseum. We stood at the spot where Julius Caesar was killed. And above the crowd noise and the hawking of the vendors, we heard a bird song. "Sounds like a wood thrush," said Kate.

"Caesar must have woken up with the sounds of those birds," I said.

We paused and watched the crowds milling about, seemingly everyone taking everyone's picture, as if immortality could be captured digitally. We marveled at the blocks of stone beneath us, smoothed by countless centuries of feet. The enormity of human comings and goings was overwhelming, and yet long before the popes and the Caesars, and even Romulus and Remus's arrival at the Tiber, there were the songbirds.

I smiled at Kate and put my arm around her. "You know, when you think about all the lives in this place—come and gone, each person, feeling the swell of their own importance, busying along, having to get somewhere, do something—it kind of puts things into perspective, don't you think?"

"What perspective?"

"You know, our lives, me surviving one year, not knowing if I'll get another, the whole thing."

"You're fun to travel with," she teased.

"Now you know how I feel," I tossed back, because she's often the one to jolt me back to reality by bringing up the cancer stuff. We started walking again, arm in arm, silently acknowledging our acute awareness of the vulnerability we both felt while blending into the happy crowd of visitors in this ancient place.

Now, we look out our window in the castle at the undulating green hills in the soft, misty twilight. From above comes the scratching feet of birds on the castle's roof. I take Kate into my arms and look in her deep blue eyes. "You know what you are, don't you?"

"No, what?"

"You're my castle's keep."

◇◇◇

Several days later, we are walking the narrow, twisted streets of the hill towns of Montefalco, Bevagna, Assisi, Todi, and Orvieto, where the sights and sounds bleed together into a chiaroscuro of startling shadows, dark nooks and crannies suddenly punctuated by bright blue sky or an arch that opens to the green countryside sprawling below. Each town is dominated by a piazza, with either a *chiesa* (church) or a *duomo* (cathedral). The mixture of modern commerce, rushing tourists, and ancient stillness is as compelling as in Rome. We feel as if we have parachuted onto a different planet, alone and content in the throngs. We are awed and humble and deliciously happy.

I sit for an hour at the tomb of St. Francis, who died in 1222. Kate wanted to shop, and I need to sit. My heart is filled with awareness that this one man inspired centuries of people with his simple message of embracing poverty, living in simplicity, and following the precepts of his famous prayer: *Oh Divine Master, grant that I may not so much seek to be consoled . . . as to console. To be understood . . . as to understand. To be loved . . . as to love.*

The crowds stand in reverent silence by the stone sarcophagus. I watch and wonder at how much the simple teachings of Christ and a man like St. Francis have been bastardized by the relentless human hunger for power and hegemony and control throughout the history of the Christian Church. And yet, eight hundred years after St. Francis's death, people still come to visit his remains.

After Kate retrieves me, we go to see the frescoes by Giotto in the little chapel. "He was the first to create perspective in paintings since Roman times," Kate says. "See the way the buildings become smaller. He created a play between foreground and background." I am churched out and only make a token acknowledgment. "You are such a philistine," she says.

On the way out, I buy a biography of St. Francis. I am busy trying to not to notice that the ache in my gut is getting worse. Throughout our visit to Assisi, it demands my attention with increasing pain. Kate is so happy and relaxed that I can't bear to tell her. Privately, I think about what would follow from a call to Dr. Hochberg: the decision to fly home immediately, the emergency PET scan, the likely bone marrow transplant, the chance that either the treatment will kill me or simply will not work.

Surprisingly, I feel a growing sense of acceptance: *que será, será.* Not my old friend denial, but real acceptance. Somehow being surrounded by this extraordinary pulse of history helps me put my life in perspective. I have so much to be grateful for, the richness and blessings that have been showered upon me—a blessed marriage, remarkable and tender sons, a satisfying life's work. If I'm lucky, this pain won't get worse. I have another PET scan already scheduled next month. So far, I've had three clean ones. Having clean PET scans is like finding buoys when you're sailing in the fog. For a moment you are safe and know where you are before you plunge back into the impenetrable murk, still a long way from safe harbor.

"What are you thinking?" asks Kate, in the midst of a simple lunch of pasta, cheese, and prosciutto in an enclosed garden restaurant.

"Just how surprised I am about how wonderful this is. I never would have expected to enjoy walking through these hill towns and seeing these churches as much as I have."

She smiles lovingly back at me. "I am truly happy." She reaches her hand across the table.

I take her hand in mine. "Me, too," I say, telling the truth, but not the whole truth.

◇◇◇

We arrive at the Hotel Rodeo in Scarlino Scalo. We are joining a group for a sailing expedition. This adventure is why we're in Italy.

The graying hair, wrinkled faces, and balding heads belie the animated, excited conversation among the twenty of us seated at a long table. We are a weathered band of adventurers, mostly accomplished people committed to leaving the world a better place. Some know each other well; many are meeting for the first time. We have six-degrees-of-separation conversations and invariably learn that we went to the same school, have friends in common, our children know each other somehow, or we have similar careers and politics, mostly of the do-gooder variety. What defines us more than anything is our generally privileged back-grounds, our age (sixties), and our passionate enthusiasms. Many casually mention health issues, such as knee replacements, back surgeries, angioplasties, and many mention the loss of friends, but it is with a mix of bowing to the inevitable and fierce defiance. This is a "Do not go gently into that good night" crowd.

This group will sail hard, scale peaks, investigate ruins, eat and drink well. I say to Kate as we weave up the stairs, "Screw cancer. Let the good times roll."

"I just want to get into bed," she says.

A week later, strong wind squalls, slashing rain, and dead calms are interspersed throughout the night of our sail from St. Stefano to Ponzo. It is an adventure. Dawn reveals a nasty storm system looming ahead of us. The mountainous island of Ponzo on the horizon is enshrouded by thick, dark clouds and slashing sheets of rain. The sky and the ocean around us have that sickly greenish hue. We have our sails down and we're motoring through the eerie calm that often precedes a bad squall. We are staring at the gloomy scene when Kate, pointing to the sky behind us, says, "Hey, look at that." It is bright blue. The clearing weather is right behind us.

"It's our metaphor," Kate whispers.

"What are you talking about?"

"You know, I told you months ago—us being like a small boat sailing right on the edge. We don't know if we're going to be hit by the squalls or if the clearing wind is going to blow the storm through and we'll be in blue sky and sunshine. I think it's going to clear. It's like a sign that you're going to be okay."

"For Chrissakes, Kate, you know how I feel about magical thinking, signs, portents, omens. Who knows what's going to show up on my scan? Do we always have to be talking about it?"

Kate's face falls. She turns away. "Would anyone like some coffee?" she asks the rest of the crew. They are enthusiastic and she slips away to go below and make some brew. I feel like a shit. Sometimes we can tease each other about the big "C" and sometimes we can't. I have to tell her how worried I am.

From Elba, to Giglio, to Ponzo, to Ischia, Capri, and finally Naples, the days and nights of sailing, hiking, touring, and feasting bleed into each other. My stomachache waxes and wanes, varying between pain and muted ache. I finally confess my worries to Dr. Kate. It scares her and I feel much less frightened and alone. After that, we have whispered check-ins about my stomach "awareness" in our tiny aft cabin, but at least we are in the fear together. I am so grateful for how steadfast and loving she's been throughout this year. My Dr. Kate.

Now our trip is over and we are headed home. Shortly after taking off, the Alitalia 757 bringing us back to America banks sharply. Suddenly I can see all of Rome spread out beneath me, with the Tiber a ribbon of sparkling gold weaving through the heart of the city. I catch a glimpse of the Coliseum and St. Peter's. Then the city is gone and there is a patchwork quilt of lush greens and rich dark browns. Springtime in Italy.

Kate

IT IS HARD TO BELIEVE IT HAS BEEN A YEAR SINCE DAVID'S DIAGNOSIS. I am deeply grateful he is still here and seemingly doing well. The decision to go to Italy was made months before in the spirit of "cherish this time," not quite believing we would ever get here. It is wonderful. We walk through the countryside together, eat in small hill towns, and savor the light, the landscape, and the kind people we meet.

I am excited and even happy when we meet our friends at the Hotel Rodeo to begin our sailing adventure. By day we explore the islands in shifting groups renewing old acquaintances and getting to know those of our fellow travelers who are new to us. Each night we congregate on different boats or go ashore to eat in one of the local *ristoranti*. Eating the superb food is a sensual experience. As we listen to the lyrical beauty of spoken Italian, it is once again as though we have been whisked off to another land where cancer does not exist.

At least until David mentions his abdominal pain. He tries to say this casually, but I can see the fear in his face. We are sitting alone in a tiny stone-walled courtyard eating lunch. The sun filters through the vines that weave through the trellis overhead. The ever-present knot in my stomach tightens. He wonders out loud if we need to call Effi. I look at him, searching for some sign of illness. I grill him about every conceivable symptom. There is nothing except the dull ache in his abdomen, where his liver is, a place that could easily be invaded by tumor. I decide we should wait.

Over the next few days, as we visit the beautiful islands, I watch him, looking for any overt sign of illness. I question him over and over about how he is feeling, how bad the pain is on a scale of 1 to 10, keeping a running tally in my head of his previous answers. When he reports his pain is better, I relax for a while, convincing myself this cannot be a recurrence. Sometimes, hours go by without worry. When his pain is worse, however, I am barely aware of my surroundings. As hard as I try not to, I drop into my bleakest thoughts.

David's death has never been an abstraction for me, either the emotional toll or the physical reality. I know about the finality of death in my life. I know the profound yearning to be able to say one last thing or see them just one more time (as though it would ever be enough). Equally real is the image of David's death. I have seen so many patients die, witnessing the animus or soul or spark leave a person's face, that profound moment when life ceases.

The idea of being a widow is also vivid for me. Watching my mother's grief after my father's death, when she was forty-eight, is seared into my being. She adored my father. He was her refuge, her teacher, her support in just the same way David has been for me. She was an immensely strong woman. She continued on, after my father's death, working very successfully in the world of New York Madison Avenue advertising, continuing to have friends and parties, to be engaged and interested in the world, to laugh. But when she was alone at home, her deep loss and loneliness were transparent. Until she died twenty-two years later, she never went on a serious date, saying always, "I am still married to your father." We visited often, and it was always at the moment of leaving, of hugging her and saying good-bye that her intense loneliness was so evident in her face. It never changed no matter how many years went by. To this day I never say good-bye to our children without remembering Mother in that moment.

Over my years in practice, I have taken care of many women who have lost their husbands. I have watched each struggle with this profound loss, each continuing their lives with courage and grace and each expressing to me the pain of their grief. They talk about coming home after a trip and how sad it feels to walk into an empty house. They describe sleepless nights, the deep loss of closing a home of forty years, the friends who don't call because they are no longer part of a couple, the pain and the longing. I always feel a special tenderness for these women, who keep going, keep living, keep giving to their friends and children. When I ask how they are doing, their faces break and their eyes fill. The loss is never far away.

Quite recently I saw a long-time patient for follow-up of her chronic medical problems. As always, she asked me how my husband was and told me again that she prayed for him every night. I felt the same sense of gratitude I did whenever patients ask about David. Their care and concern about me feels like a balm. Her husband was diagnosed with lung cancer a few years earlier. Initially, he had done well, but six months ago she told me he'd had a recurrence and was being treated with radiation and medication to control it. She was back for another visit, and she told me her husband was not responding to treatment. He was in constant pain, and his doctors had started him on some other type of chemotherapy with little hope of success. She was preparing herself for his death. They had been married fifty-six years.

"How are you doing with this?" I asked.

She shrugged, looking composed, as so many patients do, despite intense fear or anxiety, or worry, thinking somehow they should be brave.

"Are you talking with anyone about this? About how hard this is?" I pressed.

She paused and then said that one of her sons had flown in from the Midwest and they had had dinner with several of her other children. She said that after everyone had left, he stayed behind and said, "Mom, we have to talk about the elephant in the room. We have to talk about Dad's dying." As she described her son's concern, she began to cry.

"I don't want to live without him," she wept to me. "I don't know how I can have a life if he is not there." She was sobbing, her shoulders shook. "How will I sleep? I figured out that I have slept next to him over twenty thousand times. I cannot bear it. Loneliness is like a physical pain. I don't want to live like this." She was almost shouting.

I felt rocked. I had said those same words to myself so many times. Tears filled my eyes as I listened to her. Here was another woman who would go on, doing what she had to do, loving her children, seeing friends, keeping the brave smile, and living with an almost unbearable loneliness. I hugged her, wishing I could protect her from what lay ahead.

In the bad times, when I try to imagine how I will keep going if David dies, I think of my mother and I think of all the widows I have known. On the one hand, it is clear that somehow one does keep going. But at such cost. I have many friends whom I like and enjoy, but I have no one that I have ever leaned on in the deep, connected way that I have with David. From my days in high school when I could not talk about my overwhelming grief to the later time when, because of a demanding job and my family, I had no time to make outside connections, I have never really learned to depend on anyone but David for emotional support. When David has to be in the hospital overnight, I, too, hate sleeping alone.

I lie in bed at night imagining living alone in a small house. All I can see is my mother, by herself and sad. I cannot see a way to find joy. I am terrified of relying too heavily on my children. I do not want to burden them, and yet their presence is the only thing that I can imagine bringing comfort. I look ahead, seeing them coming to visit, bringing their wives and children. I imagine being happy in those moments, and then I see them leaving, and once again I am my mother. Who does one talk to about all the insignificant happenings of the day? Who does one cry with? Who will be there when I am on my knees screaming for help?

It is as though I live in parallel worlds. On the one hand I am having a fun and relaxing time with friends in a beautiful environment. On the other, I am in a panic. Oddly, it is not unlike being a doctor. I have learned to pause outside the patient's room. I close my eyes momentarily, take a deep breath, and think about the person I am about to see. It almost feels as though I shed the garment of myself as I walk in the room to bring my full attention to my patient. It is a handy skill. In a similar way, I am mostly able to shed my fear, although I cannot entirely ignore the elderly women in black who walk down side streets, shop in markets, or sweep their stoops.

SUMMER 2006

David

I AM WEARING MY DAD'S GREEN DARTMOUTH BLAZER. IT IS WAY TOO big for me, partly because he was always taller than me and partly because I'm now even smaller than I normally have been. I am standing at the family plot, facing my Treadway cousins; my aunt Jane; my sister, Lauris; my son Michael; and a few old friends of my father's. They are waiting for me to say a few words at this interment service on what would have been Dad's ninety-second birthday.

They must have had to dig the damn thing with a jackhammer, I remember thinking forty years ago, as I watched my dad kneel on the frozen ground at the Treadway family plot and put the cardboard box with my mom's ashes into the little black hole. It was the dead of winter, February 8, 1966, three days after my mother's suicide. Dad, Lauris, and I were there. Lauris was already going psychotic. On the ride to the cemetery, with Mom's ashes in the backseat, she thought Mom was talking to her through the music on the radio. I had to put her in a mental hospital later that day, on my way back to college.

Someone has cleaned all the family's headstones for the occasion, and there's Dad's, right next to Mom's:

Martha C. Treadway	Richard F. Treadway
March 5, 1918–February 5, 1966	June 5, 1913–March 26, 2006

Last year at this time, I was lying in a hospital bed, expecting to die soon. Now my dad is gone and I am still here. I look at Michael. He must be wondering when he'll be saying a few words over my grave.

Tears well up. They probably think I'm choked up about my dad. I wish I were.

I don't know what to say. I look out at my siblings and cousins and begin: "I am really, really glad to be here . . ."

◇◇◇

On the way back to Boston, Michael and I stop at the Publick House, the colonial inn in Sturbridge that my parents owned when I was a child. In the old restaurant that first opened in 1763, we look over the menu that has barely changed since I was eight years old. It's easy to imagine my mother and father, brothers and sister, and me sitting around these old mahogany tables fifty-five years ago. I suddenly feel truly ancient, as aged as my dad, and yet as vulnerable as that eight-year-old boy from long ago.

I look across at Michael as he studies the menu. I want to see how he's feeling about his big move to Vanderbilt and starting up a new life in graduate school and living with Anna. He's made a lot of changes in this year. Moving home really allowed him to start his life over. Kate and I are relieved to see him so happy, settled, and secure. "So, Michael, how are you doing with the enormity of what's ahead of you? Moving, Nashville, graduate school, Anna, the whole thing?"

There's a long pause. Maybe he doesn't want to have a big talk. I'm certainly not going to push it.

"Dad, you always get me to talk about me, but you haven't said a word about what it was like, after everything you've been through, to stand there today at your parents' gravesite. How are *you* doing?"

His question touches me deeply. By the time I was fifteen, because of my mother's mental illness, I was thrust into the role of being my dad's confidant and caretaker. I was always the one who asked him, "So how are you doing, Dad?"

Now here's Michael really asking me with obvious caring how I am doing. And it doesn't feel inappropriate. He's not a boy like I was. He has become a man. "Your wanting to know how I am feeling means the world to me." I start to tear up. "After all, that's usually my question."

Michael reaches over and pats me on the shoulder. "Maybe, one of these days, Dad, you'll get that we care about you as much as you care about us."

"It's hard for me to know that."

"I know. You're kind of stupid on the subject."

Our shared chuckle feels like a hug.

Michael

ANNA LOOKS AT ME FROM HER SPOT ON THE COUCH IN HER SOMERVILLE apartment. "You know, if it doesn't work out, we'll both be okay," she says.

The light in the corner casts a shadow over her eyes, making their normally sparkling green appear flat gray. It has been a lazy Sunday, and we are lounging in front of the TV watching a movie. Anna likes to talk during movies, regardless of whether they are good. It is a trait I find only intermittently endearing, but given this comment, I lose interest in what is happening on the screen. "What do you mean?"

"I mean, it *will* be okay," she repeats. "You'll get on with your life, and I'll get on with mine."

"But, I want it to work," I say, offering reassurance in the hopes of receiving it. We have been dating for a little over six months. Shortly into our relationship, I was accepted to a PhD program in clinical psychology at Vanderbilt University in Nashville and decided I would go. Anna was halfway through her PhD program in molecular genetics in Boston. The past month and a half have been fraught with difficult conversations about whether we should try to make something of our young relationship. We have tentatively decided that Anna will take a year off from school and come live with me in Nashville, getting a job in her field. It is a plan as exciting as it is fragile.

"I want it to work, too," she says. "I was just saying . . ." Her voice trails off and she turns her attention to the movie.

I feel confused and betrayed. On the one hand, I know that what she is saying is literally true: neither of us will take our own lives if our relationship ends. But it still seems unfair, like she is breaking some unspoken pact. Neither of us feels that this is simply a fling. Since our first date when we went to the *Symphony Fantastique*, we have been inseparable. Anna first said the words "I love you" less than a week later. In less than six weeks, Anna was whispering that she wanted to marry me when we were curled up in bed, and I always enthusiastically agreed, squeezing her ever closer. We spent the following months in a romantic idyll. I felt like I finally was ready to make a life with someone. And it seemed that she felt it, too.

Yes, we have some challenges, and strong emotions don't predict the outcome of a relationship. But why would she make that comment? It seems so blunt and hard. What happened to thinking I was the most special, wonderful person she'd ever met?

As she stares at the screen, I turn her comment over in my mind. I've never subscribed to the notion that we all have a single soul mate. I know Anna is not the only person I could end up with, nor am I for her. There are likely thousands of other people with whom we could find happiness, security, and partnership. But that isn't the point. Part of being a loving partner, I think, is to convey a certain sense of specialness. To say "I choose you," even when you both know that it could be otherwise. It's not that you choose someone because she is special and unique, but she *becomes* special because you have chosen her, because you'll share your life with her. Pointing out that we would survive a breakup seems irrelevant, and more than that, it feels mean.

Why did she bring this up now, when things are going so well? Maybe, I console myself, she is feeling anxious about it all. After all, she is risking a lot more than I am. We both had agreed that any chance we had of making this relationship work in the long run would require the up-front investment of living together for a year. If it does work out, then we can manage whatever long-distance situations lie ahead in the future. Eventually Anna will have to return to Boston to finish school, probably long before I am done at Vanderbilt. So who can blame her for feeling stress, or for even wanting to comfort herself with the reminder of the worst-case scenario. "We will be okay." Maybe that isn't such a bad thing to say after all.

For all the doubts she may be having, I am not. For the first time in what seems like forever, things are going really well for me. I took a big risk leaving the world of finance to change careers. I was accepted at one of my top choices for a PhD program. I met Anna, who is the antidote for all the pain and frustration of my relationship with Kristin. And most important, Dad seems to be doing better. He is about to be completely done with treatment.

Anna is watching the movie. The images reflect in her eyes, making them sparkle. I love looking at her eyes, especially when she isn't aware of it. I marvel at how often they change color. "I choose you," I softly say, and kiss the top of her head. She looks up at me and smiles, and returns to the movie. I can't tell if she heard me.

Kate

DAVID AND I ARE DRIVING TO MGH FOR HIS LAST METHOTREXATE infusion weekend. The drill has become familiar. We call Ellison 14 at 7:30 on Friday morning to get a bed assignment. When we arrive at the hospital later that morning David goes up to the floor, has his IV placed, and begins receiving the large amounts of fluids he needs to be able to wash out the methotrexate, which otherwise will be toxic to his kidneys. Aside from having to urinate every half hour, David tolerates these weekends, at least physically, reasonably well. With medication, he has only a mild sense of nausea, mostly when he thinks about eating. By his March admission, just looking at the MGH menu would make him nauseated. It is a relief to think this is the last.

In retrospect, I am amazed at how well David has gotten through this year. I was so worried about how hard all the procedures and treatments would be for him. He has always hated medical things, even having his pulse taken, much less having blood drawn. Yet remarkably, he handled the needles and drugs most of the time with good humor and only minor griping. As much as I have complained about it over the years, David's ability to detach has gotten him through a tough year. I am also aware of how often that skill has allowed him to be there for me. I know how hard that must have been and what an act of love it was for him. Now we just have to get through the next PET scan. It is scheduled right after Sam's graduation next week.

David

"WE SHOULD HAVE CALLED FOR A RESERVATION EARLY, LIKE EVERYONE said," Kate says again grumpily. The four of us are plowing through dinner at Sam's favorite Chinese restaurant. Kate had started bugging me about reserving rooms at the Archer House in Northfield for Sam's graduation more than a year ago. I said I would do it but then I completely forgot about it, which is why we're spending the night in a tacky motel off the interstate, twenty minutes south of town.

"I'm sorry, hon, but I was distracted this time last year, as you may recall," I say somewhat defensively, recognizing immediately that my effort to be light came out as sarcasm.

"Whoa, Dad, you've got to stop playing the cancer card." Sam's tone had an edge in it, too.

"Sam, stop getting on my case."

"Dad," quickly intervenes Michael, "Sam's not trying to be mean. It's just none of us want to be even thinking about the cancer tonight."

"It's true. You guys have put up with a lot with me this year," I say trying hard to rally. "And I am really, really, proud of you guys." Kate reaches over to me and takes my hand.

"You haven't done so badly yourself, big guy," says Sam.

"Well, thank you, Sam," I respond, holding back my tears.

◇◇◇

Sam's standing in the long line of seniors wearing his black cap and gown with the tassel dangling over his eye. Kate, Michael, and I are so happy to be here and are so proud of Sam. And perhaps Sam's proud, too, because he passed his math comps and is graduating. Carleton hasn't been a great experience for him. Given that Carleton is a very expensive school, I was a little disappointed also. And I know that Sam feels that judgment. But today, I feel free to just enjoy his day. Right after the ceremony, we're packing him up and he and I will head west to Seattle. He will live with my brother, Jim, and work in the just-opened Hotel 1000, one of Jim's hotels. Sam will be a bartender and intern at the highest level in the hotel business under Jim's tutelage. If he's interested, he will be the fourth generation of Treadways to be in the business. My dad would have been pleased.

Kate

WE ARRIVED IN NORTHFIELD A FEW DAYS EARLY TO HELP SAM AND his roommates clean up the house they have lived in during their senior year at Carleton. It was one of a row of similar houses, each with a small common area, a kitchen, and four bedrooms. Each had a small yard and an outdoor grill. They are quite attractive for campus housing.

Having been through a moving-out with Michael at Columbia, I asked Sam for weeks to start the clean-up before we got there. Sam assured me that he and his roommates had been picking up for days, but there is still a horrifying accumulation of dirt and grime. Heaven knows what it looked like before their "efforts." All the parents pitch in while our offspring pack their belongings. I feel as though I should be in a biohazard suit as I attack the upstairs bathroom, though I suspect I have the easier job after I see what the two moms in the kitchen are working on.

Graduation day is unseasonably cold and gray with the ever-present wind of the Minnesota prairie. As I scan the sky, I pray it does not rain. I did not bring an umbrella, and the graduation is set up outside on the quadrangle lawn. David is cold and tired. Because we had been on the Parent's Council before David became ill, we had seats near the front and could actually see. David is relieved not to have to search long for a seat. He sits down heavily, looking frail and drawn. This is in stark contrast to how well he seemed last month in Italy. Maybe it is a response to his recent methotrexate. Or maybe it is the bronchitis he has developed. It's a jolt to see him look as he did months ago. But we are all here. I feel deeply thankful.

As I watch Sam walk across the outdoor stage, diploma now tucked under his arm and a grin of satisfaction on his face, I am filled with conflicting emotions. On the one hand, I am proud of Sam and the young man he has become. He is a truly kind and decent person, with humor and a strong sense of his own values. On the other hand, I know Carleton has been a mixed experience for him and that he does not feel that he used it as well as he might have. He has come to the end of his college career with no clear direction. I worry that he feels he has disappointed us. I have tried to reassure him on this point many times.

I certainly made a hash of my undergraduate experience, and I didn't even go to my graduation. David and I were married in our senior year, and neither of us went. It took me five years to find my way to what I ultimately wanted to do. My hope for Sam is that he will find something that he cares about passionately, that helps others and that makes him happy. And, of course, I hope he will find someone he loves and who will love him. I hope he can actually enjoy the process of exploring the possibilities of how to build a successful life. For now he is moving to Seattle, where he will live with his uncle Jim and work in a high-end bar downtown. He had enjoyed working part-time as a bartender in Northfield, and this plan gives him some time to decide on his interests.

I had the same worries about Michael when he graduated, but now he seems to be on a path that feels right for him and that he is happy about. He is looking forward to starting his PhD program at Vanderbilt, is pleased about the neuroscience program, and is feeling he has finally found his path. He has found a wonderful young woman who is everything he has ever hoped for. Anna is bright and enthusiastic. She is planning to move to Nashville to be with him. I have never seen Michael in love in this way before. Remembering not only Michael's wandering path but David's and mine as well reassures me about Sam.

Michael

THE THREE OF US—MOM, DAD, AND I—ARE SITTING AT SAM'S graduation under a sky that, anywhere else, would be described as partially cloudy, but in Minnesota, is considered partly sunny. The ceremony is being held on a small lawn with a covered stage and podium for distinguished guests. Family members are to the right of the stage, with rows of seats in the center reserved for members of the class of 2006. The graduates wend their way along a wooded path, their caps and gowns creating a sense of solemnity that, while appropriate to the occasion, is at odds with my brother's natural exuberance. As the graduates march to their seats, we catch a glimpse of Sam just as he sees us. He leans outside the line and flashes us a beaming smile that breaks through the rows of drab gray robes.

As we have gotten older, Sam and I have grown closer. I am increasingly impressed by the person he has become. Every time I turn around, some new facet of his personality seems to have emerged, not slowly, as I would have expected, but fully formed. Like the time when I was suddenly aware of his talent for socializing. We were at a party with a lot of strangers of all ages, and I watched Sam comfortably work the room like a seasoned politician. I'm not sure when, how, or where he acquired those skills. He was phenomenal—friendly, setting people at ease. He kept an eye on the room to make sure everyone was having fun. Just like our father.

I am relieved that now there is a chance that Dad will survive and that he and Sam will have whatever time they need for their relationship. Sam's decision to deny the seriousness of Dad's condition may actually work out okay. In a way, Dad's cancer forced him and Sam to acknowledge the problems in their relationship that were never out in the open before.

That's true for me, as well. In a strange way, Dad's battle with cancer has been a gift. I have rediscovered how much more important family is than whatever success I earn. And the biggest gift of all is that I learned this lesson without losing my father. It is as if life has given me a warning shot across the bow. And add to that, the gift of finding Anna. It is, indeed, miraculous; as if, dare I say it, cancer was just what our family needed.

We all have developed a habit of responding to life's incessant inconveniences and challenges by saying "It's not cancer." Everything else seems insignificant compared to losing Dad, and the new perspective keeps us in a near-constant positive mood. How can I possibly care about any of the petty issues that have consumed me, now that I have been given my father back?

And yet, sometimes I feel that maybe it has ended too quickly, that I got off too easy. I wonder if the lessons we have learned will stick. Or maybe we really haven't learned anything it all. Maybe it hasn't been a "growth experience" but just a shitty thing to go through without benefit. Maybe, for all its drama and intensity, the journey of my father's cancer and my year spent living with him wasn't that much different from any other. I am still me, and my dad is still my dad. Maybe that is good enough.

Sam

GRADUATION WAS A BLUR JUST A COUPLE HOURS AGO, AND NOW MY DAD and I are about to hit the road. It feels like I'm being rushed out of school. Although in many ways I'm glad to be done with Carleton, I'm crushed to be saying good-bye to my friends. Moments ago my few closest friends and I were cursing the tragedy of graduating. We have no idea when we'll see each other again. It's also terrifying to leave the security of college. Not that my professors ever made me feel safe. It was the safety of being in a structured institution, where you know where you're next meal is coming from, you know someone else is footing the bill, and you know who your friends are: a somewhat nicer version of prison.

"So, which route should we take?" I ask my mom amidst my tears.

"I think that going up through North Dakota is where all the fun things are, like Rushmore and the Badlands, but I'm really not sure. You should check a map before you get on the highway." My mom reaches in and tries to give me an awkward hug. "I'm sorry to leave you while you're so upset. I'm sure you'll feel better soon."

"Thanks, Mom. I hope you and Mike have safe travels home."

"We will, and we will see you soon enough. Don't worry." I don't tell her that not seeing them soon isn't why I'm upset. I'm leaving my friends. I turn to my dad in the driver's seat, wipe my tears, and try to get psyched up for the drive out to Seattle. My Volkswagen Jetta is packed like an overstuffed pillow, with a huge duffle bag lashed to the roof. Everyone has told me that the trip will take at least four days, but I think that's rubbish. Especially because today's Saturday and my new boss wants me to be at the bar for training on Monday. We've just gotta cruise.

I'm absolutely terrified to be going to Seattle for a new job, new home, new life. It'll be good to try something new, but another summer at home like last summer would be pretty damn good as well. Minus the whole cancer thing, of course. The only reason I'm moving to Seattle is fear of the complacency that would settle over me if I moved home. I would slip into my teenage self, not wanting to get a job or really move forward. Or really move at all, for that matter. For a change, I'm avoiding the easy way out. Going to Seattle represents a challenge, striking out on my own, trying something new.

I'm already looking forward to the next time I will be able to go home again. This year I've been home an amazing number of times— five trips home since August. I told myself that it made sense because I wanted to see my friends and see Dad. But the truth is that I was homesick. Although last summer was traumatic for everyone else in my family, it actually felt good to me. I didn't really realize it then, but there was a closeness among us that I hadn't felt in years. I kept going home during the school year, wanting to feel it again. In the past, I would have been sick of my parents after so many visits home, but even now, after all those visits, I want nothing more than to be heading east toward Boston rather than west.

Northfield flies by my window. I won't be seeing this town for a long time. Good-bye, Bagel Bros. Good-bye, Las Delicias. Good-bye, Tavern. I worked there for two years. It was a great college job and a springboard to this new bartending gig. I direct my dad to the highway and leave Carleton and Northfield for the last time. Next stop: Seattle. A new chapter.

David

THE EMPTY NORTH DAKOTA PRAIRIE STRETCHES OUT BEFORE US TO the horizon. It's like being on the open ocean. So far, this road trip has simply been fun. Much to our mutual surprise, I don't have a big agenda of things to talk about. Ever since the clearing up of my stomach pain and the clean PET scan, I've actually been a little more relaxed. So hopefully it will be just a classic roadie—drive fast for long hours, listen to lots of music, and eat lots of bad fast food.

The last time I drove to the coast, I was just eighteen and with my brother Jon. It was a wild ride, our evenings punctuated by drinking bourbon and shooting at signs with his pistols as we sped into the darkness. Back then, I was just a kid on the loose who thought his wild, alcoholic, gun-toting older brother was very cool. Remembering what a mess I was as a teenager eases my anxious vigilance about how my two sons will turn out. It's a miracle I got through this first year. Nobody really expected me to last this long, so maybe, just maybe, I'm going to make it. My chances of having a recurrence are about 50-50 now, and the fact that I responded so well to the chemo suggests that if I do have to have a bone marrow transplant, I might do well. I know the experience of transplant is really harrowing and not everyone survives the treatment, but I'm applying the Sam strategy to the issue. I choose not to worry about it. But the truth is, I still privately assume that I will get a recurrence and probably die.

Somehow the thought of my own death still doesn't scare me or sadden me very much. I don't ever dwell on what I might miss: my boys getting married, my first grandchild in my arms, Kate and me retiring to a farm in Vermont. For all the anxiety and grief I feel about Kate and the boys going forward without me, it's surprising how numb I feel about myself. It's almost as if I still don't dare to care. I look over at Sam, who is intently speeding toward the sunset. We're listening to Kenny Rogers sing, "You've gotta know when to hold them, know when to fold them, know when to walk away, know when to run."

With Sam and Michael beginning new lives and Kate creating her innovative new course for incoming Harvard medical students, I have to say that the three people who are so precious to me are doing well.

Together, we've survived this year. We've fought and hugged, wept and laughed. Now, they will be able to go on, whatever happens to me. Not that it will be easy in the worst-case scenario. I worry about Kate being dreadfully lonely. I worry for Michael because he relies on me so much as his mentor and friend. And I worry about Sam because he is disappointed in himself and in me, although he won't acknowledge it. If I had been simply a jerk as a dad, it would have been easier for him. But I was a kind and loving dad who did his best. So it's hard for him to be freely mad at me despite the fact that most of my help and suggestions didn't work well for him.

My death could leave him with a shit load of grief, guilt, and anger, like I had after my mother died. The trauma of her suicide scarred me for life and damaged my children. It made me an anxious and covertly controlling parent. Every time the kids struggled or got depressed, I was scared they would have a nervous breakdown or kill themselves. I shudder to think what the legacy for Sam might be if I die and he's left with all his anger. And I don't want his children to grow up under that shadow.

"Sam?"

"Yeah, Dad."

"You've got to promise me one thing. If things go poorly, you and I will really have to be sure that we talk, before it's too late. So you aren't left with a mess of feelings that could haunt you the rest of your life."

"Are you kidding me? Here we are, driving along, having a good time, listening to ridiculous country western music in the middle of friggin' nowhere, and that's what you're thinking about? Man, you have no life."

He makes me laugh. "Guilty as charged, Sam. But seriously, we still have stuff to deal with. Believe me, I'm not any more interested in talking about it than you are. Let's make a deal. We won't talk about it anymore unless the cancer comes back."

"Dad, didn't we already make that deal on one of our other road trips?"

"Well, maybe, but your old man forgets."

"No kidding. But I don't. It's a deal. Now go to sleep. You're on in another hour."

"Okay, I surrender." I rest my head on the pillow against the window and close my eyes. For a moment, I feel they really are going to be okay.

We've had the gift of enough time. It could have been so much worse. We're lucky. No matter what happens next. And I truly believe that despite my worrying, Kate and the boys will have a shot at good fulfilled lives not haunted by my absence.

As for me, I am already playing with the "house" money, as poker players say. I have outlived my expectations. If I have the gift of many more years, I will do whatever I can to, as Effi said those many months ago, "cherish the time." In this moment, I feel content, almost happy, as Sam motors on into the enveloping darkness.

Sam

"WE COULD BACKTRACK, I GUESS, BUT WE'D LOSE A LOT OF TIME," I SAY AS we roll into North Dakota. We had forgotten to check a map, and once I looked at it, it was clear that going the southern route through South Dakota was the way to see Rushmore, the Badlands, and Yellowstone.

"If it means a lot to you, we can do it." Despite my dad's words, his preference to keep going is obvious.

"Screw it. Let's just drive."

"Yeah!" My dad gets into the roadie mood and to my astonishment cranks up the radio. He usually hates music in the car. I don't want to jinx it by making a comment. I quietly let the road and music lull us into North Dakota and Montana.

The next day we pass another sign for the East Montana Badlands. "Should we do it?" I ask.

"I think so. We've barely stopped since starting this little adventure. I bet this is going to be better than the real Badlands. Maybe we're discovering a little-known travel secret."

We're all smiles as we turn off at the exit and head into Makoshika State Park. We park on top of a small hill and look around us. It's magnificent. It looks as if large hands had raked through the sand and left a maze of crazy canyons and peaks. We get out of the car and read from a sign that the "hands" that created this landscape were actually water and that it took thousands of years to erode the crevasses.

Despite posted warnings, I start to climb to the top of the nearest butte. As I peer over the edge, the sandy ground melts away and I'm suddenly sinking into the dirt and gravel. I slide and tumble thirty yards before coming to a crashing stop at the next outcropping. Amazingly I'm fine, but I have a hell of a time trying to climb up the soft and shifting sand.

When I finally get back to the car, Dad already has found me a spare set of clothes from the trunk and is chuckling. "Can't take you anywhere, can we? You did always like to go off adventuring on our hikes in Maine."

"Mostly to get away from you guys, because I'd been stuck on a boat with all of you," I joke, as I change my pants.

"No, please, tell me how you really feel." My dad laughs. "But it wasn't all that bad, right? Our sailing trips?"

"Oh, come on, Dad. You know I like them. I just like to give you a hard time about it now and then. In fact, I was at Lake Bilsby last week before graduation and thought how nice it would be to be sailing instead of just sitting on the beach with my friends."

"It's just nice to hear that, from time to time, to know that I did something right."

We both enjoy the view for a few moments more, and then it's back on the road, westward bound.

"So, how are you feeling about your big move to Seattle?" My dad asks as we cruise through Montana. "I know you flipped back and forth before you made the decision, so what do you think?"

"In some ways, it's an easy way out for me, and in other ways it's really hard."

"What do you mean?"

I watch the greenish-brown landscape flow by the window, not wanting to talk about it but also wanting to get my thoughts clear. To find the right words. "Ummm . . . I didn't have to look for a job. Uncle Jim offered this one to me. It's not going to be that hard, given that it's just bartending. And I'm going to be living with his family. So in that light, it's the easy option. On the other hand, I won't know anyone. The city will be brand new to me. I'm even farther away from you guys and my friends than before. I'm going to be alone."

"Hmmm . . . Yes, it'll be tough, but I know you'll meet people. You're good at that."

"Am I? I don't think so. I have the same group of ten friends that I've had from middle school. I only made four good friends in college."

"But you're so social. Throw you into a room full of strangers and you do fine."

"Fine. I can talk to people. But what I crave is real friendship, and you definitely don't get that working at a bar. Maybe that's why I'm good behind a bar—I connect with people easily. I make them feel welcome and comfortable, then they pay and leave."

"Isn't it rewarding to make people feel good? That's basically what I do for a living."

"Yeah, I guess so. We'll see. Now that it's here, and I'm heading to Seattle, I'm more nervous than excited."

"Well, what do you mean by 'real friendships'?"

"You know, when you can talk without talking. Or when you get comfort from just hanging out doing nothing of importance, but it feels good. Like I love just sitting with my friends playing video games. It's not like the games are that amazing, it's more the fun of being there together. Kind of like how our family is with bridge. I'm going to miss bridge."

"You know we'll play online a lot."

"And Mike and I will continue to kick ass. But you know it's not the same. I'm worried I'm going to get lonely out there." I haven't spoken that fear out loud before. I feel it slap me hard across the face.

"Being alone is something we all have to deal with from time to time."

"Duh. But it sucks when it happens."

"Mmmm . . ." My dad appears to be really soaking in all that I'm saying. It's surprisingly nice to actually be putting words to my thoughts.

Kate

ON THE PLANE HOME FROM SAM'S GRADUATION, I TRY TO MAP OUT ALL the things that still need to be done for the Introduction to the Profession course, which is now only two months away. While most of the course is ready, there are lots of details still to be finished. It is hard for me to believe I have been able to do this over this past year. It is only with the help and support of an incredible group of colleagues at the medical school that it has come together. I know from personal experience how important the first weeks of medical school are in shaping the attitudes of students. With all the press about uncaring doctors and angry patients, I desperately want to convey medicine as I have experienced it. I am so profoundly grateful for the kindness and compassion of the doctors who have cared for David and, by extension, me. Having been on the receiving end over this past year, now more than ever I want the students to start out on the right foot, understanding that the person they are and what they know are equally important in caring for patients.

David's PET scan marking the first year after his diagnosis is scheduled this week at MGH. I think back to the beginning of this process, or more accurately to the weeks before it began. We were going about our lives, working hard, trying to find time for ourselves, worrying in the normal way about our children, paying the bills, doing errands, completely unaware of the giant wave silently heading toward us, about to engulf our lives. Once again, my anxiety grows as I wait for the PET scan. Even though David seems to be doing well, maybe it is starting all over again, just as it had a year ago. A PET scan done a week before David's arm pain would have shown lymphoma everywhere, yet we were totally unaware. So his seeming good health now does not provide reassurance. I promise myself that if things are okay, I will eat better and exercise more. I will try to return to a sense of the normal and not be consumed with foreboding. I will focus more intensively on the course I have designed and I will stay on top of my paperwork. I promise I will be better, if only David will be all right.

On the day after the PET scan, I receive a text message on my beeper: "Hi Kate, prelim scans look clear. –f." I feel a rush of relief and a sense of profound gratitude that David is here, after this long and difficult year. Perhaps I was too pessimistic, but I did not think we would get here. I say a silent thank-you to Effi. I lock the message into my beeper.

Michael

A FEW WEEKS AFTER SAM'S GRADUATION, I AM HOME PREPARING FOR my move down to Nashville. My bedroom is completely covered with my sprawling packing job as I laboriously sort through the many odds and ends I have acquired over the last half dozen years, much of which is not worth carting down to Tennessee.

"Mr. Mike," Dad calls from the other room, "how's the packing going?" Dad has been in high spirits. As much as both my parents are sad that I'm moving so far away, I can tell that they are very excited for me, and for me and Anna. It feels like a great way to start a new chapter in my life.

I look over my room, the floor of which is completely obscured. "Fine."

"You want to take a break?"

I hesitate, surveying briefly all that I have to get done in the next few days. "Yes."

"Great, let's get lunch."

I think this sounds like an excellent idea, and Dad and I make the short drive to a nearby restaurant. The restaurant, which in our family is only ever referred to as "the restaurant," is an old diner located in the small business center of our town. Growing up, Dad, Sam, and I would go there at least once a week for breakfast, each of us always ordering the same thing. Neither the food nor service ever warranted this level of customer loyalty, but at this point, it is a tradition because it is a tradition.

"So, Mike, talk to me," Dad says as a waiter brings us water. A smile creeps onto my face as the familiar ritual begins to unfold.

"About what?" I ask, priming the inevitable response.

"About you! What's going on? How you're feeling about graduate school, Anna, me, us, the family, everything?"

I take a sip of my water and decide whether I want to really talk or just bullshit. "Well, things are good," I say, opting for the latter. "Anna and I are really happy, and I'm excited about starting graduate school and finally getting this new career track underway."

"And after having left finance almost two years ago, does the move to psychology still feel good?"

I want to say yes, but the answer is more complicated. "I think it's good," I start unsurely. "I'm a little anxious about starting graduate school at a relatively late age." I expect Dad to chime in with a riff about lots of people starting new careers well into their thirties and forties. To my surprise, he doesn't.

"How come?" he asks.

"I just feel like I have a lot of catching up to do," I confess. He smiles knowingly. This isn't our first conversation on this subject. "I still worry about whether I've made the right decision. It's like this is my last chance to start over if I'm going to be successful."

"What does being 'successful' mean to you?" Dad asks in that familiar, probing way.

I'm not sure how to answer that. The only time I ever enjoyed venture capital was when the subject shifted to something other than finance. Every so often, a tired CEO would vent to me about his struggles with his kids or the stress of an upcoming business deal. I'd come to life. It made me feel as if I were doing more than just building wealth.

After a few moments of silence, my dad provides his own answer. "Mike, when I was your age, just before I became a therapist, I was in the same boat as you. For me, it wasn't about making a lot of money, but it was about being a big shot right out of college. I'd gotten involved in radical politics and civil rights. I thought I was really helping people, but the truth was that I was much more focused on playing the role of a Great Radical Progressive."

"Really?" I say with some surprise. But then again, at least he had been trying to help people. I hadn't even tried to do that. My first job out of college was working for an Internet start-up, hoping to become a millionaire by twenty-five. And when the dot-com bubble burst, I didn't go help a third-world country; I just moved over to finance.

"You've always told me you feel a calling as a therapist," I remind him.

"That's true, I do feel a calling, but it took time. Sometimes I still daydream about what would have happened if I'd gone into politics. Most of the time, I shudder at the thought, but sometimes I wonder."

"But that's the thing, Dad. I'm as focused on being a big shot as I ever was. Now I'm just betting that I'll be glad I've chosen a career that's more about helping people than about making money and feeling important."

"Well, that's the bet I made, and so far it has worked for me."

After lunch we drive back, and I resume packing. Dad goes back into his office to return some phone calls. My phone rings. It's Anna. "Hi. So I was just on the phone with my mom, and she wants to know exactly when we're planning on arriving in Nashville, because she's thinking about coming down the following weekend to help us organize and wants to book a flight. So what are we thinking? Thursday?"

I am slow to respond. I'm still thinking about my conversation with Dad. Thinking it's all a bet. "Sure," I say.

"What's wrong?" she asks gently, noticing the slight distance in my tone. Her voice is strong and reassuring.

"Nothing's wrong," I say truthfully. "Things are great."

FALL 2008:
Three Years Later

Kate

I AM HAPPY TO BE LYING IN BED. IT HAS BEEN A HARD WEEK, AND I am exhausted. I can hear Sam getting something more to eat in the kitchen. He moved back to Boston after a year in Seattle. I am so glad to have him nearby again. He is still living in the apartment with his now-former girlfriend and has come home for a few days to get away from the tension. He is working at a new bar in Boston. While he is still struggling with what he will ultimately do, he is clearly having fun right now. It seems to be a family tradition that we all search for a while before we find our path, and Sam is no exception. It is comforting to hear Sam moving about downstairs. Michael is flying in from Nashville Saturday for a visit so we will all be together for the long Columbus Day weekend.

"David?"

"Ummm?"

"Are you sure you will be okay tomorrow?" David is going to the boat tomorrow just for an overnight; one last sail before the end of the season.

"Of course I'll be all right! The weather is supposed to be great, and I'm only going to Damariscove. There is nothing to worry about. Give me a kiss and let's go to sleep."

He leans over and kisses me gently. I smile back at him.

"Good night, heart of my heart."

I know it is a sign of health that he is back to going on solo forays in the boat, but still, I worry. He is not quite back to his old self in ways that I am aware of but cannot easily describe. He is not as strong physically. Sometimes he still goes off to nap, a remnant from his illness that unnerves me. At times he doesn't quite seem the same person, some loss of quickness that makes me uneasy. But then he is back to his old self and I can put my worry aside.

Somewhere around the third year, I let myself begin to believe that David might live, that we might really be lucky enough to start thinking about a cure. I am surprised by how long it has taken me to believe David might be well. Even though I knew intellectually that once we passed the two-year mark, David was likely to survive, it took much longer to actually believe it. It has been a slow process to shed this shroud of fear. At first, it was simply a cessation of terror. Several days could go by without even thinking about lymphoma, but then a pain in David's arm, weight loss for too many days in a row, or seeing him go off to take a nap would bring it hurtling back. The only difference was that I could let go of the fear more quickly. I could remind myself that he really was doing well and actually let myself believe it. Then one day, walking through the hallway of the hospital, my syllable counting game by this time abandoned, I was aware that I was feeling happy, a feeling I had not had since David got sick. I had not noticed its absence at the time, but it made me realize as much as anything how hard these last few years had been. Although increasingly I am optimistic about the future, I continue to seesaw back and forth. I do not stay in one frame of mind for very long.

Sometimes when we sail and the air is warm and humid, what feels like fingers of cooler air come and go over the course of the afternoon, the first signs of a weather change, the cold front finally coming through hours later. That is how I feel now, as though those first tendrils of a normal life are coming back only to recede again and then return.

Although I feel I have been given my life back, I have yet to decide how I should change in response to having come so close to losing that which I hold most precious. How will I choose to live? How do David and I find the closeness in health that the threat of death brought so vividly? When I did not think we had much time left, the only thing I really cared about was being with David. The rest of my life I put on hold. I did what I had to do and nothing else.

I am slowly reclaiming my life. I wish I could say that I have changed the way I live, but in many ways I haven't. I find myself slipping back into the old routines. I still work too hard and spend long hours in the hospital or at the medical school, torn between the job I love and wanting to be home. I want to be aware of each day, each hour, each minute. But I am no more successful than I ever was. I get lost in the constant planning about what I need to do next, forgetting to be in the moment. I find that time goes by just as fast despite my desire to slow everything down and savor and appreciate all that is happening. David has the same struggle.

Even so, some things have changed. I have a profound sense of gratitude that David is alive. I am aware of, in a much more significant way, the transient nature of our lives. Effi's caution to "cherish this time" seems now like a good rule to live by, no longer a grim prognostication. The truism that love and family are the most important things in life is now seared into my heart. As a doctor, it is sometimes hard to decide how to put limits on one's practice to be there for family. It is easy to put aside one's own needs to be there for the needs of patients. It seems clearer to me now that it is possible and necessary to find a balance between my professional duties and the needs of my family. I value and cherish my relationship with David and my two sons in a deep and connected way that is more conscious than before. I have not lost the sense of profound gratitude for what we have been given. I may still get caught up in all the daily tasks and press of work, but our mantra, "It's not cancer," remains a centering phrase that helps put in perspective all the daily annoyances that used to seem so important.

I have always thought of us as a close family, but something has changed. It is not just that David's illness made us more appreciative of each other. It is that we have shared our own fears together, even Sam, in his own way. We have been able to hold each other and have been allowed into each other's hearts more deeply.

This is in stark contrast to my own family after my father died. We all grieved, but we largely grieved alone. We put on a brave front. I have mourned the loss of my father my whole life. I have missed him at holidays, have been sad that he has not seen the person I have become or known my husband and sons. I have talked about him freely to my children, telling them about how important he was to me and trying to share with them his beliefs. I have told myself that my father's death made me a better person and a better doctor. And that is true. But in the depths of my fear during David's illness I have come to realize that the woman in my imagination howling and shrieking behind the steel door was not just my adult self; it was also that lonely, unspeakably sad fifteen-year-old self. In my terror over losing David, I heard the echoes of that young girl's sadness, which has permeated my life. I have begun to understand the ways in which I and my family have paid a price for locking that young girl away. Maybe grief is not the only way to hold on to the people you love.

David and I are now in our early sixties. Sooner or later, we will face this situation again. One of us will become seriously ill. One of us will die. I believe that somehow, what we have been through together will help when that time comes.

Sam

"SO YOU'RE SAYING I SHOULDN'T DATE ANYONE FOR OVER A YEAR?" I SAY into the phone, as I sit on the couch in my dad's office. 11 p.m. on a Thursday night. It's both depressing and comforting to be spending the night at home. I live in my apartment in Cambridge with Lauren and two friends, but ever since Lauren dumped me three months ago, it's nice to get out of there whenever possible. Although, retreating to my parents' house feels lame, like somehow she's winning the breakup.

"What I'm saying is that you shouldn't date seriously. Go out and meet new people, have fun, but don't jump back into a committed relationship," Sarah replies. I haven't talked to her in over a year; I hadn't realized how much I missed her. Last week, I got drunk and depressed about Lauren and drunk-dialed Sarah but didn't reach her. So we set up this phone call. We've already been talking for about a half an hour. Mostly, I've been complaining about Lauren. Getting relationship advice from Sarah is kind of odd, because when I broke up with her, she was the heartbroken one.

"You should take some time to learn how to live on your own," she says. "Figure out what you want from life, and then you'll be able to know what kind of partner would complement your passions. Because it seems like you're very accommodating and you just adapt to the person your with. And that's not healthy."

"That's a lot easier said than done. First of all, I take a lot of comfort from being in relationships; I hate being alone. And second of all, I don't know how to find out what I'm passionate about."

"Well, you're just going to have to."

"You're right, of course."

"Thanks. So, Sam, how are you really? I know things suck right now because your girlfriend dumped you, but I mean more generally. What's different for you since we dated?"

"Wow, let's think. You and I broke up in November of 2005. Since then, I graduated college, moved to Seattle, got a girlfriend, brought her to Boston, and then got dumped by said girlfriend."

"What made you move back to Boston? Didn't you like Seattle?"

"I loved Seattle. It really is an amazing city, and I was having fun at my job. It's just that I got homesick. The couple of times I was home, I realized I needed to be able to see more of my friends and family. You know how close I am with my high school friends. And Lauren was up for the adventure of moving across the country."

"That's impressive. It's such a big move. So, how have you grown? How have you changed? If we dated again, what about you would be new to me?"

"Why? Do you want to date again?" I tease.

"No, I told you I have a boyfriend. Hypothetically, I mean."

"I don't know. I'd like to believe I've grown as a person, but I can't pinpoint specific things. That's a pretty heavy-duty question. I mean—"

"Oh wait, my boyfriend just got home. He's had a really long, hard day and I need to be there for him. It was nice to talk. We'll have to catch up some other time. Sorry I'm leaving in such a rush."

"No problem, it was nice to talk to you too—"

"Have a good night. Bye," she says as the phone clicks.

"Bye," I say to no one.

I look around my dad's office. My parents have long since gone to bed. It's too late to call up a friend. Maybe my brother is awake in Tennessee. But it feels pathetic to have to go from one phone call to the next for support. I just want someone to be there for me and give me a hug at the end of a long day. Sarah's question keeps tumbling around in my head. What has changed in the last few years? I'm twenty-four. What do I have to say for myself?

I graduated from Carleton. A great school that gave me a not-so-great college experience. I have a math degree I don't know what to do with. All I've been doing is bartending. I guess when you come out of college you can either work hard toward a career or you can just go out and have fun. Seems like I picked the latter, but if that's the case, why aren't I having more fun?

I still don't know what I want to do in life. I've never had much of a passion or commitment to anything. Naturally my father has wanted me to get help with that. But I'm confident that it will all work out. I just have to find this stuff out on my own. It just takes time, something that I have to remind myself when it comes to getting over Lauren. Dealing with a breakup always just takes time. I guess I still don't know enough about women. I really thought I was doing well in that relationship.

Relationships in general are a problem. I still snap at my parents, especially my dad. Now that he's healthy, it's just back to the same routine. Although he's been making a real effort not to provoke me. He is accepting of my failings and doesn't need to micro-analyze everything I do. He's trying to just let me live my life, which I'm grateful for. Yet somehow I still get agitated by the small things he does. Without his illness being a constant reminder to hold in my anger, my fuse has been gradually shortening back to its original length. The dumbest things will set me off. And then my dad will get that hurt expression on his face that makes my insides tie in knots. I hate to upset him, but it just happens.

I look down at my bourbon old-fashioned. Dumb. Why am I drinking alone right now? Another bad routine to have. But it's not like I can quit drinking. Wouldn't it just be hypocritical for a bartender to not drink? I have to work the long Friday shift tomorrow—2 p.m. to 2 a.m. Ugh. But at least the next day my brother will be in town for the weekend, and he'll come see me at the bar. I'll get to show off a little bit.

I head upstairs to my bedroom, jump on my bed, and crack open my laptop to shoot off a few e-mails. I look around my old childhood room, which hasn't changed much over the years, much to my mother's chagrin. Jerry Rice poster on the wall even though I don't much care about football. More books then I could ever hope to read piled up haphazardly on and around the bookshelf. My lifetime's worth of knickknacks scattered around the room, things I can't bear to throw out but yet aren't worthwhile to have with me in Cambridge. It doesn't feel right, though. The bed doesn't sag in the same places. My couch is gone. It makes me feel old. Like somehow this preserved relic of a room is taunting me. I feel like back when I lived here things were easier. I've never had many passions, but back then it didn't matter. I didn't have to know what I wanted to do with my life. I was just living day to day. Cursing homework and cherishing friendships. I was always surrounded by a loving and supporting family. I suddenly feel very alone. I don't have a plan. No passions or purposes. I don't have a girlfriend. I don't know what I'm doing. At least I have my family. Sure my brother is stuck down in Nashville, but he's still alive and well. My parents are asleep in the next room. Both of them. My dad's still here.

During my dad's sickness I'd never really realized how close he was to dying. When he was originally diagnosed, I thought he had a 75 percent chance of living, not a 75 percent chance of dying, as I later found out had been the case. At the time, I could see that he was sick, and I knew my mom was scared, but I had insisted that I did not want to be told the facts, so I would not have to feel them, either. It worked out for me. But I feel them now. I can't believe he almost died. I was alone then in my decision to not want to know the details, and now I'm alone three years later having let them creep into my awareness. I'm dealing with the issues that everyone else has been facing the whole time. They've emotionally recovered along with my dad's recovery. I'm just starting to cope.

Even though he's in the house, asleep in the room next to me, I decide to write my dad an e-mail.

Date: Fri, Oct 10, 2008 at 1:21 AM
Subject: hey dad

i'm lying in bed crying with relief that you're not dead

i know it's lame and kind of odd to say . . . but i'm really glad you're alive . . . and that we still do have time to figure each other out.

i've been in a bad mood since lauren dumped me, i'm back behind the walls that i've built up in my relationship to you . . . i don't let you in often . . . and when you try, there is a gauntlet of snappy insults you have to endure
i'm sorry
i love you
~ sam

David

THE CRESCENT MOON IS SETTING IN THE CLEAR PURPLE SKY TO THE WEST as the sun peeks up over the cliffs to my left. I'm on the *Crow* in tiny Damariscove, Maine. The island is shaped like a lobster, with a long narrow spine ending in two claws of land that form the harbor extending out into the North Atlantic. This is our family's favorite harbor on the coast. We've been visiting it for thirty-five years.

It's damn cold. It's well past the end of the sailing season, and I'm the only boat in here. Even the lobstermen have gone. I am glad to be alone on my boat. I feel an overwhelming sense of gratitude just to be here. It's been almost three and a half years since I was diagnosed. Back then, neither Kate nor I nor my doctors believed I would make it. But here I am. I'm even beginning to think about my life and inevitable death more like I used to before the cancer. Of course, I'm going to die someday. I could fall overboard and drown this afternoon or live to be ninety-two like my dad. But finally, each twitch, ache, or pain doesn't make me think, *This is it; the cancer's back.*

After my last clear PET scan in December of 2007, I began to believe that I might make it. I hadn't had a recurrence in a year and a half. My odds of surviving had gone up from 25 percent to 65 percent—significantly better than a coin flip. It was shortly after this that I entered the single-handed race to Bermuda with the plan to have Sam be my crew for the double-handed race back.

I was boldly reclaiming my life, declaring myself strong and healthy. I had sailed this race back in 1979 and almost thirty years later was going to do it again. I had also signed up for a speaking tour in Australia and New Zealand, committed to write chapters for two books, and was rebuilding my public speaking career and clinical practice. I was on a little bit of a manic high. I am sure Kate and the boys as well as my friends were worried about me. But they were all cautiously and kindly supportive.

As the time for the race grew close I became more and more anxious. Could I really do it? Was I putting myself at risk after almost dying? Was I strong enough for the sleeplessness, the storms, and the inevitable challenges of equipment failure or human error? And what if Sam were killed by a wildly gibing boom or went overboard and I couldn't get him back? One of my clients washed off a sailboat and drowned on the way back from Bermuda years ago. His mom was forever haunted. I would be permanently shattered. How could I look Kate in the eye if I lost Sam? Even worse, how would Sam survive, if I were swept over and drowned?

I realized I was desperately ignoring how I was really doing. I was a mass of heart palpitations, jangled nerves, flashbacks, and self-destructive impulses. I was in florid denial. I rolled over in bed and said to Kate, who was just falling asleep, "I can't do it. It's nuts. I'm nuts. What if something happened to Sam? I'm not strong enough to do it." I started to cry hard. She took me in her arms. I sobbed like a baby. "I can't do it. Why would I worry you and everyone for a frigging sail-boat race after everything we've been through? I've been unbelievably selfish. What have I've been thinking?"

Kate began to cry, too, as she held me.

"Have you been scared?" I asked as I sat up and looked at her.

"Of course I've been scared, you idiot."

"Well, why did you go along with it?

"Because you had your heart set on it. Because it was so good to see you excited about something again." She paused, "And, I suppose, because it made you seem all better. I don't know. Maybe it was like me going along with that workshop in Lancaster when you were so sick."

"You've been nuts in your own way about this, haven't you?

"Yes, my dear, I suppose I have. Let's just say I think you have just made the smartest, best, most loving decision in your whole life," she said. "Except marrying me, of course."

I realized I didn't know how to step back into my life. I didn't know how to be well. Instead of the race, I went on an eight-day meditation retreat. I went to learn how to live again, since I might be around for another thirty years. I needed to reclaim the normal person's delusion that we own our lives and can plan a future. It was unimaginable. Now that I was off my adventure high, I didn't seem to care about anything.

In the middle of the retreat, I was in the meditation hall with a hundred other people on cushions. There was complete silence except for the occasional cough, throat clearing, stomach gurgling, and car passing. I was deep in Samadhi concentration, paying full attention to the experience of the breath, filling and emptying in my lungs. I was free of thoughts, floating weightlessly like a space walker. Suddenly I felt a tickle on my forearm. I opened my eyes and on my arm was a ladybug—a little dot of life making its way from somewhere to somewhere. And in that moment, my arm was its path. I felt a flush of understanding on almost a cellular level that nothing separated me from the ladybug. We were just creatures making our way. I felt like I was part of the breath of the infinite universe. It was like experiencing God.

What did I learn? Nothing new. It's all 2,500-year-old wisdom. But at least for these eight days, I just was. The retreat worked. I felt healthy and renewed. I felt excited about building a new life. I had reclaimed a vision of my future. I decided I would go home and center my life on my spiritual practice. I would see fewer clients and do fewer workshops. I would meditate three times a day. I would take long walks and cherish the turn of each season. I would forgo sleeping pills, booze, and comfort food. I would go to the gym, lose weight, and get regular massages. I would bow to the miracle of each life I encountered and each moment I lived. Again, like planning the race, I was a little high. I thought I was well on the road to recovery.

And again, I was wrong. Within a month of the retreat, my pretty self-improvement projects popped like the magical iridescent bubbles that I blew when I was ten. Unexpected family visits entailed much drinking and eating out. I meditated sporadically. I worked like a dog with clients in constant crisis. The openness and vulnerability that I had so assiduously cultivated on the retreat made it more difficult to handle the pain and pressure of treating the enormous suffering and struggle in my clients' lives. I wasn't sure I could handle it anymore. I was completely out of my normal capacity to compartmentalize. After a lifetime of measured detachment, I was too much in the moment. My well of compassion felt dry. Caring for others was no longer as fulfilling. I was a tangled knot of anxiety, depression, despair, and irritability (and, as Kate would tell you, a real pleasure to be around). Something had to change.

The hardest sailing is pressing close-hauled into the teeth of a gale. You shorten sail, the boat is heeled way over, and the bow crashes into the side of each oncoming wave, and a big blast of spray hits you. The boat shudders on impact and then re-gathers its thrust and drives hard into the next wave. When a gale gets too rough to keep driving forward, you give up your course and often run before it with the wind and seas behind you. You may no longer be able to sail the course you were headed in, but you've reduced the risk. The motion smoothes out and the boat settles as it surfs down the face of the big seas. It can even be fun.

In the last six months, I've finally stopped banging into the oncoming waves of ambitious plans and self-improvement projects. I am finally accepting that recovery from cancer is hard, too. Now I'm just trying to run before the wind, ride the waves rising up behind me, and allow the motion to smooth out.

◇◇◇

I step out into the cockpit of the *Crow* and the sun is high in the cloudless blue sky. It's become much warmer for an October day. A gentle breeze is coming in from the southwest, which will give me a nice sail home. I'm pleased to realize I'm not morbidly wondering if this might be my last sail on the *Crow*.

I am learning how to live again, and our family is moving on. Michael and Sam have had some difficult disappointments and struggles. I am better at accepting that their journey is not mine and that the greatest gift I can give my sons is to love them for who they are and be with them as best I can. I am letting go of my desperate need to protect them. My sons are grown men. In reality, they took care of me. I am proud of them.

And Kate, I see her stepping forward into her life with less of the ever-present fear and underlying sadness. I don't know how I would have survived without her. She was my life preserver.

It has been much harder for all of us than we expected. But we are so grateful. We know how lucky we've been compared to those families that lose their beloved father, mother, daughter, or son and who have to go on anyway.

I have been given the precious gift of my life back. And yet I feel like a somewhat anxious toddler, experimenting with words and phrases, pulling myself up and falling on my butt, lurching forward with arms stretched out, hoping someone will catch me. I am just like the ladybug—nothing but a dot of life, making my way from somewhere to somewhere, living as if I am going to live.

I will get home about the same time Michael's plane comes in from

Nashville this afternoon. It will be great to see him. He's had such a hard time. We're going to take him to Sam's bar tonight, and on Sunday we'll all hang out at the house. I'll cook a barbecue; we'll play some cards and have a few laughs. Simple times, simple pleasures. I can't wait to get home.

Michael

LIFE IN GRADUATE SCHOOL WAS ABSOLUTELY EVERYTHING THAT I HAD hoped it would be. To be sure, there were moments when I found my new role as apprentice difficult to take; as much as I was eager to learn and excited about this new field, I would occasionally snap back into my fragile self-importance. But such thoughts have often faded almost as quickly as they have arisen. The truth is, I wasn't a big, important person in venture capital, and I probably wasn't going to be one in science, now or in the future. And that was okay.

And I loved studying the brain. I was fascinated by all the things that had been discovered and equally amazed by all the things we didn't understand. In one of my courses we focused on the chemical effects of stress on the brain. I learned that during cancer treatments, the interactions of stress hormones and methotrexate chemotherapy can be particularly neurotoxic and that many cancer survivors complained of a mental dullness following their treatment. It was disturbing to learn how destructive chemotherapy really is—killing the brain to save it. Since dad's treatment, I have found myself worrying about health—his, mine, everyone's—much more often. In the brain alone there were millions and millions of chemical reactions that had to function perfectly every second. It was daunting to think that in every moment that we are alive, so many things have to go right.

Early on I had settled on the goal of studying the neuroscience of depression; I needed to understand what was happening when people suddenly felt worthless. I have been struck by the ways in which simply growing up in my family had prepared me for this area of study: all the car-ride conversations I'd had with my dad about his patients who struggled with depression, or the various facts about biology and the brain that my mom sprinkled on us throughout our childhood. And, of course, the experiences of the last few years, when my dad's cancer had forced me to fundamentally rethink what was most important to me. All were brought to bear on my new life as a clinical psychologist and neuroscientist.

Life with Anna during that first year had been wonderful, but our happiness was to be short-lived. The night before she was moving back to Boston to resume her own PhD program, Anna announced that she didn't think she could handle a long distance relationship, and that she wanted to break up. Just like that. I was devastated. For months, I spent sleepless nights trying to understand how I could have misread Anna's commitment to our relationship. But as my initial shock and grief passed, I also came to realize that as much as I felt her actions were unfair, mine had been, too. Part of the intensity with which I had pursued her hadn't really been about her but was part of a desire to protect myself against the fear of losing my dad. I had wanted Anna and I to get married and start a new family, a family that would always be there, even if my father's cancer came back.

Now, two years later, I'm headed back to Boston for the long Columbus Day weekend. I sleep most of the flight. Mom picks me up at the airport and we drive the twenty minutes to our house in Weston, keeping the conversation light. My dad is back from the boat in time to greet me. He's tan, and his athletic muscularity has returned. Apart from the dent in his forehead, you'd never know that three years ago he had only a 26 percent chance of being here.

The next day, my mother and I go for a walk and talk about some of the revelations she's had about how her father's death has impacted her relationships with all of us. She's realized how important it was to her to keep the memory of her father alive for me, and how when I was young, she would spend so much time trying to convey to me a sense of him and how much she missed him. Her therapist asked her if she ever thought that I, as the eldest, felt it was my job to make up for her losing her father.

When my mother asks me that question, I feel as if she voices something I have known my whole life at a level so deep I couldn't see it. My answer is immediate. *Of course I thought I needed to do something. My whole life has been spent trying to be good enough, great enough, to make up for her loss.* It had rained earlier in the day, and the ground is wet beneath our feet. We walk up the hill behind our house, cross a few streets to a road that goes by a small skating pond. On the edge of the pond is a small hutch for ice-skating someone had built a long time ago. I had gone frequently as a child. We stand together silently.

"You know, Michael," my mom finally says, looking at me with her deep blue eyes. "Nothing you could have done or could do would ever keep me from feeling the loss of my father."

I freeze. I take a deep breath. Of course I know that. But it just feels so good to hear it.

On the walk back, I wonder if Mom and I would have had this conversation before Dad's cancer happened.

That night, Mom, Dad, and I go into Boston to have a drink at the new bar where Sam is bartending. In its short tenure, the bar has become a very trendy place, and Sam is gaining recognition as one of the top local bartenders. I like watching Sam behind the bar; he seems really happy. It's Sunday, typically a slow night, and Sam keeps us company while he makes cocktails for a handful of other customers. "Okay, gang, tell me what you think of this; it's called a 'Little Italy,'" Sam says, handing us each a tumbler filled with a bourbon-colored libation. I take a sip. Dad leans over to thank Sam for an e-mail.

"What e-mail?" I ask.

"Your brother just sent me a really nice e-mail. Meant a lot."

"So, guys, want to see if we can get in a hand of bridge while I bartend?" Sam says with a wink at me.

"Great, Sam, so your family can help you get fired?" Mom says, taking his bait.

"Oh, come on. If we can play at MGH, we can play anywhere," Dad says teasingly.

"Except this time when your father says, 'ooh-bee-joo-bee-joo-bee' it won't be the chemo, but too many of Sam's cocktails," Mom replies.

"Yeah, Sam, maybe you should invent a cocktail called a 'methotrexate,'" I say. We all laugh. Not because it was particularly funny, but it just feels so good to be able to laugh about it.

"So, team, being serious for a second." Dad shifts into his therapist voice. "How's everybody doing?"

"Ok, wow," Sam cuts in with a big smile, "you've been here less than five minutes and you're already doing a family check-in?"

"Hey, what do you want from me?" Dad laughs in mock-defensiveness. "If you haven't learned to expect this from your father by now, you're hopeless." I look at my father. I can't believe how lucky I am that he's here. I also can't believe how hard it is to remember that. I had always assumed that going through his cancer would have somehow fundamentally altered my sense of what was important. That I should have a new appreciation for the time when we got to be together. Like right now.

"David, will you just dry up," Mom says teasingly.

"Whatever," Dad says with a smile. "Besides, I'm still the cancer dude. I can do what I want."

"Umm . . ." Mom cuts in teasingly, "I think that maybe we shouldn't still play that card, lest we tempt fate."

"And we all know fate is pretty dumb," Sam responds.

"Okay, so no one answered my original question," Dad says with a grin.

"Ok, Pops. Fine, I'll check in," I say with a smile. "I'm doing well. And I'm glad we're all here. Do we need to say anything else?"

Afterword:
JULY 2009

Sam

FROM THE VERY BEGINNING, I DIDN'T WANT TO HAVE ANYTHING TO DO with this book. I remember when my dad first brought it up, in the spring of my senior year at Carleton. He sent out an e-mail to my mom, Michael, and me addressed "Dear fellow authors." That was a real turn-off. I was less than excited when I got his follow-up call.

"Did you get my e-mail?" he asked eagerly.

"Yes, Dad I got the e-mail."

"So?"

"I have five reasons why I don't want to be involved," I said. (Even though I hadn't even bothered to get back to him yet, I had thought out my response enough to have numbered my reasons.)

"One, I don't want to write a book or any part of a book. Two, if I were to write a book, I would not want to write down my feelings about your cancer; I'd rather write some badass sci-fi book. Three, if I did write about my feelings, I wouldn't want them to be edited, because I hate being edited. Four, I definitely don't want my feelings being published for the world to see. Five, I really don't have time. And the idea of using my free time to write this book is just ridiculous."

After reading two of my dad's three books, I knew that this was going to be all about getting in touch with feelings. I'd also read an article my dad wrote in a psychology journal about his illness that included Michael's letter to him. I thought it was really good. It made me cry. But that didn't mean we should go and write a book about my dad's illness. Just because it's unusual for a family to write a book together doesn't mean it's a good idea. Actually, it probably means it's a down right bad idea—and that's why no one has done it.

"Wow. That's pretty persuasive," Dad said when I was done.

"I know what you're going to say," I went on before he could say anything else. "'Do it as a favor to me, be part of the team,' and all that shit."

"Well . . ."

"Yeah, and then you're going to say that you're the 'sick dude' and then I'm going to feel bad. But, by my calculations, I have five reasons

234

why I'm not going to do it, and you only have one reason why I should. So I win."

"Sam, I'm going to do this whether or not you're involved," Dad said once I'd finished talking. "I really don't want to pressure you here, and you do have five very good reasons. But I worry that you may regret not being in on this, later on."

The gravity of what he was saying hit me. For a split second, I thought of the implications if I didn't do it; Dad might not be living next year. Instead of dwelling on that thought, I just conceded the point.

"Fine. I'll do it. I gotta get to class."

Now, three years later, there is a part of me that still wishes I hadn't let him talk me into it. But I also have a definite sense of accomplishment. It's no secret that I'm not good at having or meeting goals, that I'm not terribly motivated. Still, I was able to write one-fourth of a book. That's pretty cool. But what a process it has been!

I don't like to talk about my feelings the way my family does. The past three years have seemed like one long "check-in." And I'm not really a writer. I was a math major in college and now I'm a bartender. Just the act of putting words on the page has been a challenge. Most of all, I really hate editing and rewriting, and that's all that happens when writing a book. I can barely remember writing the first draft. Maybe twelve words from it made it into the book.

But I did it. We did it. We laughed and cried. We had a shouting match or two. We struggled together through the many drafts, edits, and rewrites. And, amazingly, writing this book has brought us closer together in ways I can't even name.

I didn't let myself worry about Dad's cancer when he was first diagnosed. I was too afraid to deal with it myself. Writing the book about it has been an intense second round, with all of us sharing our perspectives of that traumatic year. Now in the safety of Dad's good health, I can actually let myself experience the scarier parts of my dad's illness. Participating in the book has been like being given CliffsNotes on how to deal with what happened. It's a good start for me.

Michael

ALTHOUGH THE FOCUS OF THIS BOOK WAS ALWAYS OUR FAMILY'S RESPONSE to my father's battle with cancer, the book also covers the most dramatic and uncertain time in my personal life: my change in careers and the pain of my relationship with Anna. Combined, these experiences all provided me with a taste of how harsh life can be and how important it was for me to reconsider some of my priorities. In many ways, I feel that the year chronicled in this book marks my true entrance into adulthood.

One of the things that I believe our family's story highlights is that real change in perspective — the ability to fully appreciate the things most dear — rarely takes the form of grand epiphanies. Instead, the change comes in small, hard-fought moments of recognition. I've certainly had plenty of my own.

When we began, I was most concerned about the potentially hurtful things that each of us might reveal to other family members. Surprisingly, such moments came up rarely and were readily resolved when they did. Unexpectedly, the fiercest arguments we had were our recollections of events — not just the bare facts, but the emotional tone of an encounter or conversation. For me, this book has been a constant reminder of how every moment contains multiple points of view, each one of which are true, no matter how contradictory.

Ultimately, the best part of writing this book has been reading each other's writing. While I believe that our family knows each other's lives and stories quite well, we all learned something new through sharing our writing, and it has led to a deepening in our understanding of each other. For example, I have always known that my dad uses dissociation as a way of coping, and that he frequently responds to stressful situations by putting on a positive front and shutting-down emotionally. I could parrot back the psychobabble from an early age; the psychologically sophisticated language that I grew up using often gave the appearance of a deeper appreciation for experiences than I really had, like a man well-versed in music theory who has never actually heard a Beethoven symphony. But I didn't have a truly concrete idea of how my dad really felt. Similarly, my mother's grief following the loss of her father is something I have known since I was a little boy, but my more recent appreciation of how that grief affected me is something that came directly out of conversations Mom and I had while working on the book.

I wouldn't recommend that every family try and write a book together. I tend to agree with my brother that our family is probably a little hyper-reflective, to say the least, and that going through this process certainly isn't for everyone. But I do think that however one might choose to do it, searching out one's own story and sharing it with the people you love can be incredibly powerful and healing. Thank you for letting me share my story with you, too.

Kate

TO BE HONEST, I DID NOT WANT TO WRITE THIS BOOK WHEN DAVID FIRST began talking about it in the spring of 2006. It seemed an impossible task. First, I couldn't imagine adding this to my work life. But much more importantly, it seemed like a tremendous invasion of my privacy. I grew up with the notion that "a lady is in the press three times: when she is born, when she marries, and when she dies." This venture would definitely exceed those guidelines.

David has always been comfortable using personal stories in his teaching of therapists. He has had years of confirmation from colleagues about how valuable his own stories are and how much they resonate with the struggles that so many face. I have not had this experience in quite the same way. Although I have shared my experiences of being a physician with medical students and have had students tell me how meaningful they were, this book would entail sharing on an entirely different level. And I haven't been confident that our story would be truly meaningful to others.

David's main motivation for writing the book was to give us a template for how we might talk together while he was ill and grieve together if he died. In a way, it would be his gift to us. He also, of course, hoped it would be helpful to other families who are facing these kinds of difficult circumstances. Though I'd initially resisted, his argument won me over in the end. And frankly, there was a part of me that did not think David would survive to write it.

It was almost six months after we agreed to write this book that we sat down as a family for the first time to share what each of us had written. We gathered in our family room, all of us with laptops perched in front of us, and took turns reading out loud our first chapters.

Perhaps because I had no real expectations for our little writing group, I was not even remotely prepared for the intimacy it engendered. I would have said we were already a close family, but the act of reading aloud to each other our internal experiences was something quite different. It led to conversations about what we had each been going through that might never have otherwise have happened. After

Sam read about how he'd cried alone in his bed in the middle of the night, I asked him why he hadn't come and woken me up so he wouldn't have been so alone. He said he didn't want to upset me. This led to a conversation about how it would have helped me to have been able to help him and that talking about hard feelings wasn't the problem—it was not talking about them that was so much harder. These kinds of conversations were invaluable, given the even tougher road we knew might lie ahead.

As the book progressed, we got together sporadically to read each other's chapters. Every time, I saw how much we had grown both individually and together. I was surprised by how well we worked and how little we argued over material. It was an extraordinary experience to work with my children and husband in this way. Most of the time, I would have to say it was fun to work together despite the often hard nature of what we were writing about.

By the end of this process, something had happened. I think that both my sons, admittedly now grown men, had moved into a somewhat different relationship with us. We had worked in collaboration with each other. We had been able to hear one another's thoughts and feelings and, as a result, been able to see each other as *people*, separate from our roles as parents and children.

Writing about David's illness and about the events of my youth also helped me personally to understand how much those earlier life experiences had shaped my life and my response to David's illness. I came to understand more fully the flow of sadness that had suffused my internal adult life. Even though on the surface I was an engaged, often happy and playful parent, my children felt this undercurrent, particularly Michael. I feel more keenly than ever the truth of William Faulkner's words, "The past is never dead. It's not even past." I'd never realized quite how much it all impacted me.

It is my fervent hope that this book will do at least a fraction for our readers what it has done for me and my family. I am very aware that our story is not typical. My access to medical information and to doctors made this a very different experience for us than for those who feel that they are alone in this journey or who lack a good relationship to the doctors caring for them. In this, I know how fortunate we were. But I hope this book will provide something useful for families who are going through a life-threatening health crisis.

I do not think the book is a road map of how to travel through a difficult illness, as I do not think there is such a thing. Each person's experience is so profoundly unique. But perhaps it is enough to know one is not alone. In the end, we are simply giving our story to you to use it as you will. I hope it helps in some small way.

David

Living with cancer is like sailing in the fog. There's no distant horizon, just an enveloping, thick, wet shroud of gray. You plot your course in small increments so you don't get lost. At any moment when you catch a glimpse of a navigational aid like a bell buoy or whistle, you carefully log your location, compass course, and your distances and times in a log book. This traditional navigational technique is called dead reckoning. For my family, our book was a kind of sailing log: our record of marks made and milestones passed during that relentless year.

I had the idea for this book after I published a short article in 2005 in the *Psychotherapy Networker*, a trade journal. It was a piece about being a therapist dealing with my own illness, and it featured Michael's remarkable letter to me. To my surprise, people all over the world responded with genuine appreciation for me sharing my story as well as Michael's letter. People seemed to value our candor and vulnerability as well as the opportunity to hear both our perspectives, so I began to think: Why not a book where all four of us chronicled our experiences? Had that ever been done before by a family?

Over the next few weeks, as the idea grew in my mind, I became certain that working together in such an intense and intimate way might help us hold on to each other and truly face my illness and our experience of it together—no matter what happened. Naturally, my family was less than enthused by this idea. Sam was most outspokenly opposed, but Kate came a strong second. She couldn't imagine finding the time to write the book, and the idea of publishing our intimate personal story of our fight with cancer seemed inappropriate and intrusive to her. Michael, who had already been given very positive feedback from our article, had reservations, but was at least slightly intrigued.

However, despite their misgivings, Michael, Sam, and Kate all eventually rallied to the idea. Their willingness to participate in this endeavor has been truly extraordinary and loving gift. I know they did it for me.

We started writing in the spring of 2006, when it was still highly likely that I would have a recurrence and then bone marrow treatment. We chose to chronicle one year because many big events were coming up, like Sam's graduation, Michael's move to Nashville, Kate teaching her new course at the medical school, and the first anniversary of my cancer. And I could be relatively confident that I would complete the year.

Of course there were many starts and stops, but everyone finally settled in to the writing. Despite his stated resistance to the idea, Sam wrote fast and furiously. Kate and Michael had little time to work on it, but then would put in intense bursts of effort that created surprisingly good first drafts. Everyone learned to accept and even trust the editing process.

None of us knew that this writing project would be such a profoundly emotional experience and be a catalyst for fundamentally changing our relationships to ourselves and each other.

I remember the first time we read our writings to each other. It was Christmastime in 2006. We were sitting in our living room in front of a toasty fire. The usual teasing banter was going on, but I was very anxious. I had been reading what the others had written as they sent material to me, but this was the first time the four of us would dare share with each other.

"Well, this is so dumb, I might as well get it over with," offered Sam who, despite his loud protestations had already written much more than any of us. Sam began, and, by the time we got to Kate forty minutes later, a profound hush had fallen upon us. There was not a sound in the room but the crackling of the fire and the reader's voice. Kate read about her fears of the boys living without a father like she had. She started weeping and then all of us did.

I looked at my dear Kate and my beloved sons. I knew that, even if I didn't make it, they would find a way of finishing this book. It would be one of the ways they would hold on to each other.

◇◇◇

I have always known that Kate is the love of my life and an extraordinary doctor. But in this crisis, she had the exquisite ability to be there for me both as my nurturing wife while also applying all of her medical knowledge to ensuring that I had extraordinary care and that I could simply trust that everything that could be done was being done. I could not have gone through this without her or without the loving support of Michael and Sam.

And yet, through the writing process, I realized that Kate's grief over the loss of her father and my anxiety from mine had shaped the development of our family and been a burden for our boys. Certainly, my anxiety and efforts to "help" my sons were clearly relentless and frequently undermining. This project has led me to finally recognize my boys' manhood and embrace them and their choices for who they are as opposed to what I think they should be. I love them with an unbridled passion and now it's time to really let them go.

Truly embracing those I love for who they are and recognizing that I can't protect them from their own struggles has been one of the most important lessons I've learned from my illness. I hope this book will help you view the different members of your family as well as yourself—with all of your rough edges and idiosyncrasies—with profound tenderness and compassion.

◇◇◇

Some time ago, Kate gave me a framed quote for Christmas. It was by Philo of Alexandria.

> *Be kind,*
> *For everyone you meet*
> *Is fighting a great battle.*

I keep it on my desk. I've spent my life working with families in crisis, and I think I have been a good therapist. But now, having gone through our experience as a family, I think of all the families I have ever treated and suddenly realize how little I knew.

We are all fighting a great battle.

Acknowledgments

There is so much that we have to be thankful for and so many people who supported us along our journey. We would particularly like to thank the following people:

Dr. Ephraim Hochberg treated David with exquisite care, thoughtfulness, and kindness. We were so blessed to have him as our doctor. In addition, the staff of the Massachusetts General Hospital provided profound comfort and reassurance to David and all of us. We are so grateful for their gentle, steady hands.

We were surrounded by family and friends from all part of our lives, whose care and affection often felt like a life preserver for each of us. We want you to know how much we appreciate you.

We also had a stalwart cadre of readers: Stephen Kennedy, Jim and Jan Treadway, Lynn Miller, Leslie Lawrence, Janc Noel, Barry Dym, and Diane Fingold, who all gave steady support and great criticism. Three people should be individually mentioned: First, there was Bob Markel, our literary agent, who dared to believe in us and this project from the very beginning. Then Cindy Barrilleaux worked with the four of us every step of the way as writing coach, editor, and sometimes wise referee. Cindy's fierce and dedicated efforts helped us be as good as we could be. In addition, we've been fortunate to have an outstanding editor at Union Square Press, Iris Blasi, whose vision and sharp red pencil were able to push us to another level of effort. Also at Sterling Publishing, our thanks to project editor Andrea Santoro, interior designer Rachel Maloney, and jacket designer Elizabeth Mihaltse. We thank all of you.

About the Authors

David Treadway is a psychologist, teacher, and author who lives and works in Weston, Massachusetts.

Kate Treadway is a physician at Massachusetts General Hospital and teaches at Harvard Medical School.

Michael Treadway is currently a doctoral candidate in the clinical psychology program at Vanderbilt University.

Sam Treadway is a graduate of Carleton College and a bartender in Boston.